ENTER TALKING

Books by Joan Rivers

HAVING A BABY CAN BE A SCREAM
THE LIFE AND HARD TIMES OF HEIDI ABROMOWITZ
ENTER TALKING

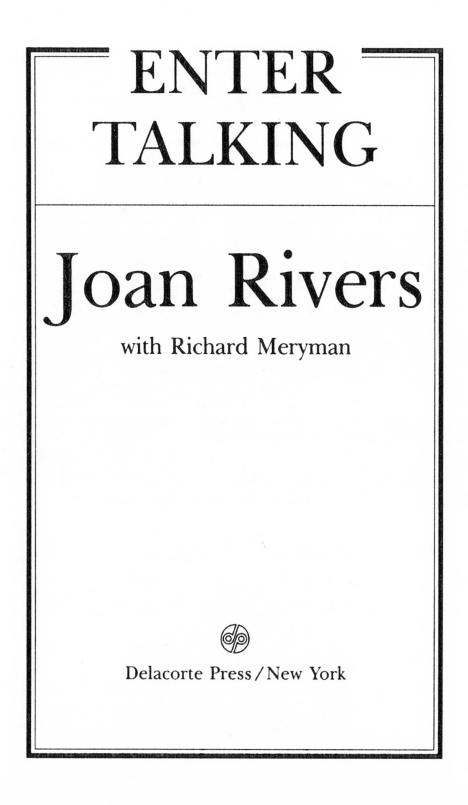

ENTER TALKING

Joan Rivers

with Richard Meryman

Delacorte Press / New York

Published by
Delacorte Press
1 Dag Hammarskjold Plaza
New York, N.Y. 10017

Grateful acknowledgment is made for permission to reprint excerpts from the following:

Portions of the lyric from "I'M JUST WILD ABOUT HARRY" by Eubie Blake and Noble Sissle. © 1921 (Renewed) WARNER BROS. INC. All Rights Reserved. Used by Permission.

Portions of the lyric from "THE MAN I LOVE" by George Gershwin and Ira Gershwin. © 1924 (Renewed) WB MUSIC CORP. All Rights Reserved. Used by Permission.

Portions of the lyric from "MR. CLEAN" by John Meyer. The song "MR. CLEAN" is Copyright © 1959 by the author, John Meyer. Used by Permission.

Portion of the lyric from "APPLAUSE, APPLAUSE." Words by Ira Gershwin, Music by Burton Lane. © 1942, Renewed 1970 METRO-GOLDWYN-MAYER INC. Rights Assigned to CBS CATALOGUE PARTNERSHIP. All Rights Controlled & Administered by CBS FEIST CATALOG INC. All Rights Reserved. International Copyright Secured. Used by Permission.

MANUFACTURED IN THE UNITED STATES OF AMERICA

FIRST PRINTING

DESIGNED BY LAURENCE ALEXANDER

Library of Congress Cataloging-in-Publication Data

Rivers, Joan.
Enter talking.

Includes index.
1. Rivers, Joan. 2. Comedians—United States—Biography. I. Meryman, Richard, 1926– . II. Title.
PN2287.R55A34 1986 792.7′028′0924 [B]
ISBN 0-385-29440-9
Library of Congress Catalog Card Number: 85-28987

To Edgar,
   who made this book happen,
      and
to Johnny Carson,
   who made it *all* happen

ENTER TALKING

1

YOU WANT TO hear stupid? Major stupid? Stand-up comic. You walk onto a bare stage absolutely alone, no comfort, no help, no script or actors to support you, no lyrics and music to give you life—just yourself saying your own words out of your own head, telling each person, one on one, the weirdest corners of your psyche. And everybody is judging your personality, judging whether you are worth their money, whether you make them happy. When they do not laugh, that silence is a rejection of *you* personally, only you. Not your mother. Not your piano player—if you have one. A thousand people in a room are saying, "You stink. You're nothing."

But here's what is even more stupid. In order to get on that stage and walk that terrible tightrope, you struggle through years of humiliation and privation, feeling like the misfit of the world. For this job you have to be nuts, but it is the craziness that makes you funny, makes you obsessed with your career. It is craziness that makes you live for that hour facing an audience which can destroy you at any moment. Yet, those are the truly happy times in my life, riding the laughter higher and higher, feeling that euphoria, feeling washed in love.

Since my earliest memories, my dream has been to make a living doing that one thing—performing on a stage—which made me feel I belonged, made me feel adored and, paradoxically, safe.

These desperate needs are the legacy of my childhood, but my anger and blame are oddly mixed with gratitude. My pain became a plus. Instead of leaving me permanently withdrawn, stunted by rage, it was in some blessed way translated into humor. Ironically, while my parents were inflicting my craziness, they were also creating my goal, the roots of my career, and the possibility of happiness.

And ultimately, despite my anger, I think my mother and father were innocent. They intended the very best for my older sister and me. But the two of them—really all four of us —were trapped by their Russian childhoods and by the sad, toxic mismatch of their marriage—the tragedy of Beatrice Grushman locked to Meyer Molinsky.

Their predicament can best be described with a memory from a Saturday when I was ten years old. That morning my mother and I had gone together to a chic furrier on Fifty-seventh Street in New York City and bought a mink coat for two thousand dollars. In the afternoon I was in my room in our Brooklyn town house and heard my father downstairs in the kitchen. I was astonished because he was a general practitioner doctor who worked constantly and was almost never home. I stopped to listen and heard the harsh rage and fear in his voice as he shouted at my mother, "You're crazy. Where do you think the money is going to come from? You're going to ruin me, put me in my grave—you and your fancy airs! Two thousand dollars! You're crazy."

My mother's voice was low, strained, fury steaming around the edges of her calm. "We can afford it. There should be good money coming in. You have a huge practice. You work without a stop. You have got to charge more. People owe you for twenty visits, but they buy a new car and drive it to your office."

"Goddamn it," my father bellowed. "You don't know what the hell you're talking about. You don't know my patients. They can't afford more and I'm sick of working so hard because of you, sick of being in debt. Do you hear?"

There was a silence. Then my mother's voice, still frigid,

asked, "If they're so poor, where do they get the money to hire private nurses?"

"Who the hell are you to run my practice! Who do you think you are! Some big lady!" My father's face, I knew, was a hot red.

"Well, you come from kikes," my mother answered, her voice steely with scorn, with loathing for his family's Jewishness, which to her, primarily a Russian, meant commonness. And she was icy, too, with her own self-contempt, her disgust at marrying beneath her. Their fights always led to this misery —and I stayed still, waiting, eyes on the floor, rigid with tension, with the fear that something awful—I did not know what—was about to happen.

The silence now in the kitchen was almost more frightening than the screaming and I moved to the top of the stairs, imagining the two of them glaring across the wall of their fury. Suddenly, my father shouted, "I'm going to call that fancy furrier of yours and he can take his goddamn coat back!" There was a banging sound, a thumping, and my mother screamed, "Don't you dare! Don't you dare!"

Panic, like an electric shock, sent me careening downstairs, tears instantly on my face as I heard my mother wailing, "Don't you dare humiliate me." She was in the middle of the kitchen, face contorted, holding the base of the phone and wildly wrenching at the cord. My father, the mouthpiece in his hand, was shouting, "You're crazy. Crazy!" He snatched the base away and turned his back and tried to dial and she pummeled him on his back with her fists. I screamed, "Stop it, stop it, stop it! Don't, Daddy," and, crying hysterically, pushed myself between them.

My mother stepped back, panting, and said, "Meyer, look what you've done to Joan," and they stopped to quiet me. My mother took me upstairs, saying, "It's nothing. Calm down. It's nothing. Just a little disagreement between Daddy and me." But I wanted to kill my father, wanted to shut my eyes and have it all go away, wanted to be able to say to him, "Here is the money. Leave my mother alone."

She told me much later that while we were upstairs, he telephoned the furrier and shouted, "I've never seen two thousand dollars in one place in my life."

In the Molinsky household money was a body of ugly emotions that dwelt with us like a fifth person—like some evil, mischief-making relative imposing himself forever, constantly agitating and souring our lives. Both my parents were almost pathologically terrified of poverty. My father dealt with his fear by agonizing over every dollar that left his hand. My mother fought off her anxiety by spending, by extracting money from my father any way she could and building a facade of affluence.

Very quickly in her marriage she established that grand style, insisting on a maid and a governess for me and my sister Barbara and moving the family into a series of apartments at better and better addresses, till finally she achieved a town house with my father's office on the street floor and big window awnings, each adorned with a decorative seal. The furnishings meant everything to my mother. I remember heavy silk lampshades, damask-covered chairs and sofa, and tables that were French antiques—if you did not look too closely. She dressed Barbara and me exquisitely—little winter coats made especially for us with velvet collars, little leggings of soft gray kid leather, black patent leather shoes and white socks, gloves, hats with a velvet band that matched the coat collar, all very English. My mother used to refer to us as "her little flowers."

Elegance was my mother's religion and her home was its temple. Everything in her domain had to be absolutely correct. The atmosphere in the house was stiff and formal, pervaded by dos and don'ts. To keep the living room a pristine salon, not even the family was allowed into it except on special occasions—as though a perpetual velvet rope stretched across the doorway. The correct spoon and fork had to be used and cocktails were never allowed at the dinner table because wine should be drunk with food. Eating was done only in the kitchen or the dining room; food never traveled upstairs. The good silver was always used, even in the kitchen, and the ketchup stood in a sterling silver holder. A wife should always be dressed and groomed for her husband, so when my father's car pulled into the driveway, my mother would put on lipstick, powder, and cologne and go down to greet him. Because a doctor should look like a doctor, she made sure he wore a tie and three-piece suit, a chesterfield coat, homburg hat, and gloves. Swearing was forbidden and children should *always* be respectful of parents. When, in a teenage rage, I told my mother, "I hate you," she wept beyond consolation and turned me away when I came to apologize.

My sister and I were expected to have flawless manners and be *ladies,* and my mother squashed any move to be outstanding, to be in the slightest way outrageous. I ached to tie my hair into a ponytail with a man's necktie and be part of a fad that swept our school. I threw a hysterical, weeping tantrum—and lost. Her final word was usually "Make yourself more, not less." Etiquette was paramount and anybody gauche enough to drop by the house casually was not received. One Sunday some relatives of my father rang the doorbell and Beatrice said, "Guests are welcome in my house only when they are invited, but when they do not call in advance we do not admit them." My father went slamming away into the back of the house while my mother and Barbara and I lay down out of sight on the floor in the upstairs den and waited until the relatives gave up and went away.

My father would have called them in, slapped their backs, insisted they stay for dinner, and maybe sleep over—"Hey, we've got a couch." But he did not dare do that and I am sure he always felt alien in his own home, like a visitor at the palace, never able to relax. He covered his discomfort with jokes. Seated at one of Beatrice's perfect tables, he would point to his finger bowl and say, "This soup looks watery."

Much later, whenever I took my parents to Le Pavillon, the best French restaurant in New York, my father would study and study the menu, though he knew no French. Beatrice, wild with annoyance, always looked at him over the top of her menu and said, "Meyer, have the chicken or the veal." After the captain in his black tie and tails finished listing the specials, my father, covering his embarrassment, would joke, "I'm just in the mood for a nice piece of gefilte fish. What kind of soup do you have?" Then he jiggled his menu and said, "And I don't see a pastrami sandwich on here." Bea's voice, like a cold knife, would flash out, "The doctor will have the veal!"

Her parties were always stylish perfection, musicales with the men in dinner jackets, no children allowed, guest lists of the most influential acquaintances she could assemble. When she asked for money to buy the right wine, my father would say, "Wine is wine. Just give 'em a bottle of Manischewitz." Though her elegant friends liked him, Bea was embarrassed by his Brooklyn bedside manner. Once he used the phrase "busted out laughing" to a company president and afterward my mother said, "Oh, Meyer, how could you say that. 'Busted out laughing'—so common!"

My mother's formality persisted even at home with her children. Hugs and kisses did not exist in our house. My independence was to her a rejection of her most deeply held values and became a battleground between us. But I understood that she cared for me beyond everything and was loyal without qualification or hesitation. She was always there for me, never away from home overnight, so I always had a listener for my problems, somebody who wanted to hear that my first-grade teacher, Miss Befler, was mean to me and went "Shhh, Joan! Shhh!" in front of the whole school at a play. Whenever my mother thought I was in the right, she would go down to the school with both six-guns strapped to her waist and raise hell—so I found out I had a champion who believed in me, who would slug it out for me, who really loved me.

I adored my mother, perhaps because in so many ways I am my mother. She died in 1976 and I still talk to her silently every day, still follow her example in a thousand different ways, still feel that the best of me comes from her. Beneath my mother's rigidity was a caring and compassionate woman who taught me that I should be aware of other people's predicaments and sensitivities. She would bring in needy children right off the street and go through my closet and give away my clothes. I would think, *Hold it, that's my snowsuit,* but knew she was being special and generous—and that I would get another snowsuit that was new.

Not only was I absorbing her values, I understood where they came from and felt sorry for her. My mother, as though telling fairy tales, described to Barbara and me her childhood in Russia in a huge dacha in Akkerman, near Odessa, where the Danube flows into the Black Sea. She told us about the parties given by her own mother, Hannah—parades of liveried waiters carrying trays high above their heads, the gold flatware, the pears filled with caviar, and outside on the green lawns, peacocks patrolling. One of them once pecked my mother, leaving a tiny scar on her forehead.

She talked about her earliest memory—lying in bed when Hannah, going to the ballet in a sable-lined coat, bent down for a good-night kiss and my mother reached up and felt the soft luxury of the fur. But her relationship with Hannah was basically formal, lacking any chance to learn to show affection. My mother said that she was really raised by a nurse who, every afternoon, elaborately dressed her and her older sister Alice and brothers, Alex and Sacha, and presented them to Hannah, the girls curtsying in their white dresses with big blue sashes and white shoes. Tea was poured from a gold tea set, and when they left, they curtsied again. When Beatrice was nearly dying of pneumonia, it was her nurse she cried out for, not Hannah.

My mother, too, grew up with mismatched parents. Her father, Boris Grushman—one of the few wealthy Jews in Russia, privileged because he sold furs, beef, and brick to the tsar for the army—was a much older, dry stick of a man who hated Hannah's pleasures and parties. But Hannah was a woman of spirit. In 1917, during the pre-revolutionary turmoil, Alex was both a radical in trouble with the authorities and a candidate for the tsar's army, from which no Jew ever emerged alive. Hannah Grushman sewed jewels into the sable lining of her coat and fled to America with her children.

In New York the jewels went quickly and Hannah worked as a midwife and took boarders into their flat. Beatrice and Alice labored all day in a blouse factory at sewing machines and when Beatrice's bed was rented to a boarder, she slept on two chairs pushed together. She had no winter coat, and when her soles wore out, she put newspaper inside her shoes.

But Hannah, proudly nouveau poor, and scorning the low-class shtetl Jews, made elegance, no matter how tattered, almost a moral defense against poverty. At dinner the shabby napkins were perfectly folded, the unmatched fish knives and dessert spoons were in the right place—and the children had better use the right fork. It was sad and crazy—my mother sewing at a machine all day at the blouse factory and coming home at night to dine with Emily Post.

Eventually, my mother's brother Alex, the ex-radical, became a successful dentist and moved the family to a big apartment on Riverside Drive overlooking the Hudson River. Hannah never had a dime in America, but Alex underwrote for her a Victorian fantasy world of servants and teak tables with marble tops, a huge Persian rug, plush draperies at the windows, and a vast chair where this now imposing lady, impressively gowned, sat like the dowager queen mother, receiving homage. My mother grew up to be the image of Hannah—

they looked alike, talked alike, dressed alike, thought alike—
and she never admitted to any person, except a little bit to
Barbara and me, that there had been one minute of déclassé
privation in her life. Incredible as it sounds, my father during
their entire forty-eight years of marriage did not know she had
ever been poor and always believed that Beatrice had been
rich in Russia and rich in America.

Beatrice and Meyer Molinsky met in 1928. He entered
her life a poor boy just out of medical school and was mightily
impressed by that Riverside Drive household—and by Beatrice, who was beautiful with dark hair against white, white
skin. He must have been impressed, too, by the nice dowry
that her brother Alex was prepared to pay. Meyer fell totally
in love.

Beatrice saw in Meyer everything that Hannah and she
believed was crucially important—the security, affluence, and
prestige that came with a doctor. He was also cute—a tall,
blond man, nicely plump, and smooth-faced with a small mustache—and she was twenty-eight years old with no prospects,
no alternatives, no other beaux, and no education. In Russia
there had been only tutors and in America just the factory.
The courtship lasted three weeks.

Beatrice and Meyer Molinsky settled in Brooklyn, where I
was born. By the time I knew her, my mother was a heavyish
woman, dramatic with almost black hair against her pale skin
and a regal air emphasized by the long dresses she preferred
and the jewelry she doted on, wearing mabe pearl earrings
even with a bathing suit. Around her neck was a good string of
pearls which she would nervously roll between her fingers,
saying "Oh, Joan! Really!" Her voice was low with a slight
Russian accent, and since English was a foreign language, she
enunciated each word precisely, carefully, rather clipped—
the way the queen mother might sound.

No matter how much money my father earned, it could never be enough to buy my mother what she had known growing up in Russia and what she wanted for my sister and me. It must have been very difficult in the beginning of their marriage when he was trying to establish a medical practice during the Depression, opening offices and falling behind in the rent and moving to a new location in the hope of finding more patients somewhere else. Once he had to skip out on his rent, emptying his office into a truck at 3:00 A.M. To eat, he sold medical alcohol prescriptions to bootleggers and bartered with patients, treating somebody again and again for three chickens. Finally, to become known, he worked free in the afternoons at the Brooklyn Jewish Hospital clinic, which charged patients fifty cents a visit. There he had an idea: If the clinic could make thousands of dollars on that fee, so could he.

Meyer went back to his own people, as he used to say, and opened an office in the Jewish Brownsville section of Brooklyn. He printed up hundreds of circulars announcing that, for the same price as the clinic, he would give private care of the best quality, and my mother, a woman of action when money was involved, handed them out on street corners and rang doorbells. In his first year, during the Depression, my father grossed over ten thousand dollars and began charging a dollar on Saturdays, and by the next year was grossing twenty-five thousand. Pretty soon he was receiving letters from competing doctors threatening to report him to the medical society for unethical advertising. But as fast as he made money, my mother spent it.

During my entire childhood, from the beginning, my father was constantly struggling to catch up to their debts, but

Barbara and I always had those governesses, had the clothes, the piano lessons, the best private schools in Brooklyn with tuitions way beyond our means, first at Brooklyn Ethical Culture School and then Adelphi Academy, where I transferred after the sixth grade.

As at Brooklyn Ethical, I endured a periodic ritual at Adelphi. I walked down the shallow half steps of the huge pink marble staircase, holding onto the high, polished wooden balustrade, my body stiff and awkward with fright. At the bottom I crossed the wide marble entrance hall toward the school office, which had windows facing into the hall, and I could see the two secretaries and the headmaster, Mr. Amos, at his desk.

I went into the office and everybody looked at me and I could tell they *knew*. I had to say, "Please, can I speak to Mr. Amos," and I was sent into the inner office and Mr. Amos looked at me and I handed him the tuition check, saying, "My mother said to leave this and could you please hold it for two weeks. Thank you very much." Added to my humiliation was the terror that he would say, "We don't want you in this school anymore."

Sometimes he answered, "Tell your parents we can hold it only one week." And whenever I passed Mr. Amos in the hall, *I* knew that *he* knew that I could not afford to be there. Of course, I believed I was the only child in the whole school who could not afford it. Sometimes, the check would bounce and I would be called down to Mr. Amos's office and he would say, "Please say to your parents that the check did not go through and we are going to redeposit it tomorrow." So I had to go home with that message, that knowledge. I always thought that I *had* to deliver those checks, that this was what Molinskys did. But I understand now: headmasters cannot yell at a six-year-old. Or an eight-year-old. Or a thirteen-year-old.

At that time my mother's allowance for food, clothing for herself, my sister, and me, money for a maid, the beauty

parlor, everything, was forty dollars a week—and you cannot
be Perle Mesta on that. Her solution was charge accounts and
my father would get the bills and explode—shouting, "You're
insane. You're spending like a crazy woman"—and close
down the charge accounts, and my mother would reopen
them and try to pay off the bills a few dollars a month. That is
how we lived; charge and payments, charge and payments,
getting way behind at Saks, way behind at Bonwit's, way behind at W. & J. Sloane.

When she gave the clerk her charge account card, it was
like roulette, and while we waited, watching the girl call the
office, I dug my nails into my palms and felt my stomach
knotting. Sometimes the girl smiled and it was all right and we
were incredulous, but more often a sealed, polite look came
into her face as she said, "Mrs. Molinsky, the credit manager
would like to see you upstairs. I'll hold the merchandise."

Then I would find myself in the credit manager's office,
writhing with humiliation, dying for my proud, dignified
mother as he told her, "You have owed three hundred dollars
since May and we cannot extend further credit." I knew he
knew that we had no right to be in that store—and we took the
elevator down, not the escalator, because we might see the
saleslady and she knew too.

Whenever my mother became desperate, she and I went
to a chic pawnshop on Madison Avenue, my mother quickly
checking the street for anybody we might know. She would
hock her four-carat ring and maybe also her "good gold
bracelet," as we called it, and pay something to each department store. We always hoped my father would not see that the
ring was gone and he always pretended not to notice.

My mother wanted M.D. to stand for Make Dollars, and
forever tried to persuade my father to be a specialist, which
would mean more prestige and more money—and she was

right. He never stopped competing with the free clinic, charging in the early 1940s only a dollar for an office visit and stuffing those dollars into his bulging pockets. At the end of the day, he piled the crumpled bills on the desk of the nurse-secretary-receptionist and said, "Flatten these and count them." He never took time off. He went back to work three days after a hernia operation and when he underwent any minor operations, he never had anesthesia because it made him groggy and groggy meant he would lose time, lose work. Our family motto was, "A good epidemic means meat on the table," and twice in my childhood there were polio scares, which was good news to us. Because of the war there was a shortage of vaccines, so my mother sprang into action and made trips back and forth to the health department, badgering them for extra vaccine, rushing back to the office—"Keep these needles sterilized. Next."

My father wanted to be the best general practitioner in Brooklyn and perhaps succeeded. He was a marvelous diagnostician and a wonderful family doctor. Saying, "Someday you'll pay me," he never turned anybody away because they did not have money. He loved his patients and, with a packed waiting room, would stand for half an hour while they talked about their children. When a patient died, he was near collapse, but also thought his patients were funny and told wild, black stories about them and did outrageous imitations: "Doctor, doctor, I was going to the bathroom and my stomach came out. Should I flush or wait for you?" He knew it was funny that Mrs. Ginsburg, trying to be elegant, had given her son the fancy name of Pierpont—and my father would mimic the way she leaned out the window and screamed to the son, "Pierponteleh, Pierponteleh, the doctor's here to take your wasser." There was the patient who told him, "Doctor, I hear a ringing in my ears," and he answered, "Better than hearing it in your ankles." My mother, who had almost no humor and knew every story ad nauseam, listened with a fixed, forced smile.

He could make contact with people on every social level, make them like him. As my mother scornfully said, "Taxi drivers want to be his friend and he wants to be theirs." I think of him standing with people and telling a joke or a story and poking them and they all laugh. He was wonderful with sick patients, jollying them out of their fears—"Ah, please, it's nothing. Are you kidding? Get in bed and don't annoy me. Take the medicine and you'll be out in two weeks. Don't take it, you'll be out in fourteen days." He would tell patients as he wrote a prescription, "These are very expensive pills, but they're worth it"—and then he would call out to his nurse in the waiting room, "Nancy, what's the Latin word for aspirin?" I learned from him something extremely important: People like you when you make them laugh.

His patients *loved* him. They brought him cakes and jars of jam and gefilte fish, and when my mother died, patients from thirty years ago sent him letters of condolence. Everybody in Queens and Brooklyn knew my father and knew the car, and he would go into a neighborhood and be surrounded like some politician. "Hi, Doc." "Hello, Doc." When he walked into a delicatessen, the owner would say, "Oh, it's Doctor Molinsky. The sandwich is on me, Doc. Are you kidding, Doc? You took care of my wife when we were broke. Don't insult me with money."

He was a star and enjoyed being a star. He took a profound satisfaction from all that love and I think was afraid to raise his prices because he thought those people would stop coming. He desperately did not want to test their love.

I believe his office was the only place my father received love. I did not see any coming from his wife and there was very little from his children. Virtually the only time we sat together as a family was at supper on Sunday nights, not in the dining room, which was inviolate, but in the pretty kitchen dining

area my mother created with a hutch and a Victorian chandelier, a patterned tablecloth on the square table and a white
glass bowl of fruit. Sitting in the wooden captain's chairs, she
would wear a hostess gown and my father would be in his suit
because he was going to make house calls later. Barbara and I,
on each side of the table, talked to my mother, who was the
one asking questions, the one who seemed to care. My father
sat there and ate, head down, reaching for food, a peasant
eater. When he slurped his soup, Beatrice would say, "Meyer,
please, a little more quietly. And put your napkin on your
knee."

He would say, "Go to hell," and put the napkin on his
knee.

If my father did not feel loved by his children, it was his
fault. Unlike my mother, he was hardly ever there for us,
never at home, never giving love. When I left for school, he
was still a lump in the bed. Six days a week he made house
calls in the morning and had office hours in the afternoon and
early evening and then made more calls. When he came home
after ten, he was exhausted. Even on Sundays, his day of rest,
there was no togetherness. During our big family recreation—
going for a drive in the car—he was constantly listening to the
radio and stopping for more house calls, schlepping up five
flights to make five dollars. I never saw him on Saturday
nights because my parents were usually invited out by specialists who wanted to be friends with Dr. Molinsky because every
time he said, "Sammy needs an operation," that meant a
referral. I must have been terribly angry that I did not have a
father.

Traveling with him was miserable. When we went to Atlantic City for a medical convention, we never stayed in a
hotel like the Haddon Hall or the Shelburne on the boardwalk. We always stayed down the street in the Copley-

Schmopley, some shabby place only two short blocks to the boardwalk, and he would sit on the beach fretting, saying, "This is costing me a fortune—and double because nobody's coming to the office."

He never brought enough money on a trip, figuring, I guess, that whatever he took would be spent. When we went to Virginia Beach, the secondhand tires kept blowing out and Barbara and I hung from the car windows listening for the next explosion—while my mother, furious, sat in the front seat saying, "I told you. I told you." We ended up stuck in Newport News with no money to buy tires, crowded into one room in a fleabag hotel worse than any place I stayed as a down-and-out performer. Finally, phoning collect, he reached a patient who wired him enough to get home. I wanted to say to my father, "Why no money, you bastard! Why not even a blank check in your wallet!"

Whenever we went to a restaurant, I knew he had only a few dollars so I ordered Salisbury steak. I never saw a lobster, unless it was alive and swimming, until I was thirty years old. After the meal there would be that ache around my heart, my hands clenched and knees pressed together while we waited for the bill, because I did not know if he had enough money and knew he would sit adding up the bill and then leave a lousy tip—so the meal always ended badly. That is why, the minute I was old enough to work, I got summer jobs at a Wanamaker's department store. I had realized that money was a way out of the prison for all of us.

During one summer medical convention at Atlantic City, I finally had cash in my pocket from selling jewelry at Wanamaker's and could take my mother to a nice restaurant, just the two of us. We had never before sat down relaxed and ordered *anything* we wanted. There were little linen napkins and she had a glass of wine before lunch and we ordered dessert. I remember taking out my change purse from my basket handbag and leaving a major tip and feeling very hot stuff. It was great being able to do that for her and I thought, *Money is power. Money is wonderful.* I have not changed my opinion.

I was terribly sorry for my mother. Even when I was little, I knew that every glass, every cushion, every matchstick, came with such finagling, such conniving, such begging. Nothing came with the slightest touch of generosity or love. She never opened a birthday present from her husband and found something wonderful. He would just hand her ten dollars. She had nothing but the house, which was a constant struggle. That was why, as soon as I started making money, I began buying her things.

I realize now that my father's anguish and anxiety about money, rising out of boyhood pain, must have been almost unendurable, cruelly beyond his control. Ironically, that childhood, which messed him up permanently, took place only a few miles from Beatrice. While she was in her dacha outside Odessa having tea with Hannah, little Meyer was at the Odessa fruit market where his mother, named Manye, wrapped oranges in tissue paper in a dank basement and sold them on the street.

The impoverished widow of a prosperous produce hauler, Manye was a cagey, indomitable survivor, a strong-willed woman who had refused to marry the man her parents picked and, when she did marry, defied Orthodox tradition and refused to shave her head. In my father's stories of growing up, the family lived in poverty in an apartment impossibly crowded with himself, three sisters, a grandfather, and a bed-ridden grandmother who sat up in bed with mixing bowls and whisks and did the family cooking—"Hey, bring me some more flour and while you're walking it wouldn't hurt if you got the salt." There was no room for Manye's second husband and their son, Harry, so they lived together downstairs. To further ease the crowding, Manye sent her eldest daughter to relatives in Brooklyn and put little Meyer in the Jewish orphanage until she could fulfill her dream and embark with her children for America.

They settled in the Brownsville section of Brooklyn and Manye sold fruit from a cart and cleaned fish in a market while the three girls sewed in a sweatshop. Meyer was the anointed student, the member who would go into a profession and lift the family fortunes. In those days the only professions open to Jewish boys were doctor, lawyer, or dentist, and Manye decided he would be "mayn zun," the doctor. What my grandmother wanted, she got. He paid for medical school with a loan from the Hebrew Loan Society and worked for the BMT subway as a conductor at night. When he was fired for falling asleep, he went back and got another conductor's job under another name.

Judging from the number of times he described two moments from that past, they must have been burned into his psyche. One was the time when he was hospitalized with appendicitis, and, unable to work on the BMT subway, he could not pay the next medical school tuition bill. He lay in the hospital night after night after night, sobbing with desperation. Finally, at the last minute, a wealthy classmate gave him the money anonymously.

The other took place in the Odessa market, when he was very young. He was there with Manye when a policeman, because she did not have a vendor's license, confiscated her small stock of oranges. Manye kept clutching at the man, wailing, "No, no, no," and I think that in some powerful mingling of memory and fear, the helpless cry always rang in my father's head.

When I was ten years old, Beatrice could no longer bear her life. She took action. She went down to Meyer's office when he was not there and raised the prices on the card posted in the waiting room: how much for a visit, how much for an injection, for a house call, etc. There must have been a battle beyond anything before, because when I came home from school, my mother had put the house in order and was gone, leaving Barbara and me a note: "Be good and I love you both. I'll come and get you when I can." That was absolute devastation, absolute emptiness. Home was no longer home —it was as though she had died. My father lowered his prices again and his mother Manye moved right in.

She was now a heavy old lady dressed in black, with sensible shoes and ankles wrapped in Ace bandages. She used a cane with a silver handle and at the neck of her dress wore a diamond pin with the initials M. M. I absolutely *hated* her. I remember we went for a drive and she was sitting in the front seat—my mother's place—which made me furious. Barbara and I were in the back and, I guess, being silly or asking for ice cream or fooling. She turned around and lifted her cane, threatening us, and said, "Keep quiet back there." I thought, *Oh, something's very wrong. Got to get fatso out of here and get my mother back.* But we did not know where my mother was.

Uncle Alex was the mediator and she returned home a week later. I came out of school and way down the street I could see her blue coat with brass buttons on it—and I rushed down the steps and hugged and hugged her and was so glad, so glad, so glad. I immediately told her all the terrible things Grandma had done, which she loved hearing.

But she came home defeated, came home believing that her only other alternative was a menial job, the fate she had married to escape and which would mean she could never have Barbara and me. Probably she was right, and I knew then that I was not going to let that happen to me. I was going to be what was called in those days a career girl and would never, never let myself be dependent on anybody—and I never have.

I wanted to be like my mother's sister, Aunt Alice, who

had the best life of any woman I knew—an interior decorator and art gallery owner, self-sufficient in fields she loved—a strong, killer lady who not only knew how to survive but did it with elegance. It was Alice who achieved genuine affluence and my mother hated her for that. Forbidden by Hannah to marry the impecunious man she loved, Alice did what was expected and found a wealthy Jewish banker named Solomon Thenen and had a Park Avenue apartment full of antiques and paintings, had silver bread-and-butter plates on her table, and gave lavish parties attended by people in the arts—the pianist Nadia Rubenstein, Mrs. Ira Gershwin, Paul Robeson, the artist Stuart Davis. And Alice had love affairs, one with a famous violinist who used to play to her over the telephone and another with the impresario Sol Hurok. My mother called the friends leeches and losers and Alice a whore and a tramp—but, of course, my mother was jealous.

Solomon Thenen never protested Alice's affairs, but I remember, when he died, she found he had quietly cut her out of his will. She was penniless in this huge Park Avenue apartment surrounded by Vlaminck, Utrillo, Dubuffet, Chagall, Sisley, Modigliani, and Mary Cassatt. But she had made it to Park Avenue splendor and she was not going to give it up. She rented the apartment, moved into a small hotel, became an interior decorator, and opened an art gallery. Within a year she was back in the apartment, still an interior decorator and renting her extra bedrooms to little Russian immigrant ladies she claimed were relatives. Sometimes, during a formal dinner party, one of these ladies in a robe and slippers would creep through the dining room murmuring, "Excuse me," and go into the kitchen to cook an egg.

Aunt Alice always had the trips to Europe on ocean liners and the face-lifts and the culture, the invitations to every art opening. The week she died, she went to an opening at the Guggenheim Museum and told me, "I saw Jackie Onassis

there. She looks terrible." Alice, dying of leukemia, was saying, "Jackie looked terrible."

I think in my family there is a strain of determination and
independence that came down through Hannah to me and to
Alice. My mother did not get it. She was very bright, but was
everlastingly mortified by her lack of education and allowed
herself to remain dependent and unhappy.

And yet, my parents really did fulfill the immigrant
dream. They built something together, moved up together,
gave each other what they needed. He gave her status in the
community—the doctor's wife. In public she never called him
Meyer; it was always "The doctor. The doctor. The doctor."

I believe he loved my mother, loved her all his life. She
was the unattainable woman he could never really own but
could be proud of, could be proud to be seen with on his arm,
proud of what she brought into his life. She gave him the
gracious home, the setting—even though it was a facade, even
though he kept saying to us, over and over, "I wouldn't mind
being poor. I'm only working for you. I could live simply. I
don't need all this."

That's why my father has always been such a puzzle to
me. My mother's mink coat was never returned to the furrier
and two weeks later he was saying, "Look at the new coat I
bought Betty. Doesn't she look great." After she died, when
people came to visit, he would say to me, "Be sure you show
them around the house." Even though he was intimidated by
it, he wanted the elegance, gloried in the proof that he had
made it in America.

I identify completely with my parents' terror, the desperation that obsessed them and tore them apart. I live with it
myself daily: the fear that you will be thrown back to where
you started. My father taught it to me and my mother taught it
to me, and I had my own lessons. I lie awake at night thinking

about it, feeling exposed, vulnerable—but feeling again the gratitude that I have what my parents missed in life—a way to be happy.

I sometimes think of the day I discovered it. In the gymnasium of Brooklyn Ethical Culture School I was a kitty cat in the prekindergarten play, a hit in a major role performed in front of a semicircle of chairs filled with grades K through three and teachers and parents. On my head was a kitty cat hat made of bunny fur with pink felt ears. Afterward, wanting to continue my happiness forever, I refused to take it off. I wore it home, wore it at dinner and in my bath, and wore it in bed that night, sitting there feeling especially pretty in my silk pajamas from Paris—ice-blue, with a lace collar and lace cuffs and crystal buttons.

I was waiting, very excited, for my father to bring up guests from the dinner party downstairs. I knew they would make a fuss over me, saying, "Aren't you darling," and be *really* impressed because on my blond curls was my kitty cat hat. I wanted to experience again the feelings of that afternoon in front of the audience—the ecstatic sense that I was a pussycat because grown-ups were accepting me as a pussycat —the sense that I could say, "I want to be somebody wonderful and walk out on stage and be the princess," and the world would say, "Yes, you are the princess." That day I found a place where I could put aside real life and rewrite the rules, redo my life.

2

I AM MYSTIFIED by people who tell me they just fell into show business, almost by accident. That contradicts everything I know about becoming a performer—certainly a comedian. You must want it so badly you will suffer anything, *anything,* just to get on a stage in front of people—be willing, again and again, to pick yourself up and keep going after you have been hit on the head by a sledgehammer. I see young comedians walk on the stage and know they will probably never make it— you either do or do not have a comedy mind, whatever that is, maybe a heightened sense of the ridiculous and the absurdity of life—but I know they will persist and persist. We are all crazy and crazed.

I think the seed of that obsession often lies in some moment like mine in the kitty hat when we realize we do not *have* to be ourselves and glimpse the secret garden of show business, the haven we think will heal our lives. I was sure that within those flowered walls I would no longer be a wimp, be the nerd in every group. I would become truly beautiful, bathed in glamour and adoration from my fans as I moved among my brilliant peers, scattering pearls before swans. When the telephone rang, it would be Laurence Olivier on the line.

The conventional diagnosis of comics holds that they are hypersensitive, angry, paranoid people who feel somehow cheated of life's goodies and are laughing to keep from crying. I agree, but think comedy is more aggressive than that. It is a medium for revenge. We can deflate and punish the pomposity and the rejection which hurt us. Comedy is power. We can be in control, can get the love and admiration and attention we bottomlessly crave—and get it from two directions. People want to be around somebody who entertains them—but simultaneously they fear us. The only weapon more formidable than humor is a gun.

My sense of being cheated by fate was all the more acute because I had tasted princesshood in prekindergarten. I had big brown eyes and long blond hair and strangers used to stop my mother on the street to say, "My God, I've never seen a child like that." It used to give my sister a complex and my mother would whisper to them, "Say something nice about the older one." When I first went to kindergarten, the teacher pinned a note on my frock saying, "Take a look at her," and sent me down to the principal's office. I was allowed into every school play, even the ones that were performed only in front of the blackboard, and won the role of the healthy tooth during National Health Week—and really *felt* that tooth. Those few years were the only time in my life when I truly lived what became THE DREAM, the only time I truly knew that I was beautiful and a star.

Then, in second grade at Ethical Culture, I was obliterated by normality. My tonsils were taken out and everything went wrong—the hair turned brown, the nose grew, the body inflated, and Little Miss Pretty became Little Miss Piggy. I was never fat to the point where people went "Oh, ugh," but the person I thought I was disappeared under chunky thighs and chunky little arms, and nobody was going "Oooh, let's take another look." That really must have whacked me out.

My mother would have saved me a lot of pain if she had told me, "Don't eat. Lose twenty pounds and you'll look great." Instead, I was loved at home and considered a good girl when I put food in my mouth. The more I ate, the cuter I became in my parents' eyes: she's adorable, watch her bloat, look at the stretch marks around her mouth. And then my mother, telling me I looked fine, would put me into my sister's old tan bathing suit at the country club and send me out on the beach, a girl already raw with insecurity. My mother *must* have thought, *Look at those thighs walking toward the water.*

When I was eleven, at the start of puberty, my mother decided it was time to change to a less progressive school—she found me writing "hows" for house. I was transferred into the seventh grade at Adelphi Academy. Before, at Brooklyn Ethical Culture, I had kept a social position among my little friends, but now I was inserting myself into a new, already frozen pecking order. I remember the first day, my heart hurting with fear as I walked up those steps, wearing a pink and green wool skirt and pink and green plaid jerkin. I must have looked like a triple-scoop ice cream cone. In the play yard at recess, one of the kids called me "fat tub of lard" and I heard "fat, fat, the water rat." I located a pebble on the ground and concentrated on it very, very hard because I did not want to cry and let them see how much I hurt.

I understood then that henceforth I was a nerd, one of the outsiders I had known at Ethical, always in the background, never one of the girls giggling together, always the one they passed a note through: "Pass this on"—"Oh, okay." When they chose up teams, they would say, "If I take Joan, you gotta take Mary," and the other person would say, "Well, I don't know if I want Mary that much." I thought if these kids talked to my friends at Ethical and found out I was really okay, was good at art and acting, maybe . . . But I realized I was stuck as the class fat kid and realized they were right—I was fat, so I hated myself even more, seeing myself as this huge thing with knees that could have fed China for a year. I felt as though everything I ate went instantly to my thighs—like a squirrel storing food in its cheeks—and to this day, no matter how thin I am, that is my image of myself.

Now that I was at Adelphi, my father drove me each

morning and often delivered me to school late. In front of the
entire student body I had to walk up the three steps to the
teacher's desk and bend over and sign the late book with my
rear end toward the room—and I knew it was a big rear end
and everybody was looking at the nerd's hips. I kept trying to
walk in sideways, because you can suck in your stomach, but I
defy anybody to suck in hips. After about a week I told my
mother I was miserable, told her that when I had to change
into my gym uniform in front of everybody, my thighs were
twice as big as Marilyn Abrams's hips and Jane Weissman's
whole body could fit in my one arm. She told me, "When they
find out you are a lovely girl from a lovely background, everything will turn around." Unfortunately, nobody ever checked
our house.

In the first three years in Adelphi, from the seventh grade
through high school freshman, I had almost no girlfriends. At
lunchtime, I never knew whether there was a place for me at a
table and always put my tray down so tentatively—not the way
Marilyn Abrams or Jane Weissman did, or Frances Rothman,
who could put her tray down anywhere and people were
happy to have her. Boys were distant, impossible mysteries. I
knew only one thing about them. I knew I had nothing they
wanted, that no boy was ever waiting for me, no valentine was
ever in the box with my name on it. I tried to convince myself
that looks were not important, that what mattered was the
inner me, but boys did not like my personality either. I was
doomed to yearn from afar, writing in my diary, "Eliot sits
near Delia in science. Of all the luck! I sit near Alice." Then,
cruel as only kids can be, Eliot wrote in my yearbook, "Ashes
to ashes, dust to dust; Joan is a girl with a forty-inch waist."
Well, that ruins your yearbook—you cannot show it to anybody.

But my great love—hopeless, passionate—was the school
athlete named Salvatore Granforte, who did not know I was
alive—unless you count a game of ticktacktoe one day at

lunch. I wrote his name on my schoolbooks and gushed to my diary, "Today Jane whispered in my ear, 'Who is Salvatore?' Oh, I just felt butterflies. All I said was, 'Just a boy.' But my heart beat a mile a minute."

School dances were always disasters. When my father arrived home from delivering me, he never took off his shoes or undressed. He waited on red alert, knowing that within an hour there would be a call saying, "Come get me." But I was a stupid optimist and each week I would forget my awkwardness, the sick misery in the stomach that afflicts nerds, and would get all dressed up again for the next dance, hoping this time I would be acceptable—only to be taught, yet again, that I was still a pig.

I remember in particular Jane Weissman's party. She was the hot girl at Adelphi, an apprentice vamp who played the guitar and was thin and had long hair that flipped under and wore lipstick and deodorant. She invited the whole class to a costume party and my mother decided I should go as a Russian girl. She put me, four feet eight and 120 pounds, into a red turtleneck and dirndl skirt and embroidered an old hat with pearls and ribbons that hung down the back. We found boots. She *really* thought I was going to a costume party and I absolutely thought I was going to be fine in that getup.

Of course, on the big night everybody else was in togas and skimpy little Daisy Mae costumes—and I marched in as Mother Russia. Nobody danced with me. When we played spin the bottle, I went into the dark room with a boy who right away said, "Let's forget this," and the next time in the room another boy took my nose and twisted it, which makes you realize you are not attractive. So I sat in Jane's kitchen and played with her dogs and called my father to come get me.

Ironically, all this time my sister and I, like two Brooklyn Brenda Fraziers, were being groomed by my mother to attract the perfect upper-class boys into the perfect WASP marriages. We were instructed how to descend the stairs with grace and elegance when we joined our admiring gentleman caller in the front hall. She taught us how to pour tea and set a dinner party table and how to eat with class, where to put our knife and fork when at rest: the knife over the fork, and when finished, side by side at twelve o'clock with the sharp edge of the knife toward the fork. She told us you could always tell about people's background by the way they buttered their bread: always break it on the butter plate, never paint it in the air on the palm. She would say, "You should be able to sit down with the Queen of England and not worry."

She gave us rules for dressing: When you are fully dressed, remove one piece of jewelry and you will be correct. She took us to Mr. Geiger's elocution studio to learn how to read aloud with expression so that we could impress with our speaking voices. She told us, "There is nothing a young man likes better than a lovely girl playing the piano or violin," and put Barbara to work on the piano and me on the violin. But to this day my collarbone is sore where I pressed down on the violin with my chin, and after six months I was switched to the piano.

I would like to say I came from a house filled with music. In fact, I came from a house filled with scales. My mother was content as long as she heard sound, so I would put the comic book in the middle of the music sheet and play scales, but if I became too engrossed in *Wonder Woman* and *Sheena of the Jungle*, she called out, "It's awfully quiet down there."

"I'm just looking up music."

My mother sent me to dancing classes and, fortunately, there was another girl in the class who was also a nerd and we developed a little strategy. We pretended we had polio— limped across the dance floor, limped to the ladies' room, limped to the coat room, so there was a very understandable reason why boys did not ask us to dance. We had polio.

But the loneliness of being an outsider, the trying and not knowing how, the hopeless sense of clumsiness, the knowledge that I was not as good as, that I was less than—all the anguish did not shrivel me. I escaped into the secret garden. I understood that acting could get me through everything. Ever since the kitty cat, I had known that whether I was thin or fat, whether or not my family was fighting, whether I had friends or did not have friends—all my problems would vanish on a stage. So I had THE DREAM, a permeating confidence that I had been born a great dramatic actress and my classmates would be sorry they had not appreciated me. I once wrote in my diary, "One day when I'm famous, I'll laugh in their faces when the boys ask me to dance and please God don't let that be too far off."

I was dreaming even in the first grade at Ethical Culture —always volunteering to carry any note downstairs to the office, because then I could come back through the auditorium and duck into the costume room just for a minute— before I had to *run* upstairs again. I remember a big room, probably because I was so little, and hanging along the walls were rows of clothes which the older girls used for school plays. I stood there running my hands over the costumes— given-away dresses, I suppose, from the twenties and thirties. I remember velvets and satins and the smell—old, musty, but glamorous, like blond ladies in jodhpurs. It was magic to me, the glorious answer to what I could be, the answer to happiness.

I pursued my acting apprenticeship in every school play. At age ten I played Pandora in Pandora's box and, when I opened the lid of the box with my back to the audience and my face hidden, I knew instinctively, "No, no, no." Miss Befler had definitely misdirected that magic moment. When I saw Margaret O'Brien in *Journey for Margaret*, we were the same age and I was very upset that she was up there on the screen and I was sitting with my mother. I thought I could have been

Natalie Wood in a second in *Miracle on 34th Street* and a knife is
still turning in my heart. I was very jealous of all the child
actresses then—Peggy Ann Garner, Elizabeth Taylor, and
even Joan Evans with her little squint eyes, who never made it.
When I was eight, I stole a thin red book with gold letters
saying *Your Career in Show Business* from the Brooklyn Public
Library, slipping it under my coat. It was instantly my bible
and I virtually memorized it, hour upon hour up on the top
floor in the Brooklyn house in a sort of playroom where
nobody went, where nobody would see me and guess my
dreams and laugh.

I knew the book was going to help me tremendously. It
had sections on radio, film, and Broadway, and I noticed the
actresses in the radio pictures were less attractive, so I projected myself right into those pictures and knew I was definitely going to be one of those women in the wonderful suits
and the big hats and stockings with seams, holding a script by
the big square microphone topped by WOR. But I also followed the book's advice on how to get into the movies. It
listed the address of MGM in Hollywood, so I mailed off a
picture of myself, frame and all, that my mother kept on the
piano in the living room. She spent days asking, "Has anybody seen the picture of Joan, the one in the antique frame?"
I did not tell her that Joan had gone to Hollywood where, at
that very moment, they must be saying, "Hey, guys, I think
we've got something here!"

My first collision with the chill truths of show business—
the first time THE DREAM was doused by reality—came
when I was twelve and sent to Camp Kinni Kinnic, which I still
think is Indian for "soak the parents." It was owned and run
by Judge Jeanette Brill, a stocky woman with short, dark hair
whom we had to call Aunt Jeanette, and by her chubby, balding husband, "Daddy" Brill. Mayor Fiorello LaGuardia had
appointed her magistrate of the family court of New York and
she went around being a great liberal and union activist—a

legend in her own eyes. She was important at the Brooklyn Child Guidance Clinic, where my mother did volunteer work, and they became friendly, a relationship which Bea, who always cultivated people she considered above her, valued enormously.

The camp was on "beautiful Lake St. Catherine" in Vermont and I hated every minute of it, hated the raft test and barely got to the raft. I hated nature walks and coming back with bites on my ankles and I was terrified of the hound-and-hare races, always sure I would get lost running through the woods looking for stupid clues on trees. I hated living six in a cabin and sharing the bathroom and hated having the counselor come around every night and say, "Have you had your BM today?" If you had not, they spooned out castor oil, which I hated.

That camp left such scars on me. They had a continuing color war—all of us divided into the brown team or the buff team, and on the night of the song contest, thinking of myself as the next Patti Page, I was singing my heart out by the camp fire with my team. Suddenly the counselor walked up to me and, loud enough for everybody to hear, said, "Molinsky."

"Yes?"

"Do you want the buff team to win?"

"*Yes!*"

"Then don't sing."

I felt the blush start at my ankles and crawl up my body until it appeared above my midi blouse and flooded through my face into my scalp and ended at the back of my neck. Ever afterward, whenever I had to sing, I always heard those words. But that night there was one great consolation. I knew that soon I was going to be a major personage, an object of awe and envy, because surely I would be cast as Snow White in the camp play.

Then, without any warning, a cast list was posted in the dining cabin. It said, "Snow White: Phyllis Bernstein." I read

down the list. "Dopey: Joan Molinsky." Dopey! He did not
have a single line, not a *word!* There were no showstoppers for
Dopey. It was my first major rejection, my first blow from the
horrors of casting, my first experience with a hurt unique to
show business. My most precious possession, my talent, was
being ignored—and ignored so unfairly by an adult world I
could not control. I knew why Aunt Jeanette had broken all
the rules, why there had been no auditions. Phyllis Bernstein's
father had donated a new curtain for the camp stage.

Emotionally, it was more frustration than a twelve-year-
old could contain, and my reaction was overpowering rage
with no sane way to release it. Scared to death, I set out to
organize the camp, agitating everywhere like a furious hummingbird—down at the dock, around the flagpole, out behind
the canoe rack, righteously passing the word—"It's not fair!
There should be auditions." I discovered I could be a leader
and my own cabin actually went on strike—"Tools down!"
Badminton rackets were placed on the court.

The camp was in an uproar and Judge Brill telephoned
my mother and told her, "Joan is a born leader, but you have
got to watch her. She could become either another Truman—
or a Hitler." Then the judge summoned me and said, "If you
are unhappy with the camp and the camp's policies, you may
leave. We have spoken to your parents and tomorrow there is
somebody traveling to New York." She was sending John L.
Lewis home to mother. When the union hit her camp, Aunt
Jeanette, the great union organizer of the thirties, the woman
who stood in front of sweatshops, who threw water on the
Triangle Shirtwaist Factory fire, who held the typewriter for
John Dos Passos—wanted no part of negotiations. We were
not called in for confabs. She broke the strike.

The next thing I knew, I was on a train to New York,
mortified but acutely disturbed by a trait I could not understand but which stayed with me the rest of my life—I could be
a leader, able to turn the camp upside down, but was unable

to be likable and have close friends. I was also aware, once again, that money was important, that if you had money, you could be Snow White. For comfort, I returned into my righteous rage—*Damn it, there* should *have been auditions!* And I told myself that in a few years, when the movie starring me was shown at Camp Kinni Kinnic, Judge Brill would be very, very sorry.

When my mother met me at Grand Central Station, I felt awful. I had let her down, disappointed her for the first time, humiliated her by being kicked out of her friend's camp. But I underestimated my mother's loyalty to me. She must have thought I was right, because she never saw Judge Brill socially again.

The only way I could feel good about myself, feel I was a winner, feel liked, and in control, was by overlaying reality with a fantasy world. Right through all the bad years I could emerge from my lumpy body like a beautiful butterfly and take flight into major melodramas, Academy Award caliber, in front of my bathroom mirror with the door locked: The Nazis are out to get us—hide the plans in your shoe and keep walking across the border; take this basket of eggs and pretend you're a little French girl—but for God's sake, don't talk; they'll know you're an American. In the mirror I would look brave and innocent; but there was death behind those eyes. At school, for days and days, I would be very cautious because *they* thought I was just a schoolgirl. They could not know the truth—until the news hit the headlines: BROOKLYN GIRL BRINGS PLANS TO ALLIES. MGM SIGNS HER FOR LIFE STORY, STARRING HER!

I allowed only one person into my dream world, Ellen Gossard, a little girl I met at camp who also wanted to be a movie star and shared my fantasies, which meant maybe they *could* happen. Together we prepared ourselves for stardom, practicing curtain calls, bowing not too low and with a certain humility mixed with warmth. We practiced giving autographs, rehearsing our mingled graciousness and condescension.

Clearly, I had to change my name. It sounded foreign to me, ugly, ordinary, the name of a plodder, loser woman. Joan Molinsky in *King Lear* just did not work. And worst of all, she was myself and I did not want to be myself. So I had J. Sondra Meredith stamped on pencils and printed on the top of cheap stationery and, with Ellen, made mock-ups of *Photoplay* and *Life* and *Look* with our pictures on the cover: J. SONDRA MEREDITH—HOLLYWOOD'S YOUNGEST WUNDERKIND. We wrote articles about ourselves: J. SONDRA MEREDITH DATING FARLEY GRANGER. For Richard Conte I stopped eating that extra doughnut and I made a Richard Conte scrapbook, drew myself into pictures beside him, and wrote captions, "She's young, but I love her and I'll wait."

There were obviously millions of moviestruck little girls buying *Photoplay* then and dreaming of stardom and Laurence Olivier. So how was I different, why did I press on and actually enter show business? The answer is the distance between a dream and an obsession. Performing became a psychological need at age fourteen, when I first experienced the full, intoxicating rush that happens onstage and all my fantasies were confirmed.

Whatever made me a leader at Camp Kinni Kinnic also happened at Adelphi Academy in my sophomore year and I became a doer with manic energy—but still not acknowledged by the other kids. To them I was permanently an outsider, a nerd doing nerd activities. I was never a cheerleader, and nobody ever stood up and said, "I nominate Joan Molinsky."

I started a school newspaper called *The Oracle*, which is in existence today—and made myself its cartoonist. I wrote for the school magazine, *The Adelphian*, and was on the yearbook staff. I organized the class plays and did the posters. Most important, I revived a discontinued school tradition, an an-

nual variety show called *The Cavalcade* and, of course, made
sure I was a featured, solo performer.

In a library book I found a monologue called *Keeping a
Seat at a Benefit* I thought was funny—a woman trying to reserve a seat for her husband and every time she looked
around, somebody sat down in it. Though it would be the first
time I was ever alone on a stage, I never had an instant's
nervousness and could not wait to get out there with my two
chairs. And then, performing, I could hear the wonderful
quiet that settles in when you are doing something well and
seriously—total silence, cotton-soft—broken by flashes of
laughter in exactly the right places. Suddenly this chubby girl
who had never been worth much attention was mesmerizing
and manipulating the entire school and faculty and all the
parents. For a moment I was the supreme princess, somebody
dazzling, somebody else. That night I wrote in my diary, "I
felt my character and didn't know I was Joan Molinsky until I
got offstage and recuperated. Golly, I feel wonderful!"

Then one day at age fifteen I was actually given a glimpse
into the secret garden—boosted up to the top of the wall,
clinging to the vines, knuckles white, arching my neck to peer
just for a moment into that dream of glamour. A little girl and
her mother took me to see Ray Bolger in *Where's Charley?* on
Broadway. Afterward we waited at the stage door for the
Saturday matinee ritual when Mrs. Bolger, sleek and beautiful, came out and invited the small herd of excited children
with parents to come backstage. Trembling with excitement, I
passed the doorman's stall on the left, with its glass box hung
with keys and the bulletin board a collage of pinned messages.
Straight ahead I could see the ropes and flats of backstage. I
felt that I was walking on sacred ground, invited into the
Vatican. I was Dorothy entering the Emerald City.

A moment later I found myself actually backstage and

everything was exactly as it should be, the scuffed wood floor, the raking wood buttresses bracing the canvas scenery flats, the worn side curtains, the slightly frayed, greasy ropes disappearing toward the cavernous roof where other flats, more sheets of make-believe, waited to descend, everything enveloped in the musty perfume of no air and no sunlight. And suddenly, there was Ray Bolger, very thin, exactly right in his yellowish makeup, the first actor I had ever seen up close, the man I had just watched onstage, and he was talking to us, inviting us into his dressing room.

We huddled just inside the door and I tingled at the sight of costumes on a rack with a man readying them for the next show. Just as there should be, light bulbs ringed the dressing table mirror and laid out on white towels were tubes and jars of real makeup that was being used and scenting the room with greasepaint—and there was a can of Crisco, which he explained was for removing the makeup because it was purer than cold cream. On one wall, smiling directly at me, was a seemingly life-sized picture of Ray Bolger as the scarecrow in *The Wizard of Oz.* So everything was exactly right here, too, and I felt as though I had died and was in heaven now with the man who had been the scarecrow.

Then Ray Bolger invited us onto the stage where the overhead lights were still on and I was afraid to breathe, afraid to say anything or do anything that might call attention to me, because maybe I was really not allowed to be there, maybe the tour was only for children with their own parents. I lurked in the rear of the group and looked at the furniture from the last scene and the seedy back of the curtain and thought that twenty minutes earlier I had been out in front of it—and when it rose again, the magic would start again.

The feel of finally being onstage was what I had expected —mystical, beyond understanding, alien to my life yet intrinsic to my life. I was the ugly duckling who saw the swans and discovered where she belonged. I felt absolutely at home and knew that if I ever became part of the theater, my life would be right; I could forget everything, have my friends, have my moments. My little girl's heart was bursting with the dream that one day I would not need Ray Bolger's permission to stand on this stage. I would be there for no other reason than because I was myself.

Of course, I fell hopelessly in love with Ray Bolger and my mother let me return almost every Saturday afternoon and wait at the stage door. I went backstage so many times he began nodding to me and saying, "Hi. Hi." My heart would lurch and I would answer, "Hi," very softly. But Mrs. Bolger was always there, blonde in her autumn haze mink stole. I was going to push her right off the stage: MRS. BOLGER KILLED BY CHUBBETTE. NINTH GRADER SITS ON HER TO DEATH.

Certain by now that I had real talent, stimulated by the *Where's Charley?* experience, I was developing a determination that added blood and bone to my obsession and gave me courage to move beyond my bathroom mirror onto the national scene. I entered the *Photoplay* acting contest—"Discover the Stars of Tomorrow." In a glass booth at the Paramount Theater arcade, I recorded a twenty-five-cent record of a Shelley Winters speech from *A Place in the Sun* when she tells Montgomery Clift that she is going to have a baby and he kills her in a rowboat. I did just one reading on this little twenty-five-cent record and the booth was not really soundproof, so in the background on the record you could hear the shooting gallery: "Bang, bang, bang."

I was picked to be one of the ten finalists and I went into the New York office and there were the nine others—thin girls with tight dresses and great legs and beautiful hair. In front of five judges ranged in front of me, I did Shelley Winters's "there's gonna be a little strangeah" speech—"I can't swim; *glug, glug, glug*"—and another speech I picked to show my

range, Henry V's speech before the battle of Agincourt—
"This day is call'd the feast of Crispian: He that outlives this
day, and comes safe home . . . ."

I came in second against those sexy girls from all over the
country. I am *very* proud of that. I won a year's subscription to
Photoplay and a watch, which is long gone. But I keep in my
drawer upstairs one of those dumb little medallions that I
stamped out for myself in the arcade: "Good luck on your
audition."

Then it happened! I was *discovered!* Well, sort of. It happened because of an acting class I joined. The sister of a
friend was a regular on a kid quiz show called *Juvenile Jury* and
she studied at the Edith Becton School of the Theater in Miss
Becton's huge apartment on Riverside Drive in Manhattan.
Without telling my parents, I took a subway up there from
Brooklyn and auditioned, reading Amy Lowell's *Patterns* with
tremendous teenage fervor. I was accepted and twice a week
for more than a year my mother actually let me travel back and
forth alone by subway after school.

This was astounding and unprecedented. My sister and I
were never allowed to go anywhere alone. Even when I played
with a friend in the neighborhood, my mother delivered me
and picked me up. When I went to the movies at the Paramount Theater with another girl, my mother dropped me off
and when I came out, to my surprise, there she would be by
chance coming down the sidewalk saying, "Isn't this lucky. We
can go home together." It took me a long time to figure out
that she had followed me into the theater, watched the movie,
and slipped out just before I did.

She must have seen Miss Becton's school as something
like an eighteenth-century girl doing needlepoint, part of my
training in womanly arts, an exercise that would teach me
some much-needed poise. And though she had no inkling that

her daughter was determined to be Jennifer Jones, she must have seen my passion, seen that she could not say no, that the battle to stop me would be too horrendous. And she loved me. To pay for the first class, she even slipped me ten dollars from her precious stash in the antique jewelry box on her bureau.

After the first class I never paid again, arriving each time panicked that Miss Becton would demand her tuition and then I would have to leave. That perceptive lady—small and blonde and softish like an old ingenue—must have sensed there was no money and tacitly in her mind made me her scholarship kid. She must have sensed, too, that those classes were everything to me, the only time I had any confidence as a person. Outside of that apartment I was a very immature fifteen, extremely sheltered, still roller skating in front of the house, tongue-tied with boys. That year, before a movie date with a boy, I prepared a list of the things we could talk about and on the way home, when I finished the list, I said, "Well, that's it," and froze into silence.

But in Miss Becton's classes, doing scenes from Shakespeare and *The Children's Hour,* I was the hot girl, more than holding my own against semiprofessional show kids who did little gigs as Broadway walk-ons and radio voices—teen-queens who arrived for class with composite photographs and makeup kits in hatboxes—while I came in with arms full of schoolbooks. Miss Becton was taking me seriously as an actress and she had a very big credit hanging on her wall—a picture of Patrice Wymore, who had been her student and had married Errol Flynn. Miss Becton told the class that they were looking for extras for a movie called *Mr. Universe* with Jack Carson, Vince Edwards, Janis Paige, and "Slapsie" Maxie Rosenbloom, the light-heavyweight boxing champ of 1930 turned actor. I played hooky from school, went to a hotel in Manhattan, applied, and got it. When I told my mother I was in a movie, she not only let me do it, but made it into a private

conspiracy, keeping it from my father and telephoning the
school and saying I was sick. For a week and a half at the crack
of dawn I got on a subway in Brooklyn alone and rode to
Grand Central where I met another girl extra, and we rode all
the way to the Sunnyside Arena in Queens.

When I walked onto that set, I was so excited, my skin
tingled. Somebody had built my fantasy and built it life-sized
—there was my camera and my make-believe set and we were
all going to play extras now. Coming from the sunlight into
the arena, I saw in the middle of the sudden darkness a brilliant pool of light, the heart of the make-believe, and I had the
incredible permission to join that light—particularly thrilling
because it was adult magic, the alluring, unapproachable
adult world till then off limits to me.

In my home children were seen, not heard, and I never
had permission to mix into adult conversations and was segregated at the children's table at family parties like Thanksgiving, or was exiled upstairs during dinner parties and waited
for somebody to come up and say hello. The closest I came to
adult opera or theater was the program my mother brought
home and gave me the next morning. My life was ruled by
permissions, sometimes granted, often refused—no sloppy
Joe sweater, no dirty saddle shoes, no chesterfield coat, no
makeup or adult clothes until age seventeen, no staying up
late. I was wildly impatient to grow up, could not wait to run
my own life.

But that turned out to be one of my fantasies. I have
never escaped my child's body and mind and still think I need
permission to enter my show business world. I am still anx-
ious every time I arrive at *The Tonight Show*, which, like all of
show business, is locked and guarded and there is a list and
you are not allowed inside unless you are on the list. When I
pull up to the guard box at NBC, I am still expecting them to
say that I cannot come through, that my name is not on the
list, that I do not belong in that world—that I am no different

from the civilians ahead of me who are being asked to turn
around and go back. But then I pull up and the sentry says,
"Hi," and I say, "Hi," and the iron gate swings open—and I
think, *Fooled 'em again,* and know that this is the only place in
the world I want to be.

Mr. Universe was a wrestling movie and the assistant director was distributing the extras around the arena, but I was not
going to sit still. When it came to movie cameras, I was an old
pro. During those years of fantasizing, there had always been
a camera right there in the bathroom filming me—or following me home from school or at my piano lesson. Cameras
were part of my life and I knew where this one was aimed
every second, and I was right there in its lens, sure I was going
to be spotted and whisked away to Hollywood. My chosen
position was close to the stars, so in this scene of an 11:00 P.M.
wrestling match, right behind Janis Paige and Jack Carson is a
sixteen-year-old child *screaming*—screaming because she is a
great actress and sky high with happiness and about to become Vivien Leigh.

The first day on the set I was dressed in one of the short-
sleeved nylon sweaters—barter from a patient who had a factory and my father did not care that it accentuated my every
bulge. But on that day the tight yellow nylon made "Slapsie"
Maxie turn around. Young, fat, unattractive, must have been
his kind of woman, because he came right over, saying,
"Hullo, hullo." "Slapsie" always repeated everything. "Do
you wanna go ta lunch? Yu wanna go ta lunch?" He had
cauliflower ears and a punched-in face with a broken nose, but
I felt right away that under the thickened skin was a gentle
soul, nothing to be afraid of—and I felt sorry for him. I sensed
he was no longer playing with a full deck, because I had seen
people walk up to him and say, "Hello, 'Slapsie,'" and he

would say, "Hello, hello," and they would walk away. But I really had lunch with him because he was somebody famous.

However, I was not dumb; I made him take some other girls to lunch too. On the way to the restaurant I let him hold my hand with his rough, calloused sausage fingers because, after all, he was a star in the film and he said, "See, it doesn't hurt. See, it doesn't hurt." We ate in a nearby pizza joint, a dark place with a bar and jukebox and some booths and I deliberately sat across from him in the booth. He talked only to me: "I'm a fighter. I'm a fighter. You know what I mean? You know what I mean? Bet you never heard this. Bet you never heard this." At sixteen I was the brighter of the two.

He did it every day, always the same, always holding my hand and asking the same questions, "Ja ever kissed a guy? Ja ever kissed a guy?" But I think he actually took this little group of kids to lunch because he only felt comfortable with children. And I know it is awful, but it was fun saying I knew "Slapsie" Maxie Rosenbloom, fun being in the inner sanctum, fun getting a little deferential treatment—"Leave her alone. She's Slapsie's girl." And it was a free lunch.

After *Mr. Universe* was over, when I was back at school, "Slapsie" called me at home and got my mother. "Hello, Ma. Hello, Ma."

My mother: "Who is this?"

" 'Slapsie' Maxie Rosenbloom. 'Slapsie' Maxie Rosenbloom. You like gefilte fish? You like gefilte fish, Ma?"

"What do you want?"

"I want to talk to Joanie. Want to talk to Joanie."

"You pervert. You sick, disgusting pervert. Don't you ever call my daughter again!"

"You like knishes?"

Slam! The first of many romances ruined.

To this day I do not understand why my mother let me do *Mr. Universe.* Throughout my childhood and most of my years struggling to break into show business, my mother had the European attitude that actors were garbage. If a girl said she was dating an actor, Bea's eyebrows shot up. Yet at the same time she sneaked me out of a week and a half of school and let me travel alone on a subway to Queens—a child who until age twenty-six was expected to call her parents to tell them where she was every minute.

This is one of the reasons why I adored my mother. Underneath her shoulds and don'ts, she did understand, did know the importance of things, and no matter how sternly she opposed what I did, she became very interested with me once I was actually involved. Much later, after I achieved some success, my mother in a dignified way was tuned into show business. When an agent came backstage, she knew enough to leave so we could talk business. "Meyer," she would say. "Come on." She, not my father, understood the problems, the tremendous pressures, that went with performing. One night after two shows I said, "I'm wiped out," and my father answered, "Big deal. You walk onstage and talk for fifty-five minutes and they pay you money." When I said I had no new, good jokes, he went, *"Awww,* it'll come to you."

Maybe from the beginning she was living vicariously and, with a different background, maybe she would have been a stage mother. Maybe, without even knowing it, she was terribly torn, half of her thinking show business was *totally* beneath her and the other half thinking it could be terrific, thinking, *My daughter could be a star; she could be my ticket out to freedom. God, wouldn't it be amazing if* . . . And wasn't it fabulous that she lived to see it happen!

She *loved* my success and would sit in nightclubs in New York and I would be on the stage saying, "I had a blind date with a dentist—and he told me to come back in six months." She would revel in the laughter—but would turn to the table next to her and say, "I'm Joan's mother. What she says is absolutely not true. Always a lovely girl. *Never* any trouble at all having dates. That's just an act she's doing."

In *Mr. Universe* I was being paid $15.56 a day, so I had my first major cash and my first real chance to let my mother know she did not have to depend just on my father for money. As usual, her diamond engagement ring was pawned and I knew she was embarrassed by her finger, so bare with just a wedding ring. I took my *Mr. Universe* money and together we went to the Brooklyn department store Abraham and Straus and picked out two guard rings—thin bands with tiny blue sapphires—which would go on each side of her wedding ring. I paid for them and was thrilled and she never removed those rings for the rest of her life. One was buried with her. The other I have worn ever since and it has never been off my finger.

3

ALL MY LIFE I have been two people wrestling in a bag. One of me is my father's daughter who inherited his peasant constitution that let him work and work and work and not go under. I have his humor and his common touch and his ability to communicate and be liked by many levels of people—and I have his unappeasable hunger for love. If I was not his daughter and he went to see me perform today, he would laugh out loud and say afterward, "Very funny. Very funny. I laughed till I almost bust." Professionally, onstage, I am Doctor Molinsky with a bow.

The other person in the bag is the Joan who adored her mother and permanently bought her standards and ambitions and tastes. If my mother, who thought no respectable person with background went into show business, saw me as a stranger onstage today, she would sit stony-faced, considering me shockingly common, a person never to be discussed. I am still so much my mother that, though I love the person I am onstage because she says everything that women think and are afraid to say, I would still never have her at my dinner table.

When I was finishing Adelphi and deciding about college, the part of me who was J. Sondra Meredith did not want to fool around with any fancy, irrelevant college. That Joan longed to start right away "playing with the big boys," my unclassy expression for going after THE DREAM, for going right into drama school at the Pasadena Playhouse next door to Hollywood. When I vaguely mentioned this course, Bea's eyebrows disappeared into her hair. She said, "Absolutely not. Are you insane? You are *going* to an Eastern college and you are *going* to get your degree!" That was that, no further discussion allowed, and my mother's Joan thought, *Right, right.* That part of me absolutely wanted to be the well-bought-up, well-educated girl who marries well, lives well, entertains well—has the box at the opera, has all the things represented by a WASP coming out party.

These values were imprinted on me a thousand ways, including guilt. My mother often reminded my sister and me that we were being given the best—the best schools, the best camp, the best unbringing—which were worth any sacrifice if they brought us the good job, the good marriage, the big house. But she let us know, too, that the sacrifices were very great—Daddy worked *so* hard. And my father had his own ways of saying the same thing. When I graduated from eighth grade at Adelphi, he wrote in my autograph book, "Always strive for advancement and your efforts, and mine, will be amply rewarded."

During the period when I was worrying about college, my mother decided it was time to move up the social scale another notch—and our neighborhood in Brooklyn was getting so tough, anyone without a police record was regarded as a hairdresser—plus my mother was tired of saying to people, "There really are some sections of Brooklyn that are very beautiful." My parents bought an impressive house in gentile Larchmont, a wealthy New York suburb—next door was the president of NBC and across the street was the president of Standard Oil. My mother told my sister and me that this was their investment in our marital futures, a home to impress the boys who came there—"your picture frame," she said. It was quite a while before I realized, *Hey, there are other people in this picture frame.*

So THE DREAM, which was still a mingling of hope and the bravado that is easy when you are sleeping in your own bed at night, was no match for my mother's training. The part of me she had created resolved to be realistic and go to college and read Ruskin and Rousseau and get the degree and become a person with a substantial background, somebody deep who could become a great dramatic actress like Judith Anderson, who was no beauty, or Katharine Cornell, who could have used a nice nose job.

My mother's Joan, the snob, wanted an Ivy League college, and with B's at Adelphi I was accepted at Vassar, Pembroke, and Connecticut College. Making my final choice, I kept on playing by my mother's book. I chose Connecticut mainly because Barbara was there and I thought maybe I *should* want what Barbara wanted. Her marks were incredibly good; she was going to *be* everything and her life was getting my mother's full approval. Barbara was having lunches at the Colony Club in New York, hanging out with girls who had debuts, dating the right kind of boys—the Yalies who had gone to Andover and Exeter—WASP, WASP, WASP. I said, "Fine! Barbara is right," and could not wait to be Betty Coed.

At Connecticut College the part of me that is my father learned what I did *not* want in life, learned it the hard way, which is the way I learn everything. At Connecticut I fantasized about those Yalies on campus and how they would spot me: "Hey! Get in the convertible!" It did not happen. I mounted a letter campaign, wrote every boy on the eastern seaboard who would write me back—guys at Harvard, Brown, Williams—and hoped to be invited to the six fall football weekends. And it worked. I got my six invitations. But every one was for the *same* weekend. I am not lucky. If I had been at the Last Supper, they would have had a guest host that night!

Connecticut was a suitcase college, and each Friday if you did not go to Williams, Harvard, or Dartmouth, you were the only person left in the dormitory. Rather than do that, I took blind dates—but I was still the snob saying, "What college does he go to?" If the answer wasn't Yale, Harvard, or Princeton, I said, "Are you kidding?" And I scorned the cadets at the

nearby Coast Guard Academy who were great marching toward you in their whites for the Wednesday tea dances, and as
they came closer, the acne on their faces looked like a braille
dictionary.

To get boys, I worked at trying to look good and bought
red rinses for my mouse-brown hair and stood in lots of lights
to bring out the auburn highlights. I had reduced down to
116, which is not bad for five feet two, and, always hopeful,
really thought I looked okay. But then one evening, wearing
my best gray flannel skirt and a cute little white blouse, I
trotted down the dormitory stairs to meet my blind date. The
guy frowned, turned to his friend, and said, "Why didn't you
tell me?" A moment like that—and there were many—rakes
every open wound and makes you feel like nothing, and I
wondered, since I was nothing, why I could not disappear.
Another time, at the beach, I was wearing a little robe and
when I took it off to go swimming, the blind date said, "Oh,
my God!"

The anguish was not just the disappointment in those
boys' faces, it was also my embarrassment—really shame—at
not being like the other girls who got the invitations, got the
votes of approval. They must have known, too, that I was
deficient. Of course, I looked for a way out and, since polio
would not work here, I brought my father's fraternity pin to
college after Christmas and wore that pin on my little blouse,
pretending it was from a guy at Johns Hopkins. Because I was
pinned, it was okay to sit alone in the dorm on the weekends,
but I was constantly on edge that some girl might go, "Oooo,
let me see," and bend close and find out that two little pearls
were missing and no wonder—because it said 1928.

The pin did not help; I remained an outsider, hungry for
acceptance, exquisitely sensitive to subtle rejections. If there
were nine girls in the room, I was the ninth. It was never *my*
room where they sat at night. Lunchtime in the dining hall was
like Adelphi all over again, putting my tray down tentatively

or, when I was the first one at the table, sitting with my face thoughtful and reflective, hoping I looked glad to be alone, as though there was no tightness in my stomach, no worry that the table might not fill up around me—while I watched the table next to me fill up, the table where Ann Marcus was.

The worst times were when three girls sat down and said hello and then gossiped together. I would try to join in a little, but soon gave up and pretended I was invisible because, since I was invisible, no wonder nobody talked to me. Sometimes in freshman year when girls went down the corridor knocking on the doors and calling, "Going to dinner. Hey—let's go," I was so embarrassed about tagging along, I did not come out, just sat very still and very silent, as though I was not there.

Trying to make some kind of an impression—even though I had no horse ribbons to hang up—I let everybody believe I was the rich doctor's daughter, which made me feel grimy, dishonest, humiliated, ashamed to be lying and playing my mother's game of keeping up the family facade. When I bought my secondhand books, which had somebody else's stupid notes on the pages, I hid the worn covers with paper jackets so nobody would know. I furnished my room with stuff from the maid's room at home and pretended I liked it that way. I acted as though I had a huge wardrobe when there were only two dating dresses—both gray flannel, of course. My ten-dollar-a-week allowance did not come every week and when I happened to go out to dinner with somebody, I pretended I was not hungry because I knew what was at the bottom of my purse—and it never crossed anybody's mind that I did not have enough money for a plate of spaghetti.

Then my parents would come up to college, looking good in the Cadillac, which I knew was bought from Stanley, a patient who repossessed cars. My mother would be wearing the mink coat that my father screamed and yelled about, and on her wrist was a diamond bracelet bought on time at Macy's and there had been screaming scenes about that too. They would take me out to dinner with some girls I asked and the whole time I did not have enough money to get to Yale for a date I had already accepted. I hated myself for playing along and joining their hypocrisy. Maybe that is why in my comedy I try to puncture the hypocrisy all around us, why it is almost a crusade with me to strip life down to what *really* is true.

At Connecticut College I learned once again that my salvation lay in the theater. I finally found a little niche, a little identity, by directing the freshman play and I loved being the cast's father-mother figure, and they bought me a present, everybody jolly and calling, "Oh, Joanie, Joanie, open this right now." It was a brass necklace, totally old WASP money, a necklace you could wear immediately to any country club of your choice. I was *extremely* pleased and I still have it.

Through college dramatics I finally, thank God, found Grace Metz, who became my best friend, and it meant everything to have a companion. We cut our fingers and merged our blood and Grace could not wait to go home and tell her German father she had Jewish blood in her.

That summer, for the first time, I learned some real compassion for my father. I worked for free in his office—a way, I thought, to contribute to my tuition. He gave the regular receptionist-nurse a six-week unpaid vacation, and I could get out patients' records and sterilize needles. I was still looking for acceptable alternatives to acting and imagined myself as young, fighting Dr. Joan Molinsky—all in white with jodhpurs, of course—doctor by day, siren by night.

I saw for myself that my father was a cottage industry, only making a nickel if he stood there and did something and then stood some more while the patient talked. Nobody would let me give injections; it was always "Where is Doctor

Molinsky? He give me my injection." But though I understood him better, I still could not talk to him. I never would
have thought to sit down and tell him I was not pleased about
Connecticut—or that I wanted to go into the theater. He
would have been touched that I confided in him, but would
not have understood, so there was no way to do it, not even a
way to start. I was a stranger with my father, a stranger, too,
with my sister. The only one was my mother, and yet the half
of me that makes my living is my father. That is so ironic.

Amazingly, I went back to Connecticut for my sophomore year, which tells how little courage I had, how weak I
was, how much the snob in me wanted the label of an Ivy
League college. But that next spring we did Christopher Fry's
play *A Phoenix Too Frequent,* and I found myself bending over
Grace Metz and sticking a mustache on her lip. I said to
myself, *Something's wrong here; this is not my dream,* and in the
middle of the next summer I transferred to Barnard College
in Manhattan on Morningside Heights. When I told my parents that it would be a lot cheaper there because I could live at
home, they were delighted.

I loved Barnard College, the sister school of Columbia in
upper Manhattan. Nobody knew there was a Yale-Harvard
game. They knew there was a Hieronymus Bosch exhibit
down at the Metropolitan Museum, and said, "Let's go to
Juilliard and hear spring music." I was not the school eccentric anymore. It was a class of 250 girls, all rebelling, and
idiosyncrasies did not make you strange, they made you chic.
Every girl was very, very bright and very, very neurotic. It was
wonderful.

At Barnard I began to be a little bit popular, a personality
in my own right, and smart girls liked to have me around
because I made quips. For the first time in my life I was

deliberately using humor the way my father did, using it to make people enjoy me and save me that place at the lunch table. And also, a funny remark and a little laughter was a way to say, "Come on, let's do it my way," and this has worked ever since. Until Barnard I had only dimly felt that power inside me. Nobody at home ever laughed at anything I said and I never did funny plays in school and never acted funny at parties—no lampshade has ever been on my head.

Only once, when I was twelve, did I get an inkling that I could control a room with humor, and at Barnard I was reaching back to that year—to an evening on a fishing trip with my father on Long Island. He went on occasional weekends with friends who gathered in Montauk at the tip of Long Island in a house owned by Captain Laub, who took them out on his boat. It was one of the very few times I was ever alone with my father and I was never relaxed in the car, worrying that I should be talking to him but having nothing to say. We had no background together. There was too much about my life he did not know. I could not say, "Let me explain to you who Mary and Joanne are and why I want them to be my best friends, but they don't want to be any kind of friends with me." And also I did not think he was interested.

But I loved waking up the next morning in that airy, three-storied gabled house, the sun reflecting off the water onto the ceilings. I could look out the dormer window of my attic room and see the water and tiny birds running like windup toys on the beach. Utterly different from my dark, cold, regimented life, it was open and sunny and free and I loved going out in the boat. My father would hold his fishing rod and go to sleep, and the other men, middle-aged lawyers and doctors in floppy hats and sneakers, helped me put the bait on the hook and let me bring in my own fish. They treated me like an equal and let me be myself and understood me much more than anybody in my child's world. I was allowed into their adult jokes, their teasing and ragging, allowed to be a little bit witty and fun to have along in a way nobody at school understood.

At the end of the day the whole crowd gathered around a huge rectangular table for Mrs. Laub's home-style dinner of big platters of pot roast and string beans. I sat next to my father halfway down the table, surrounded by men flushed by cocktails and sun, with their sunburned noses as red as their plaid shirts, their voices loud as they kidded each other and called out, "Pass the potatoes down." A doctor across from me, to be polite, asked me if I liked school; and spontaneously, instinctively, drawing on something in me absolutely brand-new, I began to speak about things so spontaneously that my mouth seemed almost disconnected from my brain. I began talking about my Latin teacher, Miss Karton, who had only three suits and three blouses and thought she mixed and matched them so cleverly we did not notice. She came back from the summer with blond streaks in her hair and claimed the sun did it, but then we watched the sun grow out. Within a minute the whole table was listening, every eye on me.

I went on, telling them that Miss Arnold was in love with the Biology teacher, Mr. Sterns, who was getting bald and combed his hair forward, and when he went out on the playing field and faced the wind, it blew his hair up and he looked like an Indian with a feather on his head. Mr. Sterns was in love with a girl in his class named Susan Kurtz, who could not stand him but figured if she crossed her legs a few times in class and gave him a little flash of thigh and knee, that would raise her mark from a B to an A, which she needed to get into Bennington College. She was in love with a senior, a football player whose number on his jersey was the same as his IQ. He was in love with Doreen, who was bright but had a nose . . . well, she would not need a fishing rod.

Now the whole table was enjoying me, giggling and laughing, faces crinkling up, eyes squishy. I could see their dental work. And my father was laughing and proud of me. I went on about Mr. Pitt, the history teacher who had this broken-down old car and in the winter went out and bought snow tires—made of snow. I talked about Miss Dogget, the dietician, who wore a hairnet—on her arms.

I felt timing inside me, knew instinctively the exact moment to pause, the instant to hit a line like punching a button to detonate laughter—and it was laughter *with* me, not at me, laughter intoxicating beyond anything. I had never known how to deal with adults, had always felt there was nothing inside my head which could be of any interest to them, but these men wanted this pathetic, fantasy-ridden kid at the table, wanted me to perform and be funny, wanted to be entertained and I was doing it. I had found out how to get my way, how to get them to say, "Sure, you can stay up another twenty minutes." By making them laugh I was in charge. It was the first time I ever had that heady feeling, the first time I found this way to be in control—and I have lived by that knowledge to this day.

At Barnard we accepted one another's dreams. You were not *going to be* a sculptor; you *were* a sculptor, a poet, a novelist, an artist. You dressed to be what you were, so right away it was okay if I was a little more actressy—which meant a longer scarf and the liberated woman's uniform of a black sweater and black skirt, though my mother forbade the black stockings and black ballet slippers. My black skirt had to make its statement to nice school shoes, but I was right there holding the rose, saying that money means nothing and life is poetry and truth and beauty—though I was just playacting that idealistic role and damn well rode to Grand Central Station in the luxury of a taxi—while my friends carried the rose into the sunset—by bus.

Three girls were making their statement by not wearing brassieres, which was major in the fifties, but I was very square, almost prim, not even swearing, and could have been the shocked old maid who goes around changing "fuck" into "book" on the subway walls. Even two years after college, when somebody on a date said something about hot thighs, I left the table and went home.

It took a long time for this mouth to open up because my mother's part of me does not say those words casually and I am terribly offended when somebody uses them to me. When I say them onstage, it's absolutely for shock value—to wake up the audience. A comic onstage must be in command, an authoritarian figure. Ladylike ways do not work for my audiences. I have to be the toughest one in the room or they will talk right through me. They have to know I am like a lion tamer who says, "If you come near me, I'll kill you."

At Barnard everybody seemed to be having sex—if you are going to write a novel, you had better have something to put on those pages—but I was into invisibility rather than liberation, into watching rather than doing. I was not afraid of sex: I was afraid of the relationship it would bring. Coming out of a family and an era when girls did *not* sleep with boys before marriage, sex meant giving myself completely to somebody, meant giving up my independence because I would be in love and therefore *totally* committed. In such intimacy I would be flinging myself wide open, and then the man could look inside me and see that nothing was there. And, anyway, I could not give myself utterly to anybody. I was spoken for— my passion was consecrated to THE DREAM, to the theater.

I was an English literature major, but quickly became the class actress who went right over to Columbia next door and took courses in Greek and Roman theater. In acting class my scenes were judged best every time and Columbia used me in all its productions: I was Juno in *Juno and the Paycock,* Lavinia in *Mourning Becomes Electra,* Emilia in *Othello.* After every production parents and friends would come back and say, "This could go right to Broadway." It's lucky none of them were producers or they would have lost a bundle.

For the first time in my life other dedicated young actors were recognizing me as one of them, letting me share their closed-off universe of the theater which to us was reality, while everything outside was foreign and superficial, irrelevant and annoying, something to be disposed of as quickly as possible. I was, at last, an insider with permission to put the white powder in my hair for Juno and feel my future opening up unimpeded, feel that yellow brick road stretching straight to Oz.

In 1954, the spring of my senior year, I again faced the choice between my two selves, between the stage and my mother. This time, there was no question. In Adelphi I had been my mother's docile daughter and had chosen college, but this time J. Sondra Meredith was going to do what *she* wanted—be an apprentice at the Westport Country Playhouse in Westport, Connecticut, the first choice of every stagestruck kid in America because it was run by the Theatre Guild, at that time the most successful and prestigious producing organization in American theater. At Westport the guild tried out new plays and anybody who was anybody—every agent, director, producer—would go up. A tiny part in a play might be yours again in New York and suddenly you were on Broadway! Westport was the Tiffany of summer stock companies in the same way that Cartier is the Tiffany of jewelry stores.

I wrote my letter to the Theatre Guild, sent in the application with my recommendations from Barnard, and got an appointment with Armina Marshall, a theater legend who, with Lawrence Langner, was the co-founder of the guild. She was a large, formidable woman and we sat in an office that was small and sunny and talked for twenty minutes about my background, what I had done, my ambitions. She must have felt my feverish commitment and energy—which is what they needed for cleaning out toilets in a summer theater. She said, "You're in." I could not believe it and felt my heart expanding, pumping excitement. It was that tingling instant when a fantasy that you know is a fantasy is magically approved and made a fact by the world. I thought, *Maybe she didn't mean it.*

My parents gave me permission to go to Westport, probably telling themselves I deserved one last fun summer before settling down in the fall to a job and the task of finding a husband. They still did not take my ambitions seriously, still thought I had no talent and that all my flings at acting—the *Photoplay* contest and *Mr. Universe*—were girlish larks. A show business career—like cancer—was something they did not recognize, did not discuss, though doubtless my mother was still saying privately to my father, "She'll outgrow it. She's just a child. She'll meet a wonderful man and get married. She'll outgrow it."

In June at Barnard I said a lot of major good-byes, all of us entering the real world to do what we had talked about doing for two years. My friend Marge Avery, the daughter of the abstract artist Milton Avery, was off into the art world. I was off to be a major force on Broadway. At home I packed my tin Kinni Kinnic trunk full of summer clothes, cosmetics, and acting books and shipped it to Westport, prepared now to end up in the Theatre Guild's first Broadway production of the fall season—"And introducing J. Sondra Meredith, right out of Barnard, a bursting star."

Well, I could not follow that trunk. These feet could not get to Westport, could not even get me across my bedroom. In my girlish room—painted pale pink over the wallpaper, a round blue barrel chair piped with pink, a pink French-type bureau painted with blue flowers—I lay on my French bed with its carved pink and white headboard and burrowed under the big white organdy coverlet, huddling, very fetal, very frightened, my brain flashing *actress* while every cell in my body screamed, *Don't go.* In the clutch J. Sondra Meredith was still no match for my mother's imprint and my mother's doubts became my own doubts and my brain churned with terrors, with premonitions of failure. Maybe competing against the best kids in the country, I was not talented, maybe Barnard had been only a friendly cocoon which meant nothing, maybe everything I had ever imagined for myself was a silly dream, maybe I would be throwing my life away. Whenever my mother stopped by my room, she would say, "It's your life," obviously not meaning it. If one person had said, "You can do it; yes, you can," I would have been on my way.

I was due at Westport on a Monday. I telephoned on the Monday and said my uncle had died—which was true. They said, all right, come up Wednesday. I stayed on that bed, all my dreams and determinations turning soft from wondering, from doubting, from asking myself, *Do I truly* want *to be an actress?* With the two Joans in collision, I could not decide, did not know what I wanted. Finally, I told myself I *had* to be sensible, had to be an adult now and do what I knew was right, which meant doing what I was supposed to do. That meant to get going in real life—and real life was: I am a college graduate, so stop fooling around and go out, find a job, and find Mr. Right.

On Wednesday I called Westport and said I still could not come. The man said it was getting too late, the other kids would have taken hold and I would be the outsider and it would not work. That was the final, decisive word—*outsider.* I said, "I can't." I had my mother call and say please send the trunk back. In the end it was an almost conscious choice to preserve my childhood fantasy and keep my secret self-image out of danger.

It was a major, major decision. It changed the course of

my life, turning me away from making a life in the theater. At Westport, I would have gone into the theater world at the top and probably, with luck, moved from there into the Actors Studio. I might today be a working actress, might be Lee Remick—yet to this day I still waver, still am not *sure* whether I have that degree of acting talent. I am still undecided about Westport.

What I did do was go into New York to Forty-second Street, walk up one flight, and take a course in typing and shorthand. That certainly was real life.

The theater was forsworn and Joan Molinsky, her mother's daughter, was in charge and she did very well. I found a real job with a real future at the Lord & Taylor department store. I was in the executive training program and they started me in the publicity department and I received three raises in one year, which was unheard of. I slimmed down and went from Porky to Petunia on my way out of the pen. I poured my crazed ambition and energy into that job and even on New Year's Eve was at Lord & Taylor doing my markdowns alone in the vast, silent stockroom, an eerie, creepy place as I walked along the narrow passages between the long racks of clothes, crossing off the old prices and putting on the new ones. At any moment "it" could get me and stuff a dress down my throat and nobody would ever hear. But going home, it was dramatic to be Joan Molinsky, girl buyer, at ten o'clock on New Year's Eve, walking alone to Grand Central Station. Little did those couples coming toward me know they were passing the future president of Lord & Taylor.

I was hired away by Bond Stores to be the fashion coordinator of their entire national chain, the youngest, I think, in the history of the world. I was in charge of all the men's and women's fashions, the fashion shows, and the window displays for their stores all over the country—$150 a week in

1955—and I was twenty-two. I bought a hat to look older and when they offered me a secretary-assistant, it was tough to hire her, because the girls who walked in to be interviewed were killers—chic thirty-two-year-olds, and thin. Finally I found a girl who was nineteen and a half and five feet tall, so two midgets were running Bond's fashions, but the other one was not allowed a hat.

Now that I had jilted the stage, I was ready for earthly love. It came to me in 1956 in the person of David Fitelson, who I met again as he ate lunch with his best friend, Aunt Alice's son, Allan Thenen. I had known David and had a crush on him since girlhood when I went to Aunt Alice's big Sunday night supper parties and Allan was allowed to invite his friends from the Little Red School House. I thought David Fitelson was breathtakingly cute, but to him I was only Allan's fat cousin hanging on the fringes and nothing passed between us except "Hello"—"Hello."

But when we saw each other that day at lunch, he was carrying a script from the Theatre Guild, where he was working, and the chemistry was instantaneous. This was the first time he had ever noticed me and to me it was like being in love with a football star and suddenly one day the star turns around and goes, "Well, hello." I could not believe that he was asking me out, could not believe it when he said he loved me, could not believe that he said to Allan, "Your cousin's my girl." It was very, very heady.

Grown up, David was dark with deep brown eyes, dark curly hair, symmetrical, flexible features, and a muscular body. He looked like Dane Clark, the movie star, and was strikingly masculine and bright and wild and exciting and adored by women. Exuding self-assurance, certain that the world was going to be his, he knew he was dynamite because he had been dynamite all through school and college. Now a maverick who put art ahead of everything, he had an air of bohemianism which was irresistible to me because it was so

exotic to me, so forbidden. When a boy in those days dressed
in a dark green wool shirt and corduroys with no necktie, no
socks—that was heavy and really spitting in the eye of society.

Everything we did together was an adventure, things that
seemed glamorous because I had never been allowed to do
them—like going to his parents' summer house in the winter
and making do with fireplaces. But we spent most of our time
together in Greenwich Village, operating out of his parents'
house, walking the streets, going on Sundays to Washington
Square to join the zoo of humanity that gathered to hear
impromptu folksingers. We sat for hours holding hands in
beatnik coffeehouses and strolled the lines of paintings along
the sidewalks during the Village Art Fair.

But mostly we talked. David was a would-be poet and
maybe a playwright who was working at the Theatre Guild
and pursuing a degree in history at Columbia University—
and the first boy who ever assumed I had read books and
understood them and could talk about them knowledgeably.
He was also from a middle-class Jewish family and we discussed how profoundly we were misunderstood and talked
with fervor and impatience about our futures, about the possibility of getting married, about my acting career and his plan
to be a teacher until the poetry engulfed him and took over his
life. Being a poet, he was burning with intensity, suffering
deeply from his sensitivity to every nuance of life. Such free-
floating angst was very appealing to me because I could be the
comforter—consoling a major American poet.

His father was the attorney for the Theatre Guild and one
of New York's most important theatrical lawyers, so to be with
David was to be at the edge of the theater at its highest level.
Going into the Fitelson house in the Village was walking into
my fantasy life, a Chagall and a Matisse in the living room, a
Henry Moore sculpture in the garden, bookshelves everywhere—books, books, books—and on the table a silver cigarette case from Mary Martin and next to his father's bed were

the new scripts he was reading. We delivered Christmas presents to Josh Logan's house. We sat down to dinner and there was Elia Kazan or Nancy Walker launching names around the table—Gadge, Marlon, Monty, and "Judy's drinking again." I felt entirely inferior and retreated into myself, not saying six words, glad that I was invisible, sure I was chewing my lettuce too loudly.

In that house was everything that was not in Larchmont—unshakable security, money, warmth, comfort, culture, and a complete understanding of living with the arts—everything I ached to be part of and what David seemed very much part of, as though his parents were pleased to have a son who was a poet and was not making a living, as though that came with having an original Toulouse-Lautrec on the wall.

My parents thought David was nothing; they knew he could not support me, which was a very big phrase: "How can he support you? Who cares what his father is? What's the son?" They thought he was terribly moody, which he was. He was a poet. When he arrived at my door with bare ankles, my mother would not let him in the house and that, of course, only made the relationship more romantic, more exciting, more a long-drawn-out frenzy—David, after we had had a fight, sitting in his Volkswagen at the end of the Larchmont driveway at four in the morning hoping I would come out.

Or I would call a cab to pick me up at ten o'clock at night to catch the 10:32 train to New York, which would get me to the Village and David by midnight. My mother would say, "You can not go out at this hour. What will the neighbors think!" and her lips would thin down to nothing with anger. And I would say, "I don't care what the neighbors think! I'm going!" and I waited for the cab in front of the house while my mother, with the front door locked, watched from behind the curtain of her upstairs bedroom, grief-stricken, because she knew she had lost control of me, and hoping I would ring the bell and come back in.

David was my first sexual experience and I was not ready for it emotionally, could not handle the excruciating intensity laced with guilt. I needed a confidante I could ask, "Am I doing wrong? Am I doing too much?" I needed a mother, but it was unthinkable to Bea that a good girl would sleep with a boy before marriage, or even speak of sex. In my mother's lexicon bed meant a place to sleep and put coats on during a party. I turned totally to David—and there was nobody there, either. He was full of his own insecurities, consumed by his own problems, so I was left to fend for myself, lonely, confused, and racked by feelings I could not control or understand—crazed with emotion.

I thought that once I found the right man and gave myself to him, he and I would be transfigured, all problems vanishing, all faults and cares swept away because life would then be wonderful and romantic and terrific and thereafter I would have a strong man who could solve everything and take care of me—like a giant agent. But gradually I realized that David could not even take care of himself, could not take charge of his own life. He was not the driven artist I wanted. He was not printing and publishing his poems himself, not shoving them down everybody's throat, not really writing all that much. He was a dilettante perfectly willing to live in a garret because he thought there was money in his future. I did not want to be married to the mad poet of the Village and kept talking to him about studying law. I wanted him to be his father. That would have been ideal for me.

We fought constantly, which for a while only added to the excitement of the romance. He was volatile; I was volatile. He was dramatic; I was more dramatic. I did not know when to keep quiet; he did not know when to keep quiet. There were incredible highs, incredible lows. After our first huge fight he came up to Larchmont and said to me, "I wrote an elegy," and I was very impressed. He wrote another after our second big fight and then our third. Eventually, he had a two-volume set. He made Shelley, Byron and Milton look like slackers.

Our fights were really explosions of my anger at his lack of drive, but the trigger was always money. Once, coming into New York to drop me at Grand Central Station, we stopped for gas and he had no money. He was taking the entire summer off, not earning a dollar, and without the slightest sign of shame, was letting me pay. I was furious at what that symbolized. We were second generation kids, going to his family's beautiful country home in New Jersey, eating at their fabulous town house in the Village, but sooner or later we would have to go out on our own, and he did not have money even for gas. This was *not* the pillar of strength who was going to take care of me. This was a boy absolutely willing to sit home and be the poet while I went to work and earned the bread.

I said, "You're twenty-two years old—you should have money for gas. If you don't have any money, don't take the summer off, get a job."

He said defensively, "I need time to think and find myself. I don't know what I want to do yet."

I said, my voice rising, words like my mother's coming out of my mouth, "Well, it's time you decided. You've had your fun being the great bohemian. Now go to law school. Your father's firm is Fitelson & Mayers. Change the name to Fitelson, Fitelson & Mayers."

"I don't want to be a lawyer," he answered. "I am a poet. That is what I am. That is my life. You are the last person to be asking me to change."

By now I was turned toward him in the tiny car, speaking like a gatling gun at his set profile. "I am not asking you to change. Be a lawyer-poet. An accountant-poet. A dentist-poet. Or if you've got to be a poet-poet, write wonderful poetry and sell it to Hallmark—do anything rather than live off your father."

"Take it easy," he said, his voice maddeningly calm. "You

don't understand. These things take time. If I get my doctor-
ate I can be a poet and a professor and that's a good life—at
Columbia the professors get free dental care."

Now, in a paroxysm of frustration, both wildly in love and
disgusted with this man, I was hitting myself with my fist again
and again on my hipbone. The fight was actually not about
David's ambition. I was crazy, shaking with rage, because he
was the love of my life and I wanted him to go out and
conquer the world for me, take twelve jobs, cut off his arm and
prove that I was the love of *his* life too. And if he *really* loved
me, he would cut off *both* arms. There was no limit to my need
for proof, because I did not believe I was worth his love. How
could *I* be the love of anybody's life!

As David slowed for a traffic light opposite Grand Central, I lashed out, "You're a lazy rich-man's son waiting for the
inheritance," and I flung open the door and leaped out of the
still moving car. I rushed into Grand Central Station, got on
the train for Larchmont, and sat there shaking. My life was in
pieces. Because I was from a home where you absolutely did
not sleep with a boy until you were married, I had given myself
totally to David and now must take myself back totally. This
was the end forever and ever. I would never see David again. I
had to build a new life and only someday—*perhaps*—would
another man be possible.

Suddenly, David sat down next to me. It was a pinnacle of
romance. He took my hand in both of his and said, "You're
not leaving me. We are locked together."

"Leave me alone," I said, not withdrawing my hand.

"You can walk out on me thirty-five times," he said, bending toward me. "You can spit in my face again and again—but
you're not getting rid of me ever. I won't let you go."

"Where's the car?" I asked.

"On Forty-second Street. I didn't even have time to take
the keys out."

"Don't be silly, it's all over, it's ridiculous," I said, thinking, *This is wonderful, this is Heathcliff and Catherine. And he's probably writing a poem to me in his head—to a Jew—on a railroad. This is big time.*

He told me all the reasons why it was not over—that we loved each other, that we were artists together—and I was saying by the time we reached Pelham, "I love you too. Oh, God, I love you too," and we got off and went back to find the car.

But ultimately I was smart enough to tell myself, "I've got to get out of this." I had learned how all-encompassing, how forever, how exciting the first love is—and there is nothing else like it. But I had also learned the flip side—how painful it is, how devastating, how exhausting emotionally. If you love the wrong person, there is a point where you *must* walk away, no matter what it does to you. I have noticed that my friends who married the first big love from Yale or the first love from Princeton broke up fifteen years later—when they realized the big love snored.

All the time David and I were together, he had been worrying about being drafted. A friend of his father's knew someone who knew someone with connections in the military who told him, "You go on down, son, and take the physical and don't worry, the fix is in." So David went down and took the physical and afterward called up. "Guess what . . ." The fix was *not* in. And the infantry! Cheap blow! Not even special services.

I knew if I waited till he came out of the army, I would be finished. I knew that if I was available, I would marry him and he would destroy me. I knew that I would have to be the strong and stable one so he could be the star, knew that we could not continue on this emotional binge, and if we were to get off it, I would have to capitulate and give up everything. I would have to earn the living while receiving too little emotional nourishment from David. I knew that eventually there would be other women and I would end up frustrated and used and discarded. But I also knew that the physical attraction between us was so intense, so overwhelming, I could not resist him. Lastly, I knew I had six weeks during his basic training to escape by getting married: "Joan, here is your task."

At my job at Bond Stores I met the son of the merchandise manager. His name was Jimmy Sanger, in his middle twenties, round face, blond hair receding slightly at the temples, crew cut, nice dirty white bucks, that old gray flannel look of any guy cheering at the Yale-Columbia game. He was the royal prince and we were the buzz of the store: "Mr. Sanger's son is talking to Joan Molinsky. Mr. Sanger's son is eating with Joan Molinsky." When he proposed to me, we had known each other only three weeks.

I decided, here is a man who is well-off, adorable, a Columbia graduate, cute, cute, cute, and a businessman. I thought, *This is reality. This is absolutely right.* My sister was saying, "What are you waiting for? He's terrific!" My parents were delighted, saying, "Darling boy—good family—crazy about Joan." Molinsky women did not marry for love, but I would not be making my mother's most basic mistake. Jimmy came from a substantial family and he was slated for success and money, so I could have a better life than my mother and maybe eventually Aunt Alice's life. I could be rid of hysterical scenes with David and crawl into a safe place, a nice, solid, sane relationship—plus a maid, a pretty apartment, a mink coat, and a country club—and children I would not have to carry on my hip, the way I would have with David.

I told Jimmy I wanted to get married immediately—and knew instantly it was all wrong. He was stodgy and stolid and I was never going to fit—or want to fit—into his world. And I was still in love with David.

Before the wedding I took a tranquilizer, the only one *ever* in my life, but I knew what was expected of me and was going to do it. The ceremony was held in my Aunt Alice's Park Avenue apartment, with banks of flowers and a strolling violinist, a very classy wedding that read well in *The New York Times*. In the reception line, in full drag in a gown from Martha's, which is a "veddy" elegant store on Park Avenue, I said to my cousin Allan, "Can you believe I'm doing this?"

What *The New York Times* did not mention was that at the end of the ceremony we sacrificed the rabbi. For an altar, Aunt Alice had an antique music stand, eighteenth century, with two candles burning on each side which used to light the sheet music. The rabbi reached through the candles to bless us and the big hanging sleeves of his robe caught fire. My bridesmaid, Nancy Heath, was very impressed: she had never been to a Jewish wedding before and did not realize that you burned up the rabbi at the end, that he made a total sacrament you could never undo.

A few weeks after the wedding David Fitelson came back from basic training. The first phone call he made was to Larchmont.

"David who?" my mother said.

"David Fitelson."

"Joan's married." Click. She hated him.

Our marriage license turned out to be a learner's permit. I had perpetrated another Molinsky mismatch. Life became a series of fights. Neither one of us had known what we had married. I found myself living with the boss's son, an ordinary, agreeable guy without much humor, rather taciturn, the only child of a very strong father, a bit of a Mama's boy but very stubborn, very set in his Mama's-boy ways. It was a shock to him that I wanted anything my way and everything I did annoyed him. I quit Bond's and went to work as assistant buyer at the Franklin Simon department store. He was not happy that I had a job and that I enjoyed it, trying to do this, get there, working late when he was a strict nine to fiver. He was furious that he had an ambitious wife. He wanted a hausfrau, always there to comfort him. He was saying, "I want to be the boss"—and look who he was saying that to. But I gave up my job to please him and stayed home and let him rule the household.

The fights went on, fights about what I wore, about our social life, which was entirely with his family, about who ran the checkbook, about my being a homemaker, about my ambition, about his ambition, which was not much. When the money was not coming in fast enough, I took a free-lance job writing a catalogue for a children's clothes manufacturer, working at home doing the little descriptions under the pictures and laying out the samples on the floor and furniture. Jimmy came home and wanted to know what I was doing. I said, "I'm earning extra money. I can make $300."

He yelled, "Goddamn it, I support my wife. I make the money around here," and kicked the clothes across the room.

But his mistake was as big as mine. I must have been a lulu. When Jimmy showed traits I did not like, I thought, *No, no, no, I planned to marry Mr. Perfect.* I did not want to see that he had problems or troubles. If he was a neurotic rich man's son, I was a neurotic idiot. Since I had cut myself off from performing, I refused to attend the theater and Jimmy would get theater tickets and I would not go with him. I must have become one moody bitch at home, feeling like a prisoner, depressed, trying to be happy and not being happy—the great martyr.

But I really tried in my marriage to Jimmy, really wanted it to work, wanted to do my duty. I had made a bargain and was damn well going to honor it. At my suggestion Jimmy and I went to a marriage counselor, but nothing changed and the fights continued. After a month, the counselor said I did not have to come anymore and Jimmy should come every day. To me that was saying, *"You are not wrong, he is wrong."* I thought, *That's it. I'm out.* I went home to Larchmont and felt forty years come off my shoulders, and understood how the condemned man feels when they tell him, "Muggsy, the warden just called and you're not going to burn tonight."

Two weeks later I agreed to meet him at the Biltmore and he had lost fifteen pounds and I thought, *Look what you have done to somebody. That suffering is all your fault, your responsibility.* He asked me to try again and I did. But nothing changed, the fights continued, and I left for good after six months of marriage. I think Jimmy's mother was thrilled. She went around our apartment with a red crayon and marked all the furniture JOAN'S, JIM'S, JIM'S, JOAN'S, JIM'S.

I found out from my relationships with David and Jimmy: Never look for a man to do it for you. Nobody else will ever have *your* ambition, will ever hand your success to you, so you had better go out and achieve it yourself. Unless, of course, you get somebody *really* big: "Dear, you go buy the company today. I'm tired."

We had the marriage annulled on the basis that Jimmy did not want children and had not told me. My case was heard in divorce court and my parents came with me. In every case ahead of me, people were testifying that they had broken down the door and found their wife or their husband in bed with somebody else, and the judge always asked, "Where were the clothes?"

"On the chair, Your Honor."

"Thank you. Next case. . . . Where were the clothes?"

"On the chair, Your Honor."

"Thank you. Next case. . . . Where were the clothes?"

"On the chair."

I started to laugh in court. Somebody should say chaise longue or sofa. My mother and father thought it was very inappropriate for me to be laughing and said I was not taking the breakup of my marriage seriously enough. Little did they know what the end of my marriage meant to me. It closed the door, not just on Jimmy Sanger, but on ever being Mrs. Westchester and Mrs. Doctor's Wife and Mrs. Normal Citizen in society.

Again I lay on my bed at home for most of a week. I kept saying over and over to myself, "I really tried. I really tried to be what my parents wanted me to be. I really tried to be what they had brought me up to be. But it did not work."

My mother kept coming in and saying, "Now, of course, you'll go back to Franklin Simon. Or maybe you could go back to college and get an M.A."

I listened to her and said, "I don't know. I don't know." And I really did not know. But I did. I knew that if I ever got myself out of that bedroom, I was not returning into the same world. Finally I told my mother, "I'm going to take a shot at what I've always *wanted* to do and should have done in the first place." And that was it. From that day on I have never had a permanent job.

4

ON THE FIRST day of my show business career—a winter morning in 1958—I walked down to the Larchmont train station and took a train for New York. It was not the Twentieth Century to Hollywood, it was a ride I had taken a thousand times with my mother on girlish excursions to the big city. For conquering Broadway, I chose my good wool coat, a striped dress with a white Peter Pan collar, my mother's purple and black shawl, little white gloves, and hoop earrings under my short, bobbed hair—and checked my makeup thirty-five times. Around my neck, for luck, was the brass necklace given to me by the cast of the freshman play at Connecticut College for Women. If the girl I was that day consulted me now, I would say, "Honey, become a teacher." There was no way she was going to be a Carson show hostess, no way that Oscar de la Renta would ever lend her dresses, and Mrs. Reagan would certainly never sit beside her.

In Grand Central Station I went straight to a little photography booth, where I inserted a dollar, and as the light flashed, composed my face into what I imagined to be a full range of expressions—quizzical, provocative, sad, idealistic, motherly, whimsical, disturbed, soulful, sexy, sophisticated—all windows into the fires of talent that burned beneath that black and gray dress.

Carrying my sheet of ten poses, I headed west on Forty-second Street toward the theater district and a newspaper stand where I could buy *Show Business* and *Actors Cues*, which listed producers and shows that were casting: "Off Broadway: *Our Town* to be done in St. Christopher's Church basement.

Cast breakdown includes Mrs. Gibbs, fiftyish, Emily . . .
Non-Equity." Or maybe, "John Smith looking to expand his
list of clients. Especially interested in seeing character ladies,
leading men and ingenues, Equity and non-Equity. Experience preferred." I sat in Howard Johnson's with a cup of
coffee and marked the places I would go that day—and began
a routine which went on intermittently for seven years.

Some offices were in beat-up brownstones on side streets
in the West Forties and Fifties above stores selling discount
appliances, records, and cheap shoes, and above Greek and
Italian restaurants. The sidewalks were trashy obstacle
courses of huge boxes being unloaded from double parked
trucks—of groups of Hasidic Jews, all in black as though
steeped in perpetual mourning and carrying their cases of
diamonds to and from gem booths—of decrepit ancients from
the SpeeDee messenger service carrying envelopes stamped
RUSH—of brisk young executives in three-piece suits saying to
their companions, "I've got a squash court at five o'clock"—
and sashaying secretaries, looking from the front as though
they had been shot in the back by two rockets.

Other offices were in shabby Broadway landmarks like
the Brill Building and in worn-out hotels like the Wellington.
Some were in narrow old office buildings and you rode up in a
small, rattly self-service elevator that never stopped level with
the floor—always with a guy delivering coffee in a brown
paper bag. Or they were in transitional apartment buildings,
several agents sharing a secretary and each taking a dingy
room with a lovely view of the air shaft and moving in and out
as their precarious futures rose and fell. On the way down the
hall through the cooking smells, you passed a door with a sign
on it, STOP THE WORLD LIMITED, and on either side was a bike
and a baby carriage.

All the agents' offices were like third-rate employment
agencies with worn board floors and scarred, creaky wooden
chairs along one wall. Perched on those chairs were desperate

actors, trying to look snappy, but wearing their single, once fashionable outfit of cracked, down-at-the-heel shoes polished a thousand times, pants shiny from wear and a thousand pressings, jackets with the linings hanging down below the bottom. They were the underbelly of the profession, the non-union, non-Equity never-will-be's, living on the fringe, living on hope.

The only jobs they could get were off-Broadway crumbs and even then the producers' first choice would be an actor with legitimate credits. So these lineups were defeated, not just by lack of talent, but by the catch-22 of our profession: They could not be in a Broadway production unless they had an Equity Union card—and the only way they could get a card was by being in a production. Among them, dressed in the clothes of my wealthy marriage, I felt like Martha Washington come to visit the slaves.

Presiding over this scene like a tyrannical headmistress was the secretary behind a beat-up war surplus desk. These were middle-aged New York women, basically nice, but basically tough and very powerful because they held the first key to your career. They decided who to keep out and who might make money for the boss and should be allowed into the sanctum. Every trick had been tried on them and they were having none of it, so if you got on their bad side, you would never get in to see the "big man." Very early I saw a pushy mother with a child thrown out by a secretary. "Out! And don't come back!" And lovely little Mary's pictures came right out of the file and into the mother's hands. I'm sure the mother had screamed about something outrageous—like wanting the check for a commercial the child had done six months ago.

I was always terrified—always afraid of everything, of being rejected, of making a fool of myself, of being laughed at, afraid of offending the secretary so she would send me out of the office. I walked into those anterooms very carefully and slowly. If you have ever seen a person walking forward—who is walking backward—that was me. My stomach was tight and half sick with embarrassment and fear. I could barely lift my eyes to look at the secretary and then immediately looked away as I almost whispered, "Excuse me, is it possible to see Mr. Tobey today?"

It was almost impossible to go into those seedy waiting rooms and tell a secretary who is chewing gum, "I'm terrific," when she does not think you are terrific—and you think she may be right. My talent, whatever it might be, was such a special thing to me that I could not verbalize it to these people. I did not want to say, "Here is my dream," and have them say, "Poo, poo, poo." I have never learned how to tell somebody something good about myself; that should be a secret they must find out.

If I made it past the secretary, I would have to sell myself all over again to the agent, and if he liked me, he would send me to a producer who would judge me again compared to a hundred other girls. This was now my life and continues to be my life, constantly reselling myself, constantly being appraised.

I remember on my first day there was a girl ahead of me who had a portfolio—zip, zip—and here were her pictures with beautifully mimeoed résumés pasted on the backs, while I stood there with my ten poses for a buck inside my little manila envelope. Slowly I learned the ropes, sitting on those rickety chairs and waiting with other actors who told me how to write a résumé—which meant how to lie.

You made it a dream sheet of the roles you had longed to get. Carol Burnett, starting out, put down Blanche DuBois in *A Streetcar Named Desire.* Ruth Buzzi actually made costumes and had herself photographed as the characters she ought to have played. When you named a theater company, it was out of town—or out of business—so nobody could check. If you listed a movie credit, you put down an epic because nobody could prove you were not in a crowd scene. Special skills were important in case somebody was booking for a commercial— "I played King Lear and I inhale." You wrote down horseshoeing, just in case somebody was doing a blacksmith commercial: "Hey, you know that girl who walked in here the other day? I think she's a horseshoer. Yeah, here it is. 'Horseshoeing.' Call her."

I put down that I was five feet three and a natural blonde. I claimed membership in all the theatrical unions and listed every play I had done at Connecticut College and Barnard— plus *Snow White and the Seven Dwarfs* at the Kinni Kinnic Playhouse in Vermont. I had two movie credits: *"Mr. Universe— avid wrestling fan"* and *"The Ten Commandments—a Jew."*

I added three spurious commercials—Ivory Soap, Parliament Cigarettes, and Six-Month Floor Wax—plus a radio show at WKOX in Eugene, Oregon, where I had done "a series of old and original scripts." I claimed to have observer status at The Actors Studio and to be studying with Herbert Berghof. And I listed my skills:

Tango Charleston	Fox Trot	Big Apple
Smoke—inhale, exhale	Drive	Field Hockey
Swim and Float	Arm Wrestle	Calligraphy

This charade has been enacted for as long as there have been actors. Everybody in the business knows that résumés are mostly lies and no legitimate producer looks at them—or, if they do, they know instantly which are the lies. Nobody ever says, "Oh, I'm going to hire you because I see you were in so-and-so." If you have a big credit, they already know it.

The second thing I needed was an eight by ten glossy photograph of myself—even though it was often tossed in the wastebasket as soon as you left an agent's office. I asked everybody for the cheapest photographer. I knew I did not want a four-picture composite: Joan Molinsky laughing, Joan Molinsky straight, Joan as a dancer, Joan dressed as Chuckles the Clown. I wanted myself looking upward at a distant horizon, at a distinguished future. It was very important to me that agents and producers see that here was the serious youth of the theater, that here was the next level coming up to push out Julie Harris. I wanted the air of Joan of Arc and a soupçon de Cordelia.

That didn't quite work out. I achieved a girl with a mustache and a couple of puckies on my cheek and the twenty-five dollars did not include retouching, nor did it include the negative. So I took the print to a copy place and had a negative made, immediately losing one generation of quality. Fortunately, the mustache became lighter—which took care of the retouching. I had a hundred copies made and glued résumés on their backs.

I also learned that you must have a place to hang out and make the friends who gossip about what plays are being cast and what types are wanted. The comics hung out at Hanson's Drug Store on Seventh Avenue at Fifty-first Street, and no self-respecting actor or actress went there except to buy stage makeup. You would see those unemployed idiots in the rear and hear laughter coming from the booths, and you bought your Max Factor Clown White and went out. You never thought about them. What did they have to do with theater? They were just nightclubs.

The B & G was the place for me. It was on Seventh Avenue across from the Taft Hotel—a long, narrow room poking straight into the building with a counter in the shape of an S curve and no booths. It was the hangout for people just starting—would-be actors, would-be comedy writers, and the comedians who could not afford even the fifty-cent minimum at Hanson's Drug Store, but people a little more ambitious and spirited than the actors I sat with in agents' offices. I first met Linda Lavin there and Dom DeLuise.

At the B & G for a fifteen-cent cup of coffee, you could sit all day—but you had to leave the counter girl a quarter. For twenty-five cents, she was your friend and that was important because she could be nasty. If you got up to make a phone call, even though you said to somebody next to you, "Save my stool," she could wipe your place clean and let another person sit down.

I came in about ten o'clock from Larchmont and went right to the B & G to talk with my friends about acting, about making the rounds, about somebody's secretary and the gossip of the street—feeding on rumors. "Gee," they would say, "so-and-so is seeing girls for a Robert Sherwood play in New York," and a group of us would run up there. Half the time, the secretary had never heard of it—"What are you talking about?"—or else, "Oh, that was cast two weeks ago." Or, "Do you have an Equity card?"

If there was nothing going on at the B & G, I crossed to the Taft Hotel with my little bag of dimes to use the phones because the B & G had only one phone and there was always somebody on it. I called agents to see if there was a part open or for a job as an extra—or I called my mother in case somebody had phoned the house. Unemployed actors and actresses know (a) which hotel lobbies have phone booths that are usually empty and (b) which hotels have clean toilets. The Astor had great toilets.

Then I checked *Show Business* and *Actors Cues,* though two thirds of their ads were useless. You went in and the secretary said, "Oh, no, no. That's a mistake. We're not looking for girls with camel's hair sweaters. We're looking for a man who's a camel trainer. They got it wrong."

"Oh, okay, but can I . . ."

"What?"

"Can I leave a résumé and a picture here?"

"No. We're not accepting new people."

My first essential piece of stage expertise had nothing to do with the stage—it was the craft of ingratiating myself with those stolid, cynical secretaries so that eventually, after a long time, they would *finally* say, "Let us know if you're in something," which was the first rung up the ladder. It took me months to learn how to drop in and say, "Boy, it's cold. I was having some coffee and thought you'd like some too—and if you want to go to lunch, I'll answer the phone for you."

"Well, isn't that nice. Thank you."

I did *anything* to be remembered, but mostly made jokes: "Should I give you my résumé—or should I save you a step and throw it right into the wastebasket?" I did idiotic things like crawling on my hands and knees all the way from the door to the secretary's desk, and suddenly she saw this hand appear over the edge of the desk holding a rose. I found their appointment books and wrote in pencil, "Get Joan Molinsky a job. She is a good kid." When I gave them my eight by ten glossy, I'd draw a mustache on my lip, or a bubble coming out of my mouth, reading, "I need work." Every Christmas, I always had a big smile for Thelma and a little package of Here's My Heart by Avon.

If necessary, I would sit forever in that row of actors—all of us like dogs watching food. We never took our eyes off the agent's door, each of us nursing our delusion: "I'll read for a director and they'll say, 'Look at that. The one from the smallest agent got the part. Isn't it amazing?' "

Then "the man's" door would open and Mr. Tobey would come out, saying to the secretary, "I'll be back in an hour." I knew his table was not waiting for him at Sardi's and he was not going to get a big hello at Lindy's. He was probably seeing his bookie. But I would decide I might as well wait, maybe there would be another chance to see him.

These agents were not MCA and William Morris. They were always living on the edge and over the edge, always rumpled, wore neckties from Tie City and their shirts for three days, and had not paid their rent in months. The phone bill was always three months in arrears and "the check's in the mail." An actor made $21.51 a day as an extra, so agents were making $2.15 and arranging the job took eight phone calls, so his profit was $1.35. I could glimpse them peeling off a stamp when the postmark had not quite hit it and sometimes they even tried to borrow money from the actors—and always they cheated them. A movie company would phone these little agents and say, "We need 20 bodies for a scene in Connecticut." The agent received maybe a flat $500. He would pocket $300 and say, "I could only get you $10, but here's the job."

Yet these crummy agents had the second key to a career: they could send me up for bit parts on Broadway and off-Broadway and on live television and, if I got that job, I got my union card and could move to the next higher strata of agents, who handled only union actors. That would be the *big* breakthrough.

I did not feel superior and uncomfortable dealing with those men, because their world had nothing to do with me. During the day I was just playing the role of an actress in my personal movie, playing the part of J. Sondra Meredith, thespian, and then each evening on the 6:25 train to Larchmont, I was magically transformed into the real me, Joan Molinsky, Westchester girl—and schizophrenic—who descended from the train in Larchmont with its pretty streets, clean and crisp air, and even tidy garbage. Though I arrived at the station each night frustrated and depressed that nothing was happening for me, I would then see our Georgian house with its blinds and arcing driveway in front and I would think how nice it was, and that it proved I was not really the beggar who plodded all day through the New York cesspool.

I would remind myself that I really was the suburban product of the best schools who lived in the prettiest house on the street, a house that made me proud—proud of the parties there which were so festive, so lovely, proud to be from this house which showed I had a good background, proud to be somebody. Every time I went in the front door, I felt safe and reassured. That house was vitally important in my life. It protected me.

My parents, indulging what they considered my girlish infatuation with acting, were allowing me the duration of my unemployment insurance to have a good time and recover from the failure of my marriage. And then, of course, when the six months were up, I would come to my senses, see that I was going nowhere, start looking for a legitimate job and the right husband. At one of the big charity teas my mother gave at the house, she stood running her hand through my hair as she said to somebody, "Joan wants to be an actress. We've decided to let her go for six months and try it." It was Lady Bountiful letting the little debutante have her fling.

But surprise, surprise, after the last unemployment check arrived I was not saying, "This is silly. I'm going for an interview at Saks." My mother still said nothing, perhaps sure that reality and poverty would concentrate my mind. I did, however, have to earn money. Despite my diploma from the summer course in typing and shorthand, I could not convince Office Temporaries that I knew shorthand. In the typing test at Kelly Girls, I was still trying to put the paper in the typewriter when they said, "Time to stop now." So I ended up at Brown's Office Temporaries in one of those West Side buildings where you climbed six flights of stairs because it was safer than taking the elevator. Mrs. Brown was a middle-aged, stocky woman and I could glimpse a hot plate in the bathroom with lots of cosmetics and dusting powder.

Mrs. Brown liked me and accepted my word that I could type and take shorthand and for the rest of my office temp career, I was mainly from Brown's, making about eight dollars a day after they had deducted their commission. Sometimes my sister Barbara and I shared jobs. Barbara had gone through Connecticut College in three years and Columbia Law School in three years, but she was having trouble starting her own law practice, because, as she said, "In New York there are more lawyers than people."

I would get an office temporary job and go there in the morning while Barbara looked for clients. After lunch, while I made rounds, she would appear at the job and take my place. Nobody ever knew we had switched. Nobody ever noticed that there was a different girl at the desk in the afternoon, that the girl in the plaid jacket had been wearing pink in the morning. In all those temporary jobs, you are invisible, sitting right there while they talk about you—"The girl's doing it right now," "When the girl's finished with this, she'll do that." Nobody looks at your face. Nobody ever says, "Would you like a cup of coffee?" You are a nonperson.

We were only caught once. Working for a man named Herman Hanover, I was fired in the morning for spending too much time on the telephone calling agents and after lunch Barbara innocently walked in, very chipper, and sat down at the typewriter. Mr. Hanover, backing away from her as though she was an escaped lunatic, said, "Don't you remember? I fired you." Barbara said, "Oh, that's right, Mr. Hanover. It completely slipped my mind."

I was fired again by a public relations office handling a Rock Cornish game hen account. From a mountain of cookbooks, I was told to type out every recipe for chicken, changing chicken to hen, and send them out as news releases to food editors. The woman said, "Note that game hen and its trademark are always in full caps. And, please, no typos."

"Of course," very crisp.

"If you do make a typo, you are to remove the page from your machine and start over. Do you understand?"

"Of course."

Well, of course, I always made a mistake right near the

end and she always knew when I used the Liquid Paper. At the end of the day I had done five pages correctly, and, while she fired me, the woman stood there, holding the pages on her palm as though weighing them. I felt terrible because I was taking their money, but I wanted to say, "I graduated from Barnard College. Graduated with honors. I'm not a typist. I'm an actress." And then I wanted to say, "Nobody's going to eat your stupid chickens." One of her releases began, "This Thanksgiving, surprise your family with individual Cornish hens." Were they crazy? A platter of little Cornish hens? For gay Pilgrims?

At another place, I had to add columns of Social Security deductions on an adding machine—$1.43 $1.69 $1.26—long, long columns of 300 figures, and the totals never came out the same twice. I went over and over them—$1.43, check, $1.69 check, $1.26 check—and then the boss would walk in and say, "Still not right," and walk out and I would think, *Please, God, if you're going to make me a failure, fine. But don't make me a failure at something I don't want to do.*

I worked one day in a place that made very cheap plastic shower curtains. For some reason the entire office always whispered. "Good morning," "Good morning." I would say, "Where does this . . . excuse me, where does this go?" The mailman came in and I told him, "Everybody's crazy in here." But he had been trained. He said to me, "I know."

For a time I had a typing job at the National Association of Sportswear Buyers in the Empire State Building. It was on the 78th floor and visitors there unfailingly walked to the window, looked out, and said, "Gee, the people down there look like little ants." One day somebody brought William Faulkner in to get some clothes at a discount—and we all held our breaths, waiting to see what this master of the English language, this giant of American letters would do. Of course, he walked to the window, looked out, and said, "Gee, the people down there look like little ants."

In January of 1959, after about seven months of making the rounds of agents, still miserably shy, I went to a cocktail party given by my cousin Allan Thenen and met a man named George Maisel, who said he was an actor. When I told him I was an actress, the first thing he asked was, "How many relatives have you got?"

I told him I had a mother, father, sister, and a bunch of aunts and he assured me I was already halfway toward getting a part in a play called *Seawood* and tomorrow night he would be happy to take me to audition for the author-producer Armand de Beauchamp. "It's not the best production you'll ever be in and no money," he said, "but it can be a showcase." I said fine. *Showcase* is the talisman word which electrifies actors, enticing them into all kinds of absurdities in the hope that some agent will materialize and see gleams of talent. I thought fate had delivered me to my first big breakthrough.

The next evening George Maisel guided me to an old New York brownstone in the West Seventies. We were buzzed through the front door and began to climb the stairs, flight after flight after flight, six in all, and we could look back down the stairway and see banisters coiling down into the endless well. On the top landing, pinned to an unlocked door, was a piece of typewriter paper bearing the name ARMAND DE BEAU-CHAMP SCHOOL OF THE THEATER written in ink. Inside in the living room a tall, plumpish youth wearing high, heavy storm trooper boots stood behind a card table and gazed at us with pale, incurious blue eyes. I walked toward him, feeling chubby, ungainly, very nervous, and pathetically eager to be in this production.

The young man was Jim, the director of *Seawood,* and he pronounced my name carefully. "Joan Molinsky." Then he asked, "Do I know your work?"

"I did a lot of things up in Connecticut. I've done *Othello* off Broadway." I forgot to mention on campus.

He said, "Good," and inquired whether I was from this area and did I have many family and friends who would be interested in coming to a performance?

I told him yes, both in New York and New Jersey.

He made a note of that and said, "Good."

I joined the little group of actors perched around the room and sat down in an elephantine overstuffed easy chair and looked around me. *Eclectic* came into my mind. The place seemed furnished by an eccentric, impoverished maiden aunt with no taste and too much proximity to a Salvation Army store. The broken-down sofa had obviously been slipcovered to hide its shabbiness and now the shapeless beige slipcover was shabby. At each end of the sofa were lamps with rust-speckled shafts rising out of marble bases to yellowed linen shades mottled black from burn spots. There was a massive dark oak chair with dragon heads at the ends of the arms, something Armand had probably rescued from the sidewalk one jump ahead of the garbage truck on pickup day. The coffee table, once on somebody's lawn, was glass with a peeling white metal base and covered with dog-eared *Theater Arts* magazines. The rug, which might have come off a stage set for a tenement, was a color you would call blotched tan. On the faded beige-papered walls were photographs of grateful students and actors in his productions, not one of them recognizable except Tab Hunter, prominently displayed and frequently mentioned by Armand.

Suddenly Armand de Beauchamp, flamboyant till you thought he would sprain every ligament, swept into the room from the kitchen, where he had, I supposed, been recharging his genius. Tall, thin, willowy, with flowing hair, he surveyed us like an overripe John Carradine, a scarf hanging long over one shoulder, an expressive hand cocked scornfully on one hip. In a sonorous, vibrating Shakespearean voice, he deliv-

The only time in my life
I was ever a natural blonde.

I never knew Hannah Grushman, my mother's mother *(left)*, posing in the 1920s, but she was a survivor, rich in Russia, destitute in America, and then living well on money from her son the dentist. She became like an empress—with a lorgnette —and you can see the strength, the imperious-ness—no fooling around with this lady, and I think my own drive came from her.

I look at my mother's 1927 wedding picture with great sadness. The splendor of the dress is a lie, symbolizing a fantasy that could never come true. And this beautiful girl is going, without love, into a disastrous marriage. She tried to live the elegance taught by her mother, but was married to a man who pinched every penny— and she settled for a facade of affluence built on bitterness.

My father's mother, Manye Molinsky, was probably the only real love he had in his life. Manye, as a widow in Russia, sold fruit at an outdoor market, and with the money brought the family to America. She insisted that her son Meyer study medicine. The gag picture *(below)* with a cadaver head and a skeleton, he set up when he was in medical school. I do not recognize the thin young man, but I recognize my own black humor.

The two people on their honeymoon *(right)* should have met for the picture and then said good-bye. My father is so natty, my mother must have been dressing him, telling him to affect a cane.

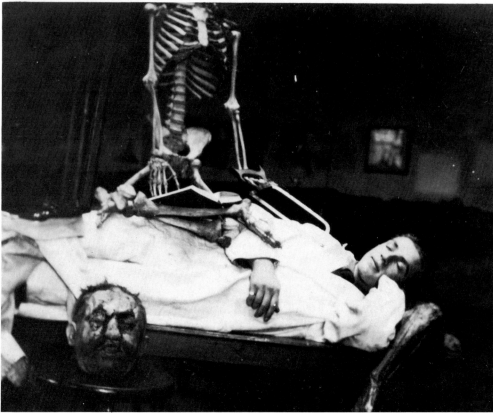

Secretly my father was as upwardly mobile as my mother and very proud of their first major car, a flashy four-door Packard *(above)*. He liked to show off my older sister, Barbara, and me *(above and right)*, all dolled up in perfect little matching outfits from Best & Co.

My father wanted his mother, Manye *(right)*, to live with us and she did, sometimes—which my mother hated. On my sister's birthday, my mother fought furiously with him about that and refused to come to the party. So this is a picture of a man torn between his wife and his mother; of a nine-year-old girl who knew that the woman she was standing next to was trouble; and of a preteen birthday girl who did not think she looked good, so she took a pair of scissors and cut her head out of the picture.

When I graduated from eighth grade at Adelphi Academy, my mother, as usual, wearing a long hostess gown, and my father gave me a lavish party in our Brooklyn town house. Watching me cut the ice cream cake *(below)* is the school hot ticket, Jane Weissman, at the far left and, seated on the right, my cousin Allan Thenen, who at that moment cared for cake almost more than for life itself.

This child knows she is a major talent and should be performing up there on the silver screen with Margaret O'Brien. So she took this picture off the piano and mailed it, frame and all, to MGM in Hollywood, expecting them to see what her mother saw—a lovely young girl instead of that round, pudgy face. She could not understand why MGM never screen-tested her, never replied, never even thanked her for the frame.

ered a brief soliloquy on our good fortune to be part of an historic theatrical event. *Seawood,* he said, was his masterpiece and its original Chicago production had launched Geraldine Page and Ralph Meeker. Unfortunately, due to prior commitments, they were unable at the moment to repeat their Chicago triumph in New York, so he would rather proceed without them and do an experimental production, free of the complications of Broadway. That way, the prominent New York critics would see in its purest form this meaningful, this major, this *great* work, receiving now its New York airing—in Armand's apartment. We all went, "Right, right."

So now that Armand had refined his play, honed it, polished it to a high luster with lapidary skill—he had assembled the finest possible group of ensemble players. I remember a skinny high school girl with a large nose and a pin that said GO ERASMUS, and an elderly woman with gray hair, a bombshell named Ingrid with a black bra under a see-through white blouse, who I found out later was the secretary for the agent, Irvin Arthur, a man who would become extremely important in my life. There was George, who was twenty and already wearing a hairpiece. His last role had been in an off-off Broadway production of Ibsen's *Enemy of the People* for which he was paid ten dollars the first week—and the second week was given the choice of being cut from the cast or returning the ten dollars. And there was chubby me.

Jim handed out "sides," which are cards with only your cues and lines, and we read for various parts. None of the characters had names, just titles. George was Man from the Sea. Lorna of the Dunes screamed for the big-nosed girl—a sort of Jewish Ondine. The gray-haired woman was going to be Old Woman and Ingrid's outfit beat me out for Prostitute. Armand was very upset and said, "I'm terribly sorry, Miss Molinsky, but there is nothing for you in the women's parts. All we have left is Man in Black."

Desperately, I said, "Why couldn't we make Man in Black into Woman in Black? She could be a lesbian."

Armand pondered that inspiration, counted the actors again, went out and checked the stairwell for latecomers, and conferred in whispers with the director—who probably told him I came from a large family willing to pay to see me, so twenty-eight bucks, his rent for three weeks, would be walking out that door. They made a quick artistic decision. How often stage history hinges on such moments. Judy Holliday replaced Jean Arthur in *Born Yesterday* in Philadelphia and became a star. Shirley MacLaine went in for Carol Haney in *Pajama Game.* Now Armand was announcing, "Perhaps we could make the role which was created for Ralph Meeker into a female part."

I said, "Fine," and we were told rehearsals would be evenings and Saturdays. Everybody—including Armand—worked at daytime jobs.

Down on the street George and I had hysterics: "So Geraldine and Ralph couldn't make this, huh? She got tired at the fourth floor and said, 'Screw this! Either he moves or I quit,' and she walked back down." But we did not care. It was a showcase.

Once rehearsals began in Armand de Beauchamp's living room, we decided that he was truly demented, that we were dealing with a banana in a cake. Like all Renaissance men of the theater, Armand was a producer, a teacher, a writer, an impresario who did everything, including direct Jim, the supposed director. A rehearsal area was created on the gray rug by pushing the dragon-armed chair, the garden coffee table, a folding wood chaise longue, and a potted palm back against one wall. Armand, in the pose of the Rodin statue *The Thinker,* sat perched on the wobbly arm of the ramshackle couch observing Jim, whose age and skills seemed more suited to a high school play than a major off Broadway production. Though he had little grasp of stage right or stage left, he had his own repertoire of affectations, throwing tantrums when the actors displeased him, stomping his heavy boots on the floor like a gay horse in a snit.

As with any great work of art, there were many tempestuous and stormy creative sessions. Every ten minutes or so, when there was a lapse in Jim's creativity, Armand would vault into action, a whirligig of cheap theatricality, a hyperthyroid Mischa Auer, running elongated fingers through his hair or waving artistic hands of agony with wrists flopping, *very* upset—"No, no! No, no"—and then clasping his temples or flinging his arms out like helicopter blades as he invoked the *New York Mirror*'s legendary columnist wailing, "Oh, God. If Winchell finds out what's going on here! If Winchell ever *knows!*" Apparently Winchell eventually did find out. Though the doctors claimed he died of cancer, his wife said it was a broken heart.

Armand would then drag Jim into the kitchen, from which Jim would presently emerge a little crestfallen but full of direction. We were being directed by Charlie McCarthy with Edgar Bergen absent part of the time.

We never saw a script and rehearsed in a vacuum, watching our little cards for the cue and then reading off our line, never really knowing the context of anything. When Armand sometimes inserted new lines—great works are always in flux —we would stir up our courage and ask him what it meant. He flapped his hands and said vaguely, "Just get into it. Interpret it." During the pauses while Armand was imparting his wisdom to Jim, we would cluster disconsolately on the rug and ask each other, "What the hell is this about?" We thought the play was an allegory because of the names, and concluded maybe it was some sort of American Beckett. I sat through one entire rehearsal and kept saying to myself, "I've read Ruskin, waded through John Stuart Mill, done *Beowulf* in the original Old English—but I don't get this." So I never watched another rehearsal, deciding it was better to come in fresh—from the kitchen.

That was where the cast sat around and talked show business and drank their containers of coffee. I liked the high school girl with the big nose who was funny and made jokes. We had immediate rapport, maybe because she seemed a tough little hustler, paying her way by working part time as a cashier at a Chinese restaurant, but still obviously vulnerable, always arriving as a package with a dark-haired girlfriend for comfort and support. Despite being the youngest person by far, she was very outgoing and at the first rehearsal came right over to me and said, "Hi, what's your name? My name's Barbara Streisand."

Even then she clearly intended to become Barbra Streisand. She was impressive, carrying at her age a full theatrical makeup kit with greasepaint in *tubes* and an Equity card earned in summer stock. Even though she was incongruous among us, so young with her Brooklyn accent, she was obviously very serious about acting and we felt a force inside her, an authenticity even in the midst of the idiocy of *Seawood.* As Woman in Black I was supposed to be in love with Barbra, but I thought that a lesbian should have other colors to her life and I tried to give myself a history, a little third dimension, and I ad-libbed a guy who had jilted me—as Ralph Meeker certainly would have done. But Armand cut it all out. What we were doing was a masterpiece, so there was no need for changes. You do not rewrite Shaw or Shakespeare, so you certainly don't rewrite Armand de Beauchamp.

We rehearsed about two weeks, courting pneumonia every minute. It was January during a cold New York winter and Armand obviously could not afford heat, so we rehearsed in coats and gloves. After rehearsals George and I sat over coffee in Grand Central Station, waiting for my train and laughing and doing imitations of Jim treating Armand like a genius. We could not believe Armand had ever coached Tab Hunter—it was too incredible that *anybody* had ever coached Tab Hunter. We also wondered how *Seawood* had launched Geraldine Page and Ralph Meeker—certainly not into a theatrical career. Maybe it had launched them from Chicago to New York because they had to get out of town.

But there was no laughter at the rehearsals because we all wanted these roles *so* much. Woman in Black meant I was *in* something, meant I was an actress, and when I made the rounds during the day, I could say, "I'm in rehearsal for an off Broadway play," and that sounded wonderful. I did not mention that it was up six flights and not so much off Broadway as over Broadway.

On opening night my father actually drove in from his office in Brooklyn to see me. I remember watching him walk up all those stairs, an exhausted man climbing six flights to see his daughter play a lesbian, a man who, when I went to college, got five dollars for each patient and the tuition was two thousand dollars. I stood looking down the stairwell, thinking, *Just the urines alone he had to do.* I could see his hat coming up the stairs and it would stop at each landing and a hand would come out and grip the banister and I could hear panting. I felt awful and sad and loving and I wished he was coming to see something wonderful.

Armand's stage, appropriately named the Garret Theater, was located in an attic above his apartment, reached by a narrow, rickety flight of stairs from the living room. The play was a one-set masterpiece and on the low platform was an indoor summer cottage subtly indicated by a table with a piece of driftwood on it and a bed. The rear of the set was the brick wall of the building. Since it was a summer play, our costumes were skimpy, which did not bother Ingrid in her black bra and gossamer blouse. If she could not sleep her way to the top, she was going to bra her way to the top.

The rest of us, waiting in the kitchen for the audience to

struggle up the last lap to the attic, tingled from both excitement and cold. It was almost a full house—fifteen of the eighteen folding chairs were occupied. I had bought seven tickets and sent them to agents, but none of them came—so there is a God. Barbra had three people and George's roommate brought a girlfriend and there had been a sign in the USO club—OFF BROADWAY SHOW. DISCOUNT TO SERVICEMEN— and three sailors came who didn't know why they were there.

Jim said, "Places, please," and we filed up the narrow stairs and waited on the landing. Those of us who had to make our entrance from a closet on stage right crossed the stage very professionally, not looking at the audience, and jammed ourselves into the closet and shut the door. The closet was small, but we all knew each other.

The actual performance is a blur—the mind protects itself. I do remember I had a big love scene where I told Barbra I loved her very much and she rejected me and I had a knife in my hand and tried to kill her and then myself. I also remember a horrendous lot of coughing, like a tubercular ward, and knowing this whole thing was insane and wanting to turn and wink at the audience, sitting there in overcoats. But I felt fine performing, did not feel ashamed, and thought I was not bad as a woman in love with Barbra Streisand. But Armand was terribly upset with me for ad-libbing and I would have been fired if he could have found anybody else who looked more like Ralph Meeker than I did.

At the intermission, the three sailors left and the rest of the audience, all twelve of them, came down into the living room, searching futilely for a little warmth. To pick up comments, Armand tried to press himself invisibly into the tiny groups—which was like King Kong being incognito at a convention of monkeys. Since there was not great word of mouth for this play, all these embarrassed audiences were friends of somebody and faced the dilemma of finding *something* to say and, after hunting around, they would assume a wise expression and say, "This certainly is an interesting concept," or "My, they certainly are doing some interesting things." When Armand rushed into the kitchen to give us instant critiques, he would report that everybody thought the play was truly interesting and then tell us, "Speak louder. They can't hear you past the first row." I wondered what was wrong—fifty percent of the audience could hear us.

There was no curtain, so we all just bowed. On opening night there was a lot of applause and cries of "Author, author" from friends of Armand's on the right side of the attic; I'd like to see the receipts for *their* tickets. My father left immediately while the cast stayed for notes. There was no opening night party.

At home that night my father said he thought the play was terrible but I was good—which was very sweet of him. The next day in *Show Business* there was actually a review and it called *Seawood* sophomoric, soap opera-ish, and ridiculous—and said the performances couldn't be evaluated because the material was so bad.

The next night—productions were on Thursdays, Fridays, and Saturdays—was like going down into the bunker with Hitler, only this was *up* into the bunker. Armand, homicidal and suicidal at the same time, assembled the cast in the living room rehearsal hall and put on the best performance I ever witnessed in those environs. Stalking the rug like Barrymore, the fine instrument of his voice alternating between fearful sibilants and booming crescendos, he lambasted us for ruining a great work of the theater, for violating the traditions set by Geraldine Page and Ralph Meeker. He had thought he had a young director who could conceptualize this great work, but he had been sabotaged and was not going to stand impotently by and tolerate shoddy performances and the violation of everything best in the theater. "If Winchell *knew!*" So he was taking over the reins and directing *Seawood* himself. All the while, Jim sat in a corner, his entire career crashed around him, an officer in disgrace whose epaulets had been ripped off. Clearly, he would have to turn in his boots because he was no longer fit to stamp them.

Armand's conception was that the play should be screamed at the top of our lungs—in a theater where the audience was almost in our laps. He kept telling us, "Bigger! Make it bigger!"—not better, bigger, and that's what he got. But even so, the insanity of theater is such that we all continued to send cards to agents and call up and say, "Could I put some tickets aside for you?"

On the next night we had ten people, some of them Armand's students assigned to come. On another night, in the second—and last—row, there was that mystery woman who inevitably appears at a showcase and the whisper always goes around, "She's somebody from Rodgers and Hammerstein's office." "That's David Merrick's secretary." "Thelma Ritter's assistant!" So, typically, we played everything to her —and at the end she reached into her shopping bag and pulled out a bottle in a brown paper bag and took a swig.

On Saturday night we had twelve, a full house, which included my father *and* my mother and, when I got home that night, they were waiting up for me in the kitchen, which my mother had done entirely in pink—including a pink refrigerator and pink stove—because she thought the color would make my sister and me look prettier. They were sitting at the captain's table with its pink linen tablecloth. My mother, very erect in the wooden captain's chair, said, "Sit down, Joan, we want to talk to you." Frightened and already angry, I faced them.

My mother started in, "Daddy and I are very concerned that you are throwing away your life on acting—a pretty girl like you, not getting any younger. Tell us you want to go to law school like your sister and we'll pay. Tell us you want to go to medical school. We'll find the money. We're not here to hold you back. But you can't waste your life. We love you and we can't stand by and say nothing."

I am sure my voice was harsh with resentment from the first second. "Acting is all I've wanted to do since I was a little girl," I said. "You wanted me to get married and get the house and the maid and I married Jimmy Sanger and it was a disaster. Your way didn't work for me, so I'm going to do it my way for a change." My mother's hand went to her pearls. In that house full of the artifacts of *their* dream, I was saying that everything they thought was important, the possessions they had married and struggled and quarreled to achieve, were wrong and they had sold out their happiness for nothing.

My father, leaning forward in his chair, said, "What are you doing this acting for? That play was the worst piece of garbage I ever saw and these people are garbage. You're crazy."

I said nothing, thinking, *They're right, but I am never, never going to let them know it.*

My mother, her lips getting thinner and thinner, said "We have supported you, sacrificed for you, done nothing but give up things—Daddy worked so hard to send you through college—and you're throwing it all away. Is this the way you are going to repay us? How can you do this to us?"

"I'm sorry," I answered, voice louder, "but I never asked you, never said, 'Do it for me.' And I'm not asking for help now. And that play isn't garbage. You don't understand. It's off Broadway and it's experimental."

"What makes you think you can be a success?" my mother asked. "You're going into a world you know nothing about, where you know no one. How do you know you have talent? Has anyone ever said you have talent? It's absolutely, utterly ridiculous. You're talented in so many other ways, why throw your life away in the one area you have nothing? Look at your sister. Barbara's a lawyer."

"I know I have talent," I said, low and throbbing. "I know

I do. I just know it. At Barnard I was the star and won out over everybody."

"Big deal," my father said sarcastically. "You were a star in college. That means bubkes. Those were not big actors, just college kids. You're kidding yourself."

"You're our daughter," my mother said, "and as long as you live in our house you'll obey our rules."

Now I was shouting—shouting them down, the way I won all my fights with them. "I don't care what you say," I screamed. "I'll leave the house. I'm going to do it *my* way. I'm going to do what *I* want." I pushed away from the table, ran upstairs, and slammed my bedroom door behind me.

The next morning my mother tapped on the door, came into the room, and sat on my bed. "We're only doing this because Daddy and I love you," she said. "We don't want to hurt you, but we can't sit by and watch you make a terrible mistake." I did not answer. I knew she was capitulating and I was relieved and frightened.

After six weeks of performances of *Seawood*, I arrived panting at Armand's door and he announced, "I'm sorry. No play. We've closed it." I went into the kitchen and got my little black dress and my makeup. On the way down the stairs I met Barbra Streisand coming up. I told her, "It's closed. There's no play."

She shrugged. "That's just as well. I got midterms."

5

UNTIL I HAD AN agent to sponsor me with legitimate producers, I would always remain part of that gray throng of perpetual outsiders haunting office anterooms—the sediment at the very bottom of show business. So the day after *Seawood* folded I immediately headed out on my rounds, trying again to impress and amuse those impassive secretaries, writing my notes that said, "This is your last warning: get Molinsky a job or you'll be wearing cement booties." But now, along with the foolery, I had a tiny quotient of confidence. Even on the absurd level of Armand de Beauchamp, I had been accepted as a professional and could say with a little throat in my voice, "I've just finished a six-week engagement in *Seawood,*" and to prove it, there was the entry on my résumé: "Garret Theater —*Seawood.*"

And now, sure enough, the months of romancing those hard ladies behind their battered desks did begin to pay off. A few said to the big man, "You really ought to see her. She's a funny girl," and I did sometimes get through that closed door into the inner sanctum. For these red-letter occasions I worked up a scene from *Cat on a Hot Tin Roof,* with a swarthy, superintense, penniless actor friend named Shelley Fromme.

One day we performed it for a little agent named Hamilton Katz. The door swung open for us and there he was, fifties, paunchy, the skin on his face loose, the folds and lines seeming to converge on the short cigar in his mouth. His eyes were tired, dead with the same defeat that was in the eyes of his clients. He took the cigar out of his mouth and gestured us into the office, which, like the cells of all such agents, suffered from the disease of grunge. The veneer was scaling off the desk, the leatherette on the chairs was crazed with cracks, the glass on the doors of the old-fashioned bookcases was blind with dust. On the walls hung the requisite gallery of endorsed photographs in black Woolworth frames—a picture of Myra and Her Trained Cockatoos inscribed "Thank you for taking me to the top." Everywhere, on every flat surface, were heaps of actors' résumés, stacks and stacks of them, someday to be filed, never to be read—and I knew that mine was already lost somewhere in that mess.

We asked Hamilton Katz if we could change into our costumes and he made a be-my-guest gesture with his cigar and positioned it again in the center of his mouth. Feeling his pale eyes watching intently, I rapidly stripped my skirt down onto the floor, yanked my sweater over my head, and put them tidily onto a pile of résumés—and told myself this was all professional, neutral, like a doctor's office. In my black slip, as Maggie the Cat, I faced my Brick—Shelley Fromme in pajama bottoms, leaning on a crutch. We began the scene, Maggie saying, "Living with someone you love can be lonelier —than living entirely *alone!*—if the one that y' love doesn't love you . . ."

With cigar smoke smogging the room, car horns honking in the street below, jet engines roaring overhead, the secretary's phone ringing outside the door, the buttons on Hamilton Katz's phone flashing irritably, it was a little bit hard to be Barbara Bel Geddes and recreate the magic we had found rehearsing in Shelley's apartment. The only spot of peace in the room was Hamilton Katz, sitting immobile and impassive, his sole sign of life an occasional twitch of the pouch under his right eye.

Just as Maggie was telling Brick she thinks he is a gay guy, the door behind us banged open and the secretary's voice announced, "It's the Con Ed matter." Hamilton Katz, interrupting his coma, motioned us out of the room with his cigar, saying, "Please step outside for a minute." So I was back again in the anteroom and the best piece of acting I did that day was to look dignified, standing there in my black slip under the unwinking gaze of a line of actors bundled up in coats and galoshes, while through the door came Hamilton Katz's voice screaming, "You shut off my electricity and I'll sue you."

When we returned inside to finish the scene, it was even harder to ignite the magic. And when Hamilton Katz's cigar actually went out and he had to rouse himself to relight it, I gave up and kind of laughed and said, "Guess this isn't our day." While we pulled our clothes back on, life surged into Hamilton Katz. Rapidly he dialed his phone and yelled into it, "Harry, I got to have the commission. Look, Harry, I got you $125; you never saw that much money before in your life. I want my $12.50. I don't want to hear troubles. That was a favor. That was the best summer stock in Jersey."

One agent—after I told him I could sing and dance— actually sent me on a cattle call for the chorus of a new Noel Coward musical, *Look After Lulu,* and that was incredible to me —my first shot at real *theater.* For that hour I was an accepted part of Broadway, going down an alley past people with scripts and saying at the stage door, "Murray Prince sent me." They checked a list and I was on it and the backstage doors opened to me and I was allowed inside onto a real stage. The talent coordinator lined us up and Noel Coward came out and was wonderful, wearing a camel's hair coat shrugged over his shoulders, just the way he was supposed to. He said, "I'm Noel Coward," as though we did not know.

He walked down the line, pointing occasionally and saying, "Yes. Yes." That finger swept past my nose so fast . . . but I did not mind. It was enough to have been sent up for a legitimate play and turned down by an English gentleman—

and I had a name I could drop at home: "I auditioned today for Noel Coward."

Another bonus from *Seawood* was my friendship with George Maisel. He had more chutzpah than I did and would say, "Let's go to the Theatre Guild," which actually meant, "Let's go ask Armina Marshall's secretary if they're hiring any extras." With George, I did get in to see a few legitimate producers, but most of the time the catch-22 was in effect: they just said briskly, "We don't take résumés; have your agent make an appointment"—at which point I was dead.

Then, in April of that year, 1958, George announced he had once again found us a brilliant vehicle for our talents, again just a showcase but full of glory and possibilities. Two young men, Noel Gayle and his lover, Clark, were pooling their pennies toward a life together in the theater, Noel working in an optometry shop, Clark operating a successful hairdressing salon. Their initial production was to be *Bernardine,* a comedy about high school boys trying to come of age written by Mary Chase, who also wrote *Harvey.*

George and I, full of the actor's invincible hope, auditioned and won roles. But in show business there are always side requirements. To be cast in *Seawood,* we had to sell ten tickets. To get his part in *Bernardine,* George had to have his eyebrows tweezed at Clark's salon because Noel Gayle thought they were too heavy. George, of course, was willing to make any sacrifices for his art, but did murmur that it was the first time he had ever had his eyebrows reviewed.

I think we were also cast as the company's token heterosexuals. For the first time I was a minority in a coterie of gays and was so unsure of myself I stuck very close to George and simply did my work, perfecting my character of an older woman who was pursued by one of the high school boys. It was easy to submerge myself because this time the production seemed professional—we had a real proscenium theater in the YMCA on West Sixty-third Street and Noel Gayle appeared to me to be entirely capable—but then Helen Keller would have been a big improvement on Armand de Beauchamp.

My parents came to opening night and brought my mother's close friend whom we called Aunt Fanny, their only trusted connection with show business. In England in the early 1900s she had been "Happy" Fanny Fields, a famous music hall star who had a major affair with the Prince of Wales, the future King Edward VII. When Fanny hit menopause, she married rich Dr. Rongee in New York and lived a fabulous life —had the butler and maids, gave small dinners in restaurant private rooms, and had a car and chauffeur waiting downstairs all day. Aunt Fanny did fine for herself; whatever the prince had taught her she remembered.

She was my mother's fantasy come true and my mother idolized Aunt Fanny, who would drive to Larchmont to have tea with her—two kindred spirits seeing themselves as truly elegant women. Aunt Fanny would say, "I would rather sit in your kitchen with you, Beatrice, than be at Buckingham Palace with people for whom I have no feeling." I hated her. Once she came over to me—I was chubby and wearing a sleeveless dress—and pinched my upper arm and said, "Flesh, flesh, flesh."

After that first night of *Bernardine,* the four of us went to the Palm Court at the Plaza Hotel. A strolling violinist serenaded Aunt Fanny as she sat there, very straight and thin, her silver-gray hair in a bouffant—Maria Ouspenskaya in a high choker crusted with pearls and a cameo. Against her chair leaned a walking stick with a mother-of-pearl handle. I felt terrific, very *theater,* very *in,* still wearing my stage makeup and costume—a pale green dress and pale green stockings and my legs were good—and I thought I had done a nice job onstage, getting my laughs from a full house, and I was mentally planning which agents should receive tickets.

When the violinist was finished, my mother leaned portentously across the table and said, "Please, Fanny, tell us. Does Joan have talent?" We all held our breath.

"Absolutely no talent whatsoever," answered "Happy" Fanny Fields.

Oh! I was destroyed! I wish I had told her, "You old bitch, you evil, mean, self-centered old lady!" But I think at that moment we were two women looking at each other, both wanting to be in the theater and, if she could not have it, I was not going to have it. In a way, she won, because that night permanently confirmed all my parents' fears and forever validated their campaign to get me out of show business.

There were only five performances of *Bernardine,* but just as Ingmar Bergman had his stable of repertory players, so the Noel Gayle Players were reassembled for another showcase around Clark. This time it was *See the Jaguar* by N. Richard Nash, a brooding, dullish allegory in blank verse which had bombed on Broadway in 1952, so it seemed natural to them to revive it off Broadway, everybody striking stances like a Calvin Klein commercial and using corn pone southern accents to mouth lines like "The world is fang and claw—man and nature—so you gotta have an iron gut!" Fortunately, Clark was multitalented and could make the transition from light comedy to serious drama by dyeing his hair dark. But this time George Maisel drew the line at having his eyebrows tweezed.

We could not use the YMCA theater, maybe because somebody there had taken a good look at *Bernardine,* so we rehearsed at night in Noel's apartment on the West Side, watched from the walls by posters of Jeanette MacDonald and Sonja Henie. I remember some very strange things on those walls, like a framed Greta Garbo footprint. By now, after

Bernardine, I was acclimatized to gay society and, no longer shy and aloof, could relax and look around me and savor it and realize that gays are terribly sensitive and vulnerable, terribly open and bright with that wicked, vicious humor I love—really their form of gallows humor. They are victims and outcasts—like Jews—and their defense is to see the silliness and outrageousness in life and laugh at it. I had never been around that before and I took to it like a duck to water. In *Jaguar* I found my girlfriends for my whole life.

I have never been truly close to women, never had great women friends—probably because we see each other as threats, competing for attention as sexual beings. I was not in competition with these gay men, but had the same interests, same goals, same humor. They were what I wished my sister had been. This was the first time anybody had ever said to me, "Wear blue. You look great in blue. Put the pin over here. Let's change your hair. Oh, it looks great. Come on, try false eyelashes."

The gays in *Jaguar* were really not there to be actors. They were there for the sex. Their theater was posturing to each other—lots of stomachs sucked in, lots of biceps tensed, lots of eyes flitting, lots of flirtations, great love affairs, traumatic breakups—lots of wonderful bleached blond heads with weepy red eyes. I could figure out the pairings by which bodies brushed during rehearsals, which coffee cups were shared, which dance bags were nestled together. When that apartment warmed up a fraction of a degree, the cast immediately felt *very* warm and everybody right away pulled off their sweaters and shirts.

None of that bothered me, but onstage there can be slight problems when the leading man is more feminine than the leading woman. When Clark could not bring himself to kiss the heroine, Noel restaged the big love scene, keeping Clark's back toward the audience—perhaps setting the modern precedent for simulated stage sex. Sometimes when Clark and I were building scenes of mythic symbolism pulsing with sexual tension, I found concentration difficult because actors on the sidelines were saying to each other, "That's adorable," and another saying, "I'm going to wear a blue polka-dot bandanna—do you think it will set off my eyes?"

Our theater, over a parking garage, was a loft where an acting coach named Eli Rill had built a little stage for his classes and rented it out at night as the Eli Rill Theater. To pay for it, Clark must have been working overtime on perms and bleaches. There was room for about sixty folding chairs but no stage curtain, and all the magic had to be done with lights. From the garage ramps below came the screech of tires on the curves and the roar of motors being gunned, so in the middle of "If I'da seen some man-juice in you, that woulda been good," we heard *vrrrooomm, vrrrooomm.* Car exhaust fumes permeated the Eli Rill Theater and I thought by the third act it would be a race whether the play had died or the audience. The entrance door to the stairs up to the loft was just at the right of the garage—so if you missed the theater door and handed them your ticket, you got a car.

The program, a green mimeographed paper stapled together, was full of the usual lies. I put my address and phone number at the beginning of the notes because if anybody wanted to get me, I did not want one instant of trouble finding this remarkable girl.

The notes read:

> Born in Cairo, Egypt, where her physician father had gone to fight a smallpox epidemic, Joan has lived in most of the principal cities of Europe. She considers Rome "my true hometown." It was there, at the age of six, that she made her stage debut in the Italian version of *Little Women.* Our delicious blond leading lady has appeared in thirty off Broadway productions, including leads in *Detective Story* and

Born Yesterday, and was the beloved Bernardine in our recent production.

But in that dumb loft over a garage, that pigsty reeking of car fumes, there was glamour. We were actors and actresses, all of us pooling our dreams. Janna, my part, originated on Broadway by Constance Ford, was a dramatic role and even if everything around me was not great, even if everybody else was wearing *very* tight jeans and soft leather dancer's shoes, I had my big speeches, my moments to shine, had my chances to live my fantasy. And working together to build this play, we accepted each other's dream selves. In that loft every one of us was a success in life—not a single failure—which is the alchemy that draws the misfits of the world into the theater. At home in Larchmont I was made to feel a failure, my expensive education wasted. When anybody telephoned to leave a message, my mother would ask anxiously, "Do you really think she's talented?" My father referred to my actor friends as "sissy boys" and made sarcastic jokes about my career. He would hand the phone to me, saying, "It's for you. Billy Rose calling."

But I suppose there was no possibility that my parents could grasp what the Noel Gayle Players meant to me. They had no idea what it was to share a goal, to do something together. We were four strangers living in a house with nothing in common, nothing to be passionate about together, no feeling of "us against them"—which is what happens in the theater. At home I never had anything like the Eli Rill Theater, never anything as intense, as fulfilling, as consuming.

Today I still love to sit at my daughter Melissa's school at night, watching them rehearse the school play. The room is dark. Sweaters are draped over chairs and the seats are folded back. Dance bags are on the floor. Coffee cups and Tab cans are everywhere. Someone, very upset, is sitting in front at a card table saying, "Line, please. Line. Do it again." Nerves are raw. People are *exhausted,* are sleeping, are whispering. There is a lot of bravery—and soft crying because the director was mean. But everything is focused on that shining spot onstage. Even on that elementary level, you are joined together to do something. It is a kind of home. When everything is over for me and I am an old lady, let me watch kids rehearse in a darkened room.

The first weekend, *See the Jaguar* went well. As usual, it was an invited audience and responsive—though the applause came at odd and unpredictable times. Barefoot in a red calico sun dress, I was the daughter of a man who lived to hunt animals and whose dream was to have a caged jaguar at his roadside gas station. My lover was defying my father and wanted to take me away and I remember there was a cage and, instead of a jaguar, a bare-chested boy was locked inside it— the role played on Broadway by Jimmy Dean.

My moments onstage seemed to go very well, so this time I called in every single favor, contacted every person I had ever visited on my rounds, saying, "Please come and see me as Janna." It was my third production and by then I had worn them to a frazzle, so they all came on the *same* Friday night. On that night, before the performance, I peeked out from behind the sheet strung up to create a dressing room and I saw, lined up on the folding chairs, every agent and secretary I had ever romanced for an entire year. The room seemed totally filled by them, every person I thought could help me—the secretary from the Martin Goodman office, the casting girl from the Theatre Guild, the secretary from Kermit Bloomgarden's office—every off Broadway producer I had ever met. Even Strasberg's secretary from The Actors Studio.

Their presence threw me totally. They were now going to find out that I really did not have talent, that I was not good enough, that everything had been a mistake. Now they would *know.* So I did what I still do when there is somebody famous in the audience, somebody who will judge me: I became almost disabled with tension, like a violin whose strings are too tight.

During the show everything that could go wrong, went wrong. Nobody was connecting at all onstage. Doors stuck, props were not in place, lights went on and off at the wrong times. Down in the garage, in addition to the usual racket of tires and motors, somebody's car seemed to have been stolen because there were police sirens and a lot of English and Spanish voices screaming "Fuck you!" A truck must have blown up because fumes filled the theater like a fog. And during a particularly tense though understated moment of drama, a stream of fire engines, sirens wailing, passed beneath the windows . . . and passed . . . and passed—it must have been the Chicago Fire—drowning out every sound onstage. We froze and waited . . . and waited . . . and waited . . . as though we had switched from a play to a tableau.

The whole performance was like a film whose happy scenes suddenly turn evil and you realize it is a horror movie. Everything that had seemed glamorous and fun and camp turned grotesque, exposing a sorry lot of painted-up amateurs, foolishly deluding ourselves. I realized that I had no acting technique at all and was working only on emotion. When the emotion was not there, I had nothing—except my tension, which made me speed up and stutter, saying, "I'll be a tree that goes to w-w-w-w-wood: no f-f-f-f-flower and no f-f-f-f-fruit!" I despised myself utterly.

The roomful of secretaries and agents was not rapt. I could glimpse people fanning themselves with the program, could hear them shifting in the folding chairs and opening their purses to look for subway money and riffling through the program to see if this interminable play was two or three acts.

In the third act the boy in the cage must have really felt

his lines—"Let me out"—because the broomstick bars suddenly came apart in his hands. Now the poor schlep had to
hold the cage together and after my big speech about how this
boy's spirit must go free and his body with it and I'm going to
let him go now, the boy just handed me the bars and slunk
away.

At the end, with no curtain, there was a blackout and the
cast appeared together for the curtain call. Then my philoso-
phy class at Barnard finally paid off. I understood the proposi-
tion of one hand clapping.

After the curtain call I hid in the dressing room behind
the sheet. I could not face anybody in that audience—they
were witnesses to a murder I had committed and I just wanted
to get away. I had come into those agents' offices with a little
bit of panache, a little bit of style, and now they had seen me in
my underwear and I reacted exactly as I still do after a bad
performance, feeling I have totally violated my image of myself—which is the perfect performing monkey every time, the
monkey that never misses a trick.

And I am genuinely frightened that people will come
backstage and lie to me.

"Good show," they say.

"The worst," I say.

They say, "Well, the audience was a little slow."

Then I get furious and want to tell them, "Why don't you
just say to me it was a horrendous show. Don't be nice. Don't
lie." They are forcing me to be polite, too, and lie and play the
same game and they are lying because they pity me, which
says I am a loser and I cannot stand that.

Fortunately, nobody came back to see me after *Jaguar*.
While the friends and relatives of other actors were lying,
saying, "Terrific, good," I faced a mirror, as close in a corner
as I could get, taking off my makeup. I will never need to have

my skin peeled, because that night I took off three to five layers. I was too humiliated to turn around until everybody had left, even if I had to die of carbon monoxide. I was too ashamed to walk out onto Fifty-fourth Street and bump into somebody I had invited—who would be, I was sure, on the way to the Carnegie Delicatessen to enjoy a lot of good laughs at me and the play.

When Eli Rill's loft was absolutely empty, I left, knowing that I could never go back to any of those secretaries. I was not going to stand there and be told that they had seen me and that "We feel there is nothing we can do for you at this time"—get the kiss off. Never again would they laugh *with* me —which means you are intelligent and witty and they want to be your friend. Now they would be laughing *at* me—which means you are an ass, a fool, and not worth their respect. A whole year of jokes and kidding and smiles and flowers and coffee and crawling on my belly was down the toilet in one night.

For three days after *See the Jaguar,* I once again hid out in bed. The only light I saw was inside the refrigerator when I fetched the thirty chicken pot pies I ate in my room off a tray. The rest of the time I lay paralyzed by my customary black depression—so ashamed, so full of self-loathing that I did not wish to talk to anybody remotely connected with my failure. When my mother came into the room, I refused to talk to her and silently went into the bathroom and locked the door. But it was hard not to talk to myself. When I asked, "Who screwed you up?" I could not delude myself. I had to answer, "You did."

I could not forgive myself for messing up my predestined path to success, for upsetting all my expectations. I knew that the movie of my life story had to open with thirty minutes of suffering and I had willingly played my struggle scenes at office temp jobs and making the rounds, gladly acted my failure scenes with *Seawood* and Aunt Fanny. But now those were finished and *Jaguar* was supposed to be the turning point, the beginning of the next ninety minutes which showed that in spite of failure, dreams do come true. But something had gone very wrong. Here was yet another failure and the whole hour and twenty minutes was slipping away.

I was still sure that there was an actress inside me—like a thin person fighting to get out of a fat one—but there seemed to be no place to start fresh, no person I had not tried, no process that would take me from A to B to C, like an internship in a business. I was discovering that there is no business in show business and I would have to build my own ladder as I went along, and I no longer knew how. And at any moment my mother would begin her litany, saying to me, "Now that you've gotten the acting out of your system, you can get a job. And I really think you should be going to the Jewish Guild for the Blind fundraisers. You might meet some very nice young men there."

Finally, I *had* to get on that train and go back into New York. For a week I just wandered around the city, immobilized, looking in stores at things I could not afford—avoiding everybody, wondering what to do—and knowing I could walk right into any department store and with my merchandising background get a great job in eight minutes. I was terrified of starting up again at Brown's Office Temporaries now that I was no longer an actress typing to eat while my real job was darting off during lunch hour to visit an agent's office. If I was simply an office temp secretary, I would turn into a loose end and something malignant would start to grow.

I was saved then—and a thousand other times—by an ex-marine named Nick Clemente who wanted to be an actor. While rehearsing for *Jaguar*, I had gone out to dinner in

Greenwich Village with friends and one of them brought Nick, and I thought how handsome and fun he was—a big man, dark, with regular features and constantly smiling and laughing, a great audience and appreciator, very bright and street smart, very Italian in his joy in food, his expressive gestures, his zest for life. I thought no more about him, but he began cultivating me and soon I found that I needed a man who loved me and, because there was very little goodness in my life then, needed this man in particular.

He was the personification of "good." He took a goodness pill every morning and it worked and he walked around sweet and kind all day. Warmth poured from him. Everybody liked Nicky. We would be eating in some awful dump and Nicky would read the name of the waitress on her badge and say, "Louise, I know it's been a terrible day, but could you bring me a piece of pie," and the way he said it made Louise suddenly glow and bring him back a double slice. If he had any bad traits, they never surfaced in all the time I knew him.

He had humor like my father's, was able to make anybody laugh and able to find the laugh in anything, turning everything bearable no matter how awful it was. When I acquired a dreadful wreck of a car, the auto registration man said, "Don't forget, a car is a lethal weapon," and Nicky would keep repeating that, turning the horrors of that car into fun. He thought people were funny and he was a mimic—imitating his grandmother telling him in broken Italian to go to the movies to find out the facts of life. Nicky said that all he ever saw in movies was the husband and wife kissing and then there would be waves crashing on the beach—so for years, trying to be a good boy, he would not go near a beach with a date. A motel, yes. Never the beach.

But Nicky was not a goody-goody. His father had a double life. He was a house painter who also worked for the Mafia, designing and building alcohol stills, touring the upstate countryside, renting barns and shipping out the alcohol in milk trucks to legitimate liquor companies who were avoiding taxes.

Nicky became the black sheep in his family by leaving school at fifteen to go on the stage and was much more a boy of the streets than of book knowledge, operating by instinct rather than intellect. He knew a son of a bitch when he saw one, but there was no malice in him, no mean bones—and also at that time not much ambition. He was very simple in his needs; whatever came was good enough—if it was a roll with butter, fine, hey, this looks delicious. Living in the minute, never worrying about the future, he always assumed he would land on his feet, so he enjoyed every single thing that happened, never caring that he had no money and no real job—which was fortunate because very soon I became his steady job.

It was an almost joyous relief to have a refuge in my life, to have Nicky there to pick me up for coffee after *Jaguar* rehearsals and make me laugh, to have a person with me to share winks and tell me afterward that I was right and they were wrong. He never burdened me with "I love you, I love you," and never proposed, probably because he knew I would say no. His courtship was all actions. He was my Sancho Panza and if I said, "Those windmills are knights in armor," he was there ready to fight by my side. He made it very easy for me to telephone and say, "Please, I have to go to Hamilton Katz's office," knowing he would keep me company. With him there, my life stopped being so brutally lonely; I could step up to those secretaries and say, "Here I am." Nicky made himself my courage, my drink, my stage mother, my Mr. T. The minute my mother heard his name and that he was an apprentice actor, she despised him and would hand the phone to me, saying dryly, "It's your Italian friend."

Now, wandering the city, scared and helpless, I made Nicky my therapist, sitting for hours with him in wretched Grand Central Station coffee shops, in the B & G, in Tad's

$1.49 Steak Houses telling him over and over that I was lost, that I had no belief in myself, no conviction, no self-confidence. And I always knew Nicky would say the things I needed somebody to say, knew he would tell me, "You *are* talented and terrific, and stop talking crazy. It *is* going to happen to you. You've *got* to start again. There *must* be a way." With Nicky behind me, I was able to go back into the fray.

At the B & G the would-be comedians regularly gathered in the first section of stools and I would nod distantly to them as I passed down the line to the actors' section. Sometimes when I went into a shoe store, there would be one of those comics saying, "Size, please."

I would say, "Oh, hi."

He would say, "Well, I just do this twice a week."

To me, the B & G comics and the sleazeballs I glimpsed at Hanson's Drug Store were the bottom, dressed in their too sharp outfits, white-on-white shirts, blue suede shoes, Tragedy and Comedy cuff links, polished nails, a pinkie ring with a star sapphire in it. Everybody had an ACT and everybody had PERSONALITY, saying to each other, "Hey, I got three minutes of shtick that'll kill ya. I had 'em screaming last night."

But it dawned on me that these sleazos were making rounds to agents who booked nightclubs, ones I had never seen—and these comics could actually do a little job at night and make six dollars and still have the daytime free. And clearly, if those fellows could stand up and tell a few jokes and make money, so could I. Right along I had been using laughter as my way to be special, to be welcome everywhere, be remembered by secretaries and sometimes they would say, "You should go into comedy. You're funny." Certainly cheap stand-up comedy would be easy, only a minor skill, not like *acting.* Comics did not have to shape themselves into a role, did not have to *feel,* did not work within an art form.

So, desperate, I began thinking that comedy might be the answer, just temporarily until I was discovered as an actress— or it could even, with luck, be another way into show business. I knew that Tammy Grimes, who was not moving as an actress, had put together a chichi little nightclub act, singing and being witty between numbers, and when Roddy McDowall dragged Noel Coward in to see her, he cast her in *Look After Lulu.*

One day on the street I met a model I had known when I was fashion coordinator at Bond Stores, the kind of model who shows off clothes in the department store restaurant. We talked a little and she told me about her husband, a comedian named Lou Alexander, who, she said, was making forty dollars doing four shows on Friday and Saturday at the Silver Slipper in Glen Cove, Long Island.

I thought, *My God, that is major buckeroos.* I told her I was thinking of going into comedy and she arranged for me to go out to the Silver Slipper and see Lou perform. Of course Nick Clemente took me. All the big dine-and-dance nightclubs in the Bronx, Brooklyn, Long Island, and Jersey were cheap imitations of the Copacabana. The stage usually projected out into the dance floor and was fancy with lights around the edge and had a semifabulous silver curtain which had seen better days and better acts. The show room walls were navy blue with silver trim and a tropical motif—wonderful silver palm trees, a little old but there. Circulating among the clientele would be a cigarette girl in a short outfit and waiters in white shirts, red clip-on ties, stained tuxedo pants, and little black mess jackets that did not fit because its original owner had long ago been fired. The orchestra leader had a hairpiece, and his name on the drums. The show was frequently a dance act, a comic, and a seminame singer—and the audio system rarely worked properly.

At the Silver Slipper, Nicky and I found Lou Alexander at a side table eating dinner. He was small and nice-looking and only in his late twenties. I was impressed that he received a free meal, with Jell-O for dessert. You could tell right away he was the comic—he had on a black mohair dinner jacket, patent leather loafers with tassels, a shirt with lots of ruffles, big French cuffs, and large initials on the breast pocket.

Lou Alexander was very nice to me. We sat with him while he ate his Jell-O and he told me to write down anything I wanted from his act because most of his material was borrowed too. He suggested that any lines he said as a man I could switch into women's jokes. And he made it clear that it did not happen overnight to be sitting in the Silver Slipper eating Jell-O and making forty dollars on a weekend. He told me that it was a very tough business, "but the end of the rainbow is beautiful and there should be room for a woman." I had figured that out for myself and was certain I could walk right in that door because there were not many girls who wanted to be Jerry Lewis.

Lou Alexander put us at a side table and we watched the show. He did a lot of jokes over his shoulder to the band, making them laugh—telling the piano player, "Next time play on the keys, not the cracks." He said the band used to be much bigger, but on its way from California they had been forced to go through fruit inspection. He had a routine about his girlfriend who was a hypnotist: "People say to me, 'Lou, does she ever put you under?' And I'd say, 'Yeah—and sometimes she put me on top.' " He interviewed himself as a Channel swimmer: " 'Tell me, Mr. Herring, what was it like to swim the Channel?' 'Well, as you know the Channel is twenty-six miles across; I swam nineteen miles, but I got tired and swam back.' "

I thought his act was terrible, yet people were laughing, so I decided, *If that garbage is what they think is funny, I'll give it to them. No problem.* The truth was, there was no way I could have done that act. He did a professional, slick job up there. He made the audience pay attention to him—ran the show—

looked as though he was in charge and having fun and was smooth and fast, "Hey, so where you from? Nice sweater. Where did you get it? Salvation Army? It's still got my name on it." Halfway through the act, he pulled open his bow tie to show he was *really* working. Whenever nobody laughed, he pressed on with energy. If his ego was on the line, he had learned to hide that.

I did write down one routine about a modern interpretive dancer whose every movement told a story. This gesture meant, "I love you." This body bend meant, "I am happy." Then Lou jumped up and down, which meant, "The beach is hot." I laughed and stole that. So it was a very educational evening. I was learning how to steal an act and finding out I would have no trouble making money as a comic. And Lou Alexander kindly gave me the name of a manager, Harry Brent.

THE DREAM was still to be Katharine Hepburn or Jennifer Jones—winning the Academy Award for great dramatic acting, "J. Sondra Meredith made you cry and you loved it!" —but in the meantime, after my seminal evening at the Silver Slipper, I moved four stools to the left at the B & G and began learning about a whole new world. Because the director of a play worries about costuming and lighting—and the material is prewritten—a stage actor needs only an agent. But in comedy I was going to need both an agent *and* a manager. The agent, for his ten percent, would book me into the cabarets. The manager, for another fifteen percent, if he was a good one, would concentrate on molding me into a professional comic, help me build and polish my act, consult about costumes and lights, find me an agent and fight with him to be sure I performed in the right places under the best conditions. A manager could actually create a career.

When I asked the B & G comics for names, they suggested Jack Rollins for a manager and Irvin Arthur for an agent. But obviously, before anything else, I needed an act. The B & G comics constantly talked about buying hunks and chunks of material, but I had no money, so at night, during Jack Paar and Ed Sullivan, while my mother reclined on a chaise longue and my father sat in the wing chair, I lay on the floor on my stomach with a pad and pencil. Getting an act together turned out to be very, very easy. All it took was twelve hours of TV watching. When anything seemed funny, down it went.

I took a whole routine from Dick Gautier—a son wants to be a boxer and his father is trying to argue him out of it in a stage Italian accent: "Why you wanna be a boxer? Do something a-good with a-you life, mak-a da music, mak-a da people laugh and dey cry and feel-a good inside."

The son answers tearfully, "Pop, why are you talking like that? You're not even Italian."

Then I locked myself in the bathroom and rehearsed my act, mumbling the lines over and over. When it was perfected, I marched in to see Irvin Arthur, whose name I already knew; his secretary had been Ingrid of the black bra in *Seawood.* I had my new fake comedy résumé and thought I could bluff it out. I used Ingrid as an introduction and he saw me right away. I did not know he was an important agent who supplied top acts to high-class clubs and could read my résumé and say immediately, "There is no Club Bijou in Cleveland." But he was a nice, good man and he must have seen something. I was a woman, which was very unusual. I was a college graduate, still with my little Lord & Taylor look. I was not Broadway Baby. So he told me I needed a manager and a lot of forming and should go to Jack Rollins because Jack could take a grain of sand and make it into an industry.

Jack Rollins was God to nightclub comedians and still is. His word alone could get an act a booking. At that time he was managing Milt Kamen, who was hot, hot, hot—and Tom Poston, who was The Man in the Street on *The Steve Allen Show*. He had Felicia Saunders, who was crying her heart out at The Blue Angel. He took on Mike Nichols and Elaine May when they first arrived in New York with an act that was a new, far reach in comedy. Jack Rollins almost lived in nightclubs, looking for newcomers he could form and mold. He had brought Harry Belafonte from nothing and made him a star—found him doing Johnny Mathis ballads and changed him to a calypso singer. At MCA the agents were saying, "Belafonte is a black folksinger who'll only work in Greenwich Village and that'll be the end of it." But Jack kept saying, "In three years he's going to be one of the biggest stars in the business." Jack always set time limits: "In five years he'll be an industry."

His office was in the Plaza Hotel. I went to the Palm Court, turned left at the sound of the violins, and walked to a little elevator that took me high up. When I stepped out of the elevator, I felt, "Hello, Flo Ziegfeld." There was his lovely secretary, Estelle. The furniture was Early American antiques —wonderful hutches and sideboards and dry sinks. There were primitive and modern sculptures and commissioned oil portraits of his clients—and not one autographed picture of a dog in a cape.

Jack came out right away. He gave everybody a moment. How does it hurt? Size 'em up. He has always been a solidly built man, with a flexible, fleshy face that could exude warmth, but was basically imposing in little half granny glasses. But he was also a great laugher and the picture I carry of him in my mind is bent double, laughing . . . with a cigar always in his hand. His clothes were loose, lots of dark gray flannel, heavy Harris tweeds, knitted ties. He spoke to me a few minutes and, like Irvin Arthur, was probably intrigued that here was a woman comic—and of his type, preppy and

untheatrical. There were no ruffles and suede shoes on Jack
Rollins performers, never an initial on them anywhere.

He asked if I had an act, and I said "Yes." He said, "All
right, let's see your act," and he took me over to Nola Studios,
which were on Fifty-seventh Street and had *the* great rehearsal
halls with chandeliers in some of the rooms and must have
cost at least two dollars an hour. I thought, *Who's going to pay
for this?* as we went into a big mirrored room with ballet
barres. He sat in a chair in the middle of the floor and I faced
him, not the least nervous, a happy amateur with no respect
for what I was doing. Out of my mouth came everything I had
stolen off television and Jack Rollins was warm, laughing and
nodding. But when I finished, he said, "You did that very
nicely. He smiled again and said, "But Dick Gautier does the
Golden Boy take-off better."

I could feel my face flush hot and into my consciousness
came an inkling that perhaps this new career might not be a
piece of cake. Then he gave me a little lecture. He said, "You
shouldn't be doing other people's material. Do your own
because you're naturally funny." He told me that other people's material only worked well for them, and when I knew
who I was, I would know what would work for me.

But I had enough gall to ask if he would handle me. Jack
Rollins said, "No, no, you're not ready for me yet," and told
me to keep working, keep trying, stay in touch with him, and
come back in six months. He told me I should stay in the
business. "You'll make it in three years," he said.

I was a little upset that I had not gotten a manager. One
of the advantages of bathroom rehearsals is that Jack Rollins
is going to sign you right then and there. Without his help I
did not have the luxury of slowly finding myself and I had to
get funny very fast and make a buck—and the only comedy I
could imagine then was what I was stealing. Writing a funny
joke about what I thought and felt, talking about myself onstage was unimaginable to me. To reveal myself that much, to

make myself so vulnerable, was terrifying—and my thoughts might be funny to a few friends over coffee, but that was not the humor currently making the vast public laugh.

I did what I always do. I decided they would never take me on a high level so I must pull myself slowly up through the ranks, starting at the bottom. So now I went to the bottom, to the lowest of the low. I took Lou Alexander's advice and went to see Harry Brent.

6

HARRY BRENT LIVED in the Wellington Hotel, the old shabby Wellington. I brought along Nick Clemente to ride shotgun and we walked together into the lobby, across the yellowed marble floor, past the wooden pillars blackened by a thousand coats of dirt and varnish. The worn leather chairs were ballooned underneath by rump-sprung springs. Over a door to the right was a big neon sign saying LUNCHEONETTE. Nicky said, "Unless Harry Brent owns this place, we're in trouble."

I said, "But one good thing, I'm not going to meet anybody here that knows my mother." Laughing made me feel safe. I was not going to be enveloped by the seediness that coated this world like dust.

Beyond a tattered green-brown potted palm—an urban palm that loved Broadway and would have died in Hawaii—and next to the front desk, where a clerk stood in his shirt sleeves, we saw a line of people waiting at the phone booths and along the wall were the house phones. I called Harry Brent, who was evidently not the eye of a storm of brilliant young performers because right away he said, "C'mon up." His room was at the end of a musty hall with stained walls I was careful not to touch. Nicky knocked on the tin door and it swung open and there was my hoped-for comedy guru.

Harry Brent, inclining his head of flowing white hair, was a medium height, roundish, handsomish man with sleepy eyes and a Florida tan from God knows where. He was down-at-the-heels natty, fully dressed for us in a frayed green-and-blue-plaid sports jacket and he had put on a blue knit tie because he was a gentleman. On his feet were blue socks and cracked blue imitation alligator loafers with big tassels and his white-on-white shirt had a blue HB monogrammed on the front. The French cuffs were buttoned with Tragedy and Comedy cuff links. Everything was color coordinated, a symphony . . . no, a rhapsody in blue.

When he stepped back with a flourish to usher us into his office-living room-bedroom-kitchen-reception room—his legs hit the bed. He took the cigar out of his mouth and, as though ushering us into a splendid suite of offices, he grandly said, "Come in, come in," and added, gesturing with the cigar toward a flimsy wooden chair by a rickety little table, "Sit. Please sit."

Memorizing his gestures so I could imitate them to Nicky later, praying he would like me, I took one step to the right and sat on the chair and Nicky leaned watchfully against the doorjamb. I could see past Harry Brent to the grimy window and past a milk carton on the windowsill to the air shaft. Above his head, like greasy brown streamers, extension cords converged on a plug in the overhead light. I thought, *When the phone rings, I'll bet the lights dim.*

Right away Harry Brent had to impress these two young kids off the street. As though he was a three-star maître d', he waved with his left hand and pinkie ring—more pinkie than ring—toward his kitchen on the bureau top with its toaster and hot plate and boxes of food and said, "May I offer you a small bit of nourishment?" I turned down the Fig Newtons and to be polite picked Ritz crackers and Velveeta cheese, and he did have the class to throw away the first, dried-up slice.

After leaning forward to serve me, Harry simply bent his knees and was immediately seated on the bed. In his deep whiskey voice he launched into a soliloquy about his stable of comedy acts—which turned out to be one comic named Dick Capri. Next, after pausing to reach his polished nails into a bowl of sunflower seeds on the bed and munch majestically, he called our attention to a framed bank check with "Insufficient Funds" stamped across it, hanging on the wall. It was from a young, long-ago Dean Martin, and Harry told us, "I found him, you know, I swear, God love him, Deano's on the phone to me once a month. 'Harry,' he says, 'you old son of a bitch, give me back that check. I wanna make it good.' 'Deano,' I tell him, 'leave me alone. You owe me a dinner. Okay?' "

I thought, *That's what a lifetime in show business has given this fifty-five-year-old man—a pinkie ring and a bounced check for fifteen dollars from Deano.* Aloud, I murmured appreciatively, registering awe.

At last, like a magnate behind a palatial desk, Harry said, "Now, what can I do for you?" I told him that Lou Alexander had given me his name and I was a comedian-actress looking for a manager and I listed the out-of-town clubs where I wished I had worked.

He asked to see my act, so I stood up and, with knees almost touching his, did my stolen-off-TV act while Nicky chuckled helpfully behind me. Harry sat silent and expressionless as his jaws worked and his manicured hand moved rhythmically between sunflower seeds and mouth. I performed to a spot six inches above his head, knowing instinctively that if I looked him in the eyes, *(a)* I might laugh and *(b)* he would be forced to react to my jokes and that would be embarrassing to both of us. But it was very difficult to perform full out with no response, with my audience a foot and a half from me, with my throat choking on cigar smoke, with a rising impulse to stop and say, "This is ludicrous; I just can't." But I was also desperate to have him think I was funny, desperate to have him be my manager because he could get me work, could open that door. If he refused me, there was no other place to go because this was the bottom of the barrel.

I sat down and there was a dramatic, suspenseful pause. Then Harry Brent said, "I've got a full plate. I don't need any more acts." My heart plummeted. "But I like you," he went on, nodding beneficently as I exhaled with relief. "I see something in you. I'm going to push some peas over on my plate and make room for you. But believe me, I'm not doing it for the money—you know I had Deano—I'll do it for Lou and 'cause I think there's a place for a girl comic, but it's going to be a lot of work."

"Oh, gosh, yes, sure, absolutely," I said.

"I don't like your material," he said, absorbing another handful of sunflower seeds.

"Me neither. I don't like my material either."

"You have gowns?"

"No."

"We gotta get some gowns. And, honey, you gotta have a better name. I'll work on that. People remember names. A guy named Jackie—right away you know he's funny, cute—a girl named Jackie, you gotta laugh. I'm gonna find you a name. And a logo."

"Anything you say."

"Okay, come back tomorrow. We'll start tomorrow."

Outside, Nicky and I waited until we were in the elevator in case he might hear us and then we fell on each other, roaring. "Did you see the monograms?" Nick said. "He'll never have to worry about losing anything in the laundry— except that he's probably doing his own laundry."

I said, "How many times do you think he's looked at that check and thought, Deano or dinner?" Then I said, "Nicky, I never want to go to that room alone. Promise me."

"Sure," Nicky said. "But listen, he can only help you. He didn't ask for money. You can't lose." And I thought Nicky was right. The beginner's incantation is "maybe" and I believed that maybe this joke of a man, this refugee from a Damon Runyon story, could open a show business door even a crack and I would be through it like a burglar. Jack Rollins had said, "See you in six months." Harry Brent, with his mouth full of sunflower seeds, was the only person in my life willing to sit and build an act with me, the only person who might conceivably get me a job—and a logo.

From then on, every day that I was not typing at an office temp job, I was devoutly perched on Harry's wooden chair, learning my new profession literally at the knee of my guru—while my Prince Valiant leaned patiently against the door. We could not work in the evenings because Harry moonlighted as an accordionist at weddings and bar mitzvahs—"just to keep my hand in," he said. "Just a little gig now and then."

At the beginning of every session Harry warmed us up with a few of his legendary stories about his glamorous life, telling us how he "pleasured" women—"This lady friend of mine, I pleasured her"—and saying, "I was talking to Joey the other night and I says, 'Joey, I got a new girl that's gonna knock you off your ass.' " We were left to figure out whether he meant Joey Bishop or Joe E. Lewis.

Harry Brent was one of a long procession of show business people who never used last names. He would say, "I bumped into Sammy. He's gone through hell. I told him, 'Hey, take a rest, baby. Bucks are only bucks.' His dad's not well. Wonderful guy, the old man. I used to go out with Sammy and the old man—it's a wonderful relationship. He really cares for him."

After Harry had suitably impressed us, I would produce my homework for the day—material I had stolen from television and one-liners I copied from Robert Orben joke books lent me by Harry—*The Emcee's Handbook, The Working Comedian's Gag File.* All the schlock comics used them, including Richard Nixon, who hired Robert Orben to supply ad-libs. He is still alive and a wonderful joke writer, so wonderful that some of my jokes are now turning up in his books.

Writing in the small blue exam books I still had from Barnard College, I arranged the jokes into little routines:

"Tonight I am brought to you by the product all America is talking about . . . Brand X. Sal Mineo would have been here tonight, but he's at home in bed with a bad haircut. I don't have to be up here . . . I've had other job offers but I'd hate to sell hats. On my first job I made eighty dollars . . . I sold my car to the bandleader."

Harry would sit on the bed listening, saying, "Yeah, yeah," or waving his hands, saying, "No, no, no. Look, there's a great line of Red's—I started him, by the way—he wouldn't mind us taking it." He showed me how to shade one theme into another, how to get from entertaining Japanese holdouts at Iwo Jima into Hemingway asking Gertrude Stein "What is the answer? What is the answer?"—and she says, "What is the question?"

He decided that there should be some music and song, so we assembled a routine on an unhappy wife. It opened with a soupçon of song:

> I'm just wild about Harry
> And Harry was wild about me.
> The day we parted
> I was brokenhearted,
> Left with memories . . .

Then I went into my marvelous routine:

> Harry, darling, what happened . . . it was all so beautiful in the beginning . . . I had always dreamed of someone like you . . . tall and dark with a civil service job . . . and when you called that first time, it seemed so right . . . there was such rapport going between us, you understood me so well the way you said, "Hello, tramp" . . . and then remember, darling, how you used to come over to my house. You never spoke. You just sat at my feet

and gazed up at me, then down at my feet, then up at me . . . and then, one day you spoke . . . you looked up and said, "Joan, wash your feet."

When I told my parents about Harry Brent, they glanced quickly at each other and I could see a new set of worry messages whizzing back and forth. My father breathed deeply, exhaled, and described for the twentieth time his visits as a young doctor to the Magistrates Court and how prostitutes arraigned before the judge always said, "I'm in show business." He went on, "The whole business doesn't smell good to me. I've heard about auditioning in front of so-called managers—everybody's a manager these days—and you're auditioning in this man's apartment. And we hear things on radio and television, how one out of hundreds makes a go of it in show business and the rest are terribly disappointed and very often go astray altogether because of certain pressures by so-called producers."

Right away I was defensive, shouting my litany: "Why do you always assume the worst! Why?"

"Because look what you hang out with. Look what you bring home. Scum. Look at your sister. She's a lawyer."

"Harry Brent is a professional and he thinks I'm good."

"He's either out to take your money or he's a pimp," he said, my mother nodding in agreement.

"Just meet him. That's all I ask. Just meet him."

"Okay," said my father, "let's see this big deal who can make you a star."

A dinner with Harry was arranged at Lindy's on Broadway and we met on the sidewalk—Harry in his slightly frayed camel's hair coat bought at Klein's on the Square, shrugged over his shoulders, the collar up, a white silk aviator's scarf around his neck. As though I was introducing my fiancé, I was very nervous, hoping they would like him, hoping he would not eat too much because I knew my father would have to pick up the check.

At dinner Harry had a wonderful time, chatting away between bites: ". . . when I was a kid . . . always loved the business . . . best brisket in town and, waiter, I'll have a bottle of beer, make sure it's imported . . . used to tell Frankie, known him since he was making twenty-five dollars a week in Newark . . . I prefer to work with unknowns . . . pass the pickles . . . this little lady here . . . waiter, another order of brisket . . . Deano said to me . . ."

My mother sat expressionless, frozen by culture shock, none of the food ever reaching her lips. My father, hardly touching his dinner, his eyes filled with confusion, was trying to be jolly but was paralyzed by the knowledge that he was paying. For them, it was dinner with an alien being, an extraterrestrial—this man with the pinkie ring saying hello to waiters who did not know who the hell he was. He waved to anybody famous—to a Jan Murray—calling out, "Hi, Jan. Best to Danny," and then turned back to my mother to say confidentially, "I remember like it was yesterday the first time I saw Danny. He was just a kid but killed 'em. Jesus, he destroyed 'em. I swear to God—if you'll pardon me—I pissed in my pants."

My mother's hand *flew* to her pearls.

Finally, after finishing his second piece of cheesecake, wiping his mouth with the napkin, Harry pushed back his third cup of coffee and said, "Let's talk about your little girl here. I know it's crazy, I know you're not going to believe me, but I think she's got something." My mother and father stared in disbelief. Harry continued, "I want to manage her. No fooling around—I'm not that kind, believe me."

At last my mother spoke her first words. She said enigmatically, "Well, we'll see. We'll all see."

On the drive home I could tell that my parents, against their better judgment, were impressed. They were thinking in terms of instant fame—like making instant cocoa—and Harry Brent was the first person who had ever said, "She's not crazy," and he was just professional enough for them to think, *Well, maybe this will do it for her.* In the car my mother asked, "So what do you think, Meyer? Do you think he's a good manager?"

"I don't know if he's a good manager or not," my father said. "But I'll tell you one thing, he's a damn good eater."

By this time I thought the act was pretty well set, but Harry Brent, ever the perfectionist, was only now concentrating on the nuances. He was still brooding about a stage name, suggesting and rejecting Kim, Lyette, and considering a man's name, Herman. Then he was hit by the first of his major inspirations. "The act ain't great yet," he said, but went on, thrilled with himself, hands jittering with excitement—genius does not sit quietly. "But I got the answer. You gotta have props." I was still using Dick Gautier's routine on the boy who wanted to be a boxer, so Harry decided—and it is amazing Dick Gautier never thought of it—that I should be wearing boxing gloves. So I could use a phone and drink a glass of Bromo-Seltzer, he helped me steal a Shelley Berman routine about a hung-over woman calling her host of the night before.

Then one afternoon Harry had the greatest idea of all. He said, aflutter with pleasure, "Honey, I got a great idea. I figured out how you're going to start your act. You're gonna come onstage—this'll grab 'em right away—and you're gonna say, 'Sorry I'm late, but I didn't even have time to shave,' and you're gonna take shaving cream and put it on your face and shave it off. That'll get their attention. It'll destroy 'em." He had worked that out, he said, very pleased with himself. "You'll get screams, I swear. Trust me."

He was also giving me comedy tricks garnered throughout his long career as the Flo Ziegfeld of comedy. When you finish your act, he told me, always leave your props behind on the piano. That way the audience will not forget you during the next act—you will still be present in the form of boxing gloves, telephone, shaving mug, Bromo-Seltzer. I said, "Fine," and continued to be humbly deferential, treating him like Jack Rollins in plumage. I thought a lot of his ideas were idiotic, but I did not want to hurt his feelings. And Harry Brent, no matter how ridiculous, no matter how ancient his check from Deano, was a professional and the longer we worked on the act, the better most of the material sounded to me. I was experiencing a show business truth—familiarity does not breed contempt, it breeds hope.

After a month he said, "Honey, let me see your gowns." I brought in from Larchmont my black prom dress—off the shoulder, puffed red-and-white candy-striped sleeves, tight bodice, dropped waist, sweetheart neck—and my green bridesmaid's dress from Nancy Heath's wedding. Holding them by the hangers, one in each hand, he twirled them and was very disappointed. "There's no pizzazz here," he said. "No pizzazz. Gotta pick up the light onstage. You gotta make 'em more glamorous, get sequins, maybe feathers. A Harry Brent act has to dress right. When they book a Harry Brent act they know the wardrobe is tops."

So I followed orders—went out and ruined the dresses, show bizzed the prom gown with gaudy, iridescent flower paillettes and I junked up the green dress with sequins and rhinestones—and it was good-bye to the Harvard Junior Prom and the Riviera Shore Club, good-bye to the Lord & Taylor job, good-bye to circle pins and Princeton Junction. If I was ever going to date a geek, I now had the right dresses to wear—and even more sad and awful, they looked homemade. I was going onstage like an eight-year-old girl in a small town parade throwing her baton in a costume sewed by her mother.

Harry liked them and said we were ready for the photographs. Harry himself took me to his favorite photographer and stood there, an impresario in a yellow plaid jacket, working for the elusive, subtle effect which would be my passport to stardom, rocketing me, perhaps, even as high as Dick Capri. "Bend over further. Come on, bend further," he kept saying and this was the time I almost broke down and laughed. This overweight Jewish girl from Larchmont was doing cleavage pictures! It was "Hi, sailor" time. The pose Harry chose, his enthusiastic favorite, was like every nightclub show-bill picture I had ever ridiculed. I was hunched over with toes turned in and hands on bent knees—a Rubenesque lady locked out of the rest room and frantic.

Harry saved his last, climactic touch for the final exciting day. When I arrived, his feet practically danced with excitement, the tassels on his shoes bouncing up and down. He said, "Sit down. Sit down and listen to me. I got you a name. How does this grab ya? 'Pepper January.' Now you need a logo. 'Comedy with Spice.' I buy it. And if I buy it, they'll buy it."

To Harry Brent, I said, "Fine." To Nicky afterward out in the hall, I said, "I'm going to commit suicide." But I also said, "If being Pepper January, comma, Comedy with Spice, comma, is going to mean I can work, I'll be Pepper January." It was that simple. I was trying to start in a business that did not want me, did not care about me. And now I glimpsed a way into the secret garden—the knob of a door among the ivy —and I was willing to do *anything,* no matter how absurd, how humiliating, to turn that knob. All my career I have been a snob who has sold out a thousand times.

And, indeed, Harry Brent did find me work, did arrange my first paying job in show business. He telephoned and said, "Got you a booking in Boston at the Show Bar. You're going to emcee. It's exotic dancers." The pay was $125 for a week, two shows a night, but out of that I had to give percentages to Harry and some little agent he had used to book me, and buy

food, hotel, and transportation. I did not know what exotic
dancers were and pictured some sort of flamenco dancers.

I said, "Fine, but how do I emcee?"

He said, "Break your act up. Do a little bit, introduce the
next act, then do the next bit. You'll be fine." So I did not
worry and was thrilled. Not only was my faith in Harry justi-
fied, I could now join the American Guild of Variety Artists
and get the card that meant everything, that meant I was
actually a working comic, truly in show business—and if I was
run over by a car, when they opened my wallet in the ambu-
lance, they would say, "This woman is a professional performer." The headline would say, UNKNOWN PERFORMER
KILLED, a nice headline—if you ignored the adjective.

I left for Boston on December 7, 1958. It was my father's
birthday and he took me to the station and waited with me on
the platform, which was sweet, but I could not wait to get on
that train. I was walking through a door into show business
and now THE DREAM was an even bigger dream. I was going
to be very thin and very wealthy and multifaceted, able to do
comedy as well as drama, and able to look back with amuse-
ment at the fact that I had started out as an emcee for exotic
dancers. And following my meteoric rise in comedy—"after
the first week Pepper January was held over and put Boston
on its ear, the change came when the Harvard boys started
coming around"—I would then be tapped for movies. It
would read well in *Photoplay:* "January got her first break on
her dad's birthday." I completely forgot December 7 was also
Pearl Harbor day, the date when half the American fleet was
sunk.

Harry Brent had given me the name of a cheap hotel
across from the Show Bar and I took a taxi right there and
lugged my two bags into the dirty, dingy lobby, all the props
and gowns in my college suitcase with a Yale sticker on it, a

huge Y and a big, big bulldog. I looked around at the rotting, leatherlike chairs, the blue lights, the scarred Coke machine, the candy machine empty of candy, the dirty shirt on the desk clerk in the box projecting out into the room, at the radio playing behind him—at the dirt and the dinginess and the sleaze—and thought, *Can I take this?* But I had no money for a better place—and I had to pay in advance, which says everything. I registered as Joan Molinsky a.k.a. Pepper January, so both my parents and the Show Bar could reach me. Yet even in this dump, I felt compelled to establish my show business credentials right away, saying to the guy at the desk, "I'm the emcee at the Show Bar," standing there with my Yale suitcase —Princess Grace arriving for a visit.

The tiny self-service elevator had no door and infinite variations on FUCK YOU were scratched into its walls. I huddled inside, trying to disappear, terrified that somebody would get in with me. It was the hotel you see in the movies when Clint Eastwood is down and out, and I knew I was going to be robbed and murdered. People did get in the elevator, people carrying brown paper sacks full of food, people who looked to me like drifters and prostitutes and twelfth-rate musicians and pimps and strippers.

The fifth floor hallway smelled of urine and peanuts. The carpet was ragged at the edges and along the wall was a smudgy ribbon of dirt and grease where hands had brushed for decades. Walking toward my room, I was physically scared. Any door could open and somebody would get me. Later I stole a fork and carried it hidden in the palm of one hand to defend myself.

The room, which cost about $2.50 a night, smelled of peanuts. The ragged floor, the threadbare, frazzled rug, the ramshackle chair, the decrepit TV set, the bed like a hammock covered by a stained chenille spread—every object seemed to me steeped in dirt and rubbed by numberless hands and bodies till the grime was almost shiny, a permanent patina. In the semidarkness lit by a single overhead light dangling on a chain, I recoiled at the prospect of ever touching anything and escaped with my suitcase of props and costumes to check into the Show Bar across the street.

I paused for a moment outside the Show Bar in the cold to look at the glass case containing the show bill. It displayed three nude women in G-strings with a black bar printed across their breasts and wearing sad black street shoes. In a lower corner was my picture and my billing: PEPPER JANUARY, COMEDY WITH SPICE. GOOD THINGS COME IN LITTLE PACKAGES. I was, for a second, a bit insulted that there was no censored bar across *my* cleavage. This moment was my first inkling that perhaps exotic had nothing to do with Balinese dancers with their fingers pointed out and maybe the Show Bar was something other than a crummy nightclub. I was shocked, but did not hesitate, telling myself that I had to break in somewhere and I would never do it again and this was a good idea because nobody I knew would see me.

I went into the Show Bar, a barren room with dark gray walls and tables distributed around a central bar. At one of the tables sat a small, dark, balding Italian gentleman who might be the boss. I told him, "Hi, I'm Pepper January. I'm the emcee." He did not get up. He just looked surprised and told me when to be back for the first show. Glancing around, I asked him, "Where's the stage?" He nodded toward a platform in the middle of the oval bar. "Up there on the lunch counter," he said.

"Oh," I answered, mystified, and asked for directions to the dressing room.

He nodded toward the rear of the bar where a steep, narrow stair led to the basement, much like the descent into a subway. Opening off a scabby, moldy hall was a narrow cell with a dirt-colored cement floor punctuated by matted bathroom rugs. Along the right side was an iron pipe hung with coat hangers and a rainbow line of gauzy, glittering, sequined gowns, ropes of rhinestone necklaces, long feather boas, flesh-colored G-strings, sequin-covered bras—lots of pizzazz —like a harem closet. The costumes—and the room—smelled of stale perfume and deodorant and sweat and talc.

Beyond the pole was a yellow stained sink and in a dank cubbyhole a toilet I knew I would never use. On the left wall was a long mirror, mottled where the silver was flaking from the back. Frayed stickers were glued on it—a heart with a star in it, a unicorn, an American flag. There were no lights around it, only a bare seventy-five-watt bulb hanging from the ceiling. On a narrow shelf under the mirror, laid out on several hotel towels, were razors, baby powder, jars of pancake, cold sore medicine, atomizer perfume bottles, baby oil, denatured alcohol and cotton balls, lipsticks, paintbrushes, wigs, curlers, a dish of lipstick-smeared cigarettes, eyebrow pencils, washed eyelashes rolled on pencils to recurl them, a greeting card saying, "This card can only be opened by a virgin."

I hung up my big-skirted June Allyson Jewish Princess dresses. I put my pumps to match down on the floor, well away from a row of silver-and-gold spike-heeled shoes. I spread some Kleenex from my purse on a corner of the shelf and arranged my little lipstick, my base, rouge, eyeliner, and Maybelline mascara. Miss Show Biz! I was still the happy amateur. I thought sooner or later magic was going to strike and it might as well strike tonight.

I went back to my room, on the way getting crackers from the food dispensers that were on every floor, and sat on the very edge of the greasy chair and watched TV until show time.

Returning to the dressing room, I do not know what I expected to find, but not three women absolutely naked and utterly unembarrassed. At home in the family we *never* saw each other naked. Bodies did not exist. The Molinskys were talking heads. And nowhere had I seen women with such great bodies—maybe a little beaten up but a lot better than mine—and I had certainly never seen women with everything shaved.

I tried hard to be casual and not notice that one of them was sponging gold paint over her entire body, including spreading her cheeks and bending over to dab the hard-to-reach spots in her crotch. I learned later that this was all ritual, that sitting nude on a smooth towel allowed strap marks and indentations to plump out, so the fantasy body would not be humanized by even a false hint of a scar. The gold paint was to cover what would otherwise have been a fatal blemish—an appendectomy incision.

I stopped in the doorway and said, "Hi."

One of the seated strippers, applying Vaseline to a zipper, said, "Honey, are you sure you're in the right place?"

I said, "I'm Pepper January. The emcee." While the girl continued turning herself gold, I sat down near the other two and asked, "What are the lights like onstage?" I thought that would sound very professional.

"You got two choices," said the one with the Vaseline, "on and off."

"How about the band?"

"Don't expect Guy Lombardo."

Believe it or not, I still was not nervous. I actually thought I was going to be doing my act to great applause. I saw myself as a college girl having to go through this to become a major star. I thought intelligence would carry me through. I was so snotty superior, I believed I was not intimidated, believed I did not need the approval and friendship of these tough women. They were nobody I would ever meet again.

But when I began talking to the other stripper sitting there—a dark girl, sultry, long legs, very domestic with needle and thread, replacing missing sequins and spangles—I quickly inserted my one important, impressive credential. I dragged in the fact that I had been to college. The girl looked up and said, "Oh? Where?"

"Connecticut College," I said.

"Oh," she said again, casually. "Me too." That absolutely threw me. She had spent two years at Connecticut College and could name the dormitories where she had lived. I was devastated, because she must have been very bright or had a good family background, which I had thought was *everything*. How could she have gone from those hallowed, ivied halls, that beautiful green-and-white campus, to being a stripper in the Show Bar? The tragedy of it! She had to have a screw loose somewhere or some kinky sexual drive. The idea that a stripper might have come from a home like mine was absolutely staggering—unimaginable.

Now it was time for me to get ready—and *that* was embarrassing. I had major, respectable things happening under my dress—a slip, bra, panty girdle, stockings, panties. No freedom of soul there. So I turned away and sort of hid up against my two dresses, changing my bra to a strapless bra. The show stuff came out of the suitcase on the floor, the other stuff went right in, neatly folded, but believe me, nobody was watching. I did my little makeup job and I was ready. "Why do they call it the lunch counter?" I asked.

My answer came from the Vaseline lady. "Because the group at the bar gets a worm's-eye view of my old Kentucky home."

"Oh," I said.

The gold lady came over to me and studied my black prom dress with its white paillettes. "Is this a breakaway?" she asked.

I had no idea what that meant. "No," I said. "It's my prom dress." I was beginning to pretend that I was invisible.

Miss Gold said, "Now don't forget my logo. I'm Aurora

Borealis, The Shooting Star. And I've just come off a four-month engagement at The Old Howard." I assured her I would remember. Miss Vaseline called out, "I'm Dyna Mite, The Girl with the Million-Dollar Wardrobe. Can you remember that? And, honey, you better clear the stage fast, 'cause I come out *big*, come out with feathers. I come on like dynamite." The Connecticut College girl, using folded adhesive tape had been fastening circular flesh-colored cones onto her nipples. She stood up and asked me, "Can you tell if I'm wearing pasties?" I told her, "No, I can hardly see 'em," and she was thrilled.

There was a knock on the door. A voice said, "Okay, Pep. Onstage." Dyna Mite was taking handfuls of ice from a pitcher and rubbing them on her breasts—I supposed to make them firm. Clutching my purse full of props—my towel, shaving cream, telephone, Bromo-Seltzer—and balancing a glass of water, I climbed the long steps from the basement, then the short steps onto the rear of the lunch counter, and stopped behind the little band of a drummer, piano player, saxophone, and bass. Over the loudspeaker was coming, "Boston's world famous Show Bar, The Bar That Shows It All, presents, direct from New York City, the one and only Pepper January, Comedy with Spice." I thought, *Even the bar has a logo.*

I placed the purse on the piano and stepped out into the glare of the single spotlight. A microphone stood at the center of the stage, but, certain that I would be electrocuted, I was not going to touch it. So I stood behind it in my tarted-up prom dress, clutching my shaving cream can, and looked out at the room. In the haze of smoke, like a bad painting, sat a mob of still, pale men, every one of them, it seemed, wearing a felt hat and holding a glass of beer in one hand. The other hand was out of sight under the table.

I looked down at the ring of cold, expectant eyes around

the bar below me. And there, almost at my feet, was Wally Peck, whom I had dated at Yale. The blond son of the owner of Peck & Peck was sitting at the lunch counter in his Brooks Brothers outfit, his Brooks Brothers shirt, his rep tie, his gray flannel suit. I do not know which of us was more astounded and upset.

By this time I had realized this might be slightly more difficult than I had figured. I lifted up the shaving cream can, telling myself, "I'm going to be okay because Harry said this will get a laugh." *Psssght.* The cream was cool and soft on my face. "Sorry I'm late . . ." All around the bar there was a steely silence. I could feel my heart speeding up, feel the palpitations in my chest and the sweat along my arms, coming through my hair, running down between my breasts. I pushed on, talking rapidly as I moved the razor over my face. ". . . but I'm staying at the hotel across the street and my bathroom is only semiprivate—I share it with only one other hotel." When they realized I was not going to be absolutely filthy, the noise began—first a commotion of voices, then yelling. "Get the fuck off! Bring on the girls!" Then whistling. "Take it off." From behind me came the voice of Dyna Mite. "The only way you're gonna get a laugh in this place is if you shave the other end."

I thought, *Something is* very *wrong. I'd better get Dyna out here fast. Then I'll regroup; I'll revamp. It's all right; I'll be fine.* I announced, "And now, directly from a four-week engagement at . . ." The guttural urgency of "Night Train" throbbed from the band and, remembering Dyna's warning, I ducked around her, lest I suffer the final indignity—being knocked over by a feather. I stood in the sanctuary of the rear steps, trying to calm myself, trying not to run out the door and run and run and run. But I knew I *had* to go back on, it was a job and by God, I was going to do well and not fail because this was the only way I could be a performer. If I did not walk back onto that stage, it would be the end of Harry Brent and show business.

Simultaneously, I was marveling at Dyna Mite, a lascivious Isadora Duncan circling the tiny stage, strutting, writhing, stroking her skin with fronds of purple and rose feathers, pausing for bumps and grinds that might have dislocated a less professional pelvis. On each circuit, her sensuous arm flung a spangled section of gown toward me, the gray wren with her heart still full of childhood dreams of secret gardens. From nowhere I heard in my head my grandmother's voice saying, "There is heaven and hell on earth," and here, I thought, was the hell, Dyna Mite, so used, having to titillate strange men and be judged by strange men. But I was even more shocked at how fast she woke up the audience—and so they were not a bad audience and I *had* to find a way to reach them. I said over and over to myself, "I can turn them around; I know I can." And then I comforted myself with the thought, *At least Wally Peck didn't yell, "Get the fuck off."*

I had always felt the shaving gag was absurd, but liked the routine about the hung-over woman. I decided that would save me. These men out there in the hats were drinkers; they would identify and bring their other hand from under the table and applaud. After Dyna's exit, I went out, still the stupid amateur, placing the phone and glass of water on the piano, then standing rigidly at the microphone.

> Oh, do I feel terrible . . . I think my tongue is asleep . . . and my teeth itch . . . boy, that must have been some party . . . I wonder if I had a good time . . . Let's see . . . Bromo-Seltzer . . . (I turned my back on the audience and dumped it into the glass) . . . Don't fizz . . . please don't fizz . . . (I drank and picked up the phone) . . . "Hello, George . . . say, George, do you think you could talk a little softer . . ."

I ignored what seemed to be one vast intake of breath out in the room and continued:

> I sort of have this headache and can't seem to remember much after the first five minutes . . . say, George, I didn't do anything . . . well, silly, did I? . . . the window, huh . . . completely . . .

If the men on the bar stools could have gotten at me over the bar, I would have been in mortal danger, but they had to settle for screaming and standing up and yelling, "Just get off. Beat it. Let's see the broads! Fuck off!" The place was bedlam —not the reaction I had received in Harry Brent's office-bedroom with Nick Clemente saying, "That's really good."

Terrified, my hands beginning to shake, my arms stiff with tension, I announced, "Next, direct from Montreal, on her way to Baltimore . . ." I would rather have said, "Direct from Connecticut College and I don't know how she got into this, 'cause she's really a nice girl . . . and she should be married, at home . . . or going back to get her M.A. . . . but here's . . ." However, that would not have been a very good introduction.

Somehow, I got through the rest of the show, just introducing the strippers, always being careful about the logo. I did not want to be selfish; I was not the only one with a logo. At the end, as I left the lunch counter, carrying my armload of props, one of the waitresses yelled at me, "A word of advice, kid. Don't send out your laundry." The men at her table roared. The bitch got the only laugh heard in the Show Bar that night.

I snuck back into the dressing room. The gold lady was standing with one foot in the sink, washing herself with soap and a filthy towel, the paint turning black the instant it hit the water. The other two, in negligees, were repairing their costumes. Nobody looked up. They were not embarrassed by nudity, but they were embarrassed by me. Or else I really was invisible. I brightly said, "Hi. I guess it's going to be a little rough for me. It's my first time out, but I think I can do it." More silence. I was still invisible. I changed my clothes and said, "Well, I'll see you all."

Dyna Mite, eyes on her needle, said, "Honey, I could help you. You could do a little comedy shtick while you're taking your clothes off to keep their attention—or, if you can't dance, try some little routine—maybe come out and peel a banana."

I fled, leaving my stuff there—the makeup, the props, the dresses, the Yale suitcase—and went back across the street to the hotel, where I got coffee and cheese and crackers from the machine. Food solves all problems. I decided in the second show, maybe they would go for "I'm Just Wild About Harry," especially if I could do it to "Night Train." At eleven o'clock I went back across the street. The boss was waiting inside the door. He moved in front of me. "Hey, Pepper," he said. "Don't bother coming in. You're fired."

I said, "Okay. Sorry. Maybe some other time." I turned away. I was not going to show him anything, give him any satisfaction.

I went back to the hotel, rode up in that scary elevator, walked along that dangerous hallway, went into that grungy room—and absolutely collapsed. I could not believe it. Fired! That possibility had never occurred to me. Fired! After I was promised the job for a week. I could have improved the act— fixed it—changed it. "Wild About Harry" would have worked. Fired without . . .

I was crying and could not stop. Could not stop the tears. I cried as I telephoned Nick, who promised to come right up on an overnight train. I cried as I phoned Harry Brent, who was not home. I cried while I took my dress off and in my slip paced and paced, back and forth across the room, feeling the dirty carpet, prickly as cornflakes under my stockinged feet, feeling my eyes swelling and aching, feeling my head stuffing up like a cold, feeling the tears hot on my cheeks and then falling cold on my chest.

I was seeing myself as my parents saw me, facing the truth that theater had not worked and comedy was not working. There was really nothing left, unless I became a juggler or a geek. Crossing and recrossing that rug, I flailed myself. "What am I doing? I'm ruining my life! What am I doing, talking to men with their hands in their pockets? What *am* I doing? Am I *really* right? If I can't even cut it at this level, maybe I don't have talent, maybe I *am* a loser."

I cried as I stood under the shower in the filthy tub—my feet protected with socks, the curtain open so the killer from *Psycho* could not stab me. The tears and water streamed together from my face as my brain whirled with grief and doubt. I had absolutely convinced myself that Harry Brent was my guru, that he knew this world, that the Show Bar would carry me through the secret door. I had believed I had a pact with the devil and was promised that if I did every one of Harry Brent's stupid, degrading ideas, I would soon be telling Louella Parsons, "Believe it or not, Lolly, it all began only a year ago in Boston on my Dad's birthday."

I had kept my side of the pact, done it all—and the devil had spit in my face. The payoff was not supposed to be this— to be fired by someone I considered the lowest, to be barred from a dive where women sat shaving parts I did not know people had. I was not supposed to do crap and then find I was not capable of doing the crap, find myself rejected as a performer, as a person.

Standing in that dirt-blackened tub, I no longer knew whether the thing inside me struggling to come out was talent or only an obsession. But even at that moment I could still feel it there, enormous inside me, still constantly pushing. It wanted to get out and I wanted it out—and could not find a

way to release it. I was giving birth to a baby and somebody
had tied my knees.

I was still crying when I climbed out of the shower, putting towels down so I would not have to step barefoot on the
floor, picking them up behind me, laying them out in front of
me. I had not seen any roaches but knew they were there. As I
moved about the room, sobbing, I realized that tomorrow I
had to go back to the Show Bar and get my dresses and
makeup—and then go home and tell my parents I had failed
again, admit my talent was not working, admit that they were
right and I was wrong—which would be admitting, "I am
nothing." Without a great body, without a great face or great
personality or great mind, the only thing I could have within
myself—so I could get into bed at night and say I have *this* and
it is something wonderful—was my talent.

I could not will the gasping sobs to stop and I cried while
I wondered what else there was in that machine in the hall I
could eat, cried while I brushed my teeth and combed my hair,
cried while I sat in front of the TV, watching a late-night
movie with Cornel Wilde and Merle Oberon. Then, repulsed
by the dingy blankets, I lay on top of the faded green spread
and cried into the pillow—slept and cried, slept and cried.
Sometime during the night somebody knocked on the door—
maybe the stripper who had gone to Connecticut College and
now was offering old-school comfort. But I could not talk to
anybody. I was too devastated and lay silent till the footsteps
went off down the hall. I would be a great schizophrenic; I
could easily shut out the whole world.

The next morning, still deep in despair as I waited for
Nick Clemente, I escaped into television and suddenly a
dumpy woman comic named Charlotte Rae came on and
talked about food—"It all started as a child. I developed a
curious habit . . . eating . . . and I don't mean eating, I

mean EATING!" I laughed out loud. Magically, my misery was left behind. Here was a woman who knew how to get laughs and if she could do it, so could I . . . especially with her material. Like a fire horse, I grabbed a pen and a telegram form and wrote everything down. In the midst of my anguish I was responding to the true voice of a woman speaking to women, but I was too dumb and naive to realize this was the answer for me.

Nick Clemente finished the healing. He arrived and enveloped me in his warmth, taking me to breakfast and lavishing on me all the consoling arguments I needed to hear—"Look what didn't like you—a bunch of slimies . . . you're too good for them . . . they're all losers." After an hour of his loyalty I was ready for the ordeal of retrieving my clothes from the Show Bar dressing room.

The club was closed and we banged on the door, then went around to the back and finally a cleaning man opened a rear door. We plunged down the stairs, opened the suitcase on the floor, and the two of us flung everything into it frantically, as though the Nazis were at the gate—the dresses, the makeup, the props, the green shoes and black shoes scrambled together, higgledy-piggledy. I could not endure being there. I wanted to be the incredible shrinking woman. But before we beat it back up the stairs, I wrote a note to the Connecticut College stripper—left her my phone number and said I had been called home because of illness in the family. I felt sorry for her and wanted her to feel that she had not really sunk to hell—which I knew she had—and I wanted her to know there was still a chance she could be accepted in such great places as Larchmont.

After that experience, until years later when I had a three-year contract at the MGM Grand in Las Vegas, I always, *always* cleaned out my dressing room every single night, packing up all my costumes and makeup. I never, never wanted to go through that humiliation again—never, never wanted to slink in and pick up my things in the daylight with everybody knowing I had been fired. If you just do not appear the next day, maybe there are other reasons why you are not there. Maybe Hollywood called.

Leaving the Show Bar behind, Nicky got me on the train. I took a taxi from the Larchmont station, and it was awful walking in that front door, embarrassed, a failure. I would have to tell my parents what had happened and I would be explaining to enemies, who would now have another weapon against me.

I went up to my room and unpacked until my mother called me downstairs for a snack at the kitchen table where we always conferred, sitting in the captain's chairs under the Victorian chandelier. She put a cup of cocoa on the table in front of me and sat down on the other side and at first poured on the sympathy: "It's all right—everybody gets fired. It's just as well—you shouldn't be working with those people." But that very rapidly led into: "But now you've learned your lesson. I'm very glad this happened—now you understand that you're not right for this business, you don't have the talent for it. Let's figure out what you are going to do."

"Don't say that to me," I said, defensive in my first breath. "This was just a mistake. It will be fine the next time. Of course I'm going to stay in the business."

"There won't be a next time," my mother said stiffly. "You can't deal with those kind of people, that element. All this foolishness has got to stop. You're making your father and me ill."

The litanies went on and on into the inexorable threats and screams and the pounding of my feet up the stairs and the concussion of my slamming door. That night, when my father came home to a house thick with heavy, sullen silence, he told me, "You're not getting a nickel from us."

I said, "I don't need your money." That was the day they became really, really frightened.

Even sobbing in the filthy shower in Boston, telling my-self, "I'm not going to do this anymore; I'm not going to do it anymore," I had known I would keep on going, no matter what. My parents were not going to defeat me. That night at home, lying in the luxury of my four-poster bed from the Jimmy Sanger marriage, there were still no options beyond show business. Jack Rollins had said I was going to be a success in three years. I only had two years, eleven and a half months to go. I could hold on to that.

7

ALL OF US IN comedy have had our Show Bars, our hideous low points that almost destroy us—except that we come back to have more of them—walking out on stages hundreds and hundreds of times when lights are broken, when microphones do not work, when audiences are hostile, when our material stinks. That is what makes you tough. That is what changes you from a happy amateur to a professional, tans your hide, turns you, eventually, leathery.

But the process gives terrible war wounds that are forever open, leaving you a victim for the rest of your life. If you have reached the top in comedy, you are, in your own way, a killer—but every killer is bandaged. And the anger is never out of you. Why was Totie Fields so angry? Why did her contract require twelve coffee cups, exactly twelve, in her dressing room? Because twenty-five years ago she could not get even one cup. After years of being pampered I am still angry. I am angry because of the Show Bar. Whenever I ask for an extra bottle of champagne or a new bar of soap in my dressing room, what I really want is the respect that comes with it. I am punishing Caesars Palace for the indignities I suffered getting started—for the nights I had to get dressed in filthy toilets, for all the disgusting dressing rooms where there was no toilet paper in the john, where the soap had hair embedded in it, where cockroaches ran across the dressing table, where my paycheck had $1.25 deducted for two cups of coffee. At one club the dressing room was separated from the men's room by a partition that did not reach the ceiling and I lived intimately with every smell and sound.

When the waiters at Caesars, who have never done anything to me, must say, "Right, Miss Rivers. Sure, Miss Rivers. Anything you say, Miss Rivers," I feel so guilty. I want to turn to them and say, "It isn't you guys. It's the Show Bar, where the toilet seat was broken."

I can hardly believe that *(a)* I went back to Harry Brent and *(b)* let him send me out again. But I was ready to do anything to be a performer who was not also a secretary, and Harry was not discouraged, only apologetic for not telling me to hide between shows on opening night. This time he explained the AGVA rule: If the boss fires you after the first show, he does not have to pay for the full engagement. But the minute your foot hits the stage for the second show, that is it and you get your full money. Therefore, on opening night, every beginner nightclub performer checks the stage, the lights, and the location of a good place to hide.

Harry's second booking for me was New Year's week at a place called Shaker Park in Springfield, Mass.—a strip joint paying seventy-five dollars for four nights. I was too naive to see that Harry Brent, for the commission, would have sent Mother Teresa up there—and maybe he thought that out of self-preservation I would begin to work dirty.

I persuaded Nick Clemente to come with me to Springfield and we went up by bus. That night I introduced the strippers one by one and then closed the show with my own little spot, my grand finale, the shaving, the hung-over woman, *Golden Boy,* Hemingway and Gertrude Stein, Harry, Harry—and this time nobody yelled. The audience was guys with dates and after two minutes of me, they began drinking and talking as though the show was finished, as though I had disappeared. Nick and I left fast and hid in a diner. After the second show, as I came off the stage, the boss said, "Get your stuff and get the fuck out of here." Not exactly genteel.

I called Harry. He asked, "Which show did they fire you after?" I said, "The second." He said, "Good girl. I was hoping for that." He told me I should go back every night and report for work.

The next evening, terrified that I was in physical danger, I walked up to the tall, thin, dark Italian stage manager and explained the AGVA rule. He said, "Ask AGVA, can you work with two broken legs?" But for three nights, two shows a night, I stood backstage with Nicky, both of us lepers, nobody speaking to me—not the adagio dancer who had told me about her hysterectomy, not the stripper whose husband ran the lights for her. They were scared, groveling for jobs. We all needed that money; we were all little people grubbing for pennies.

Back in New York, my case came up in front of the AGVA board and I got my pay—seventy-five dollars minus sixty-eight dollars for expenses and Harry Brent's ten-dollar commission. But Harry was embarrassed and I guess he took a long, hard look at the future of his client. He told me he was not going to handle me anymore. He said, "You can keep the act and the props, but I want the rights to the name Pepper January, Comedy with Spice. Great names and logos don't come easy."

When you are not even Pepper January then you are *truly* nothing. Now, after a year of struggle, I had passed square one going the wrong way. I was at square zero, back at the B & G with the rest of the losers, listening to useless nonsense from never-will-be comics and comedy writers. "I got a chunk here you're gonna love," they would say. "It's on mailboxes. Danny Thomas wants to buy it from me for two hundred dollars, but because I think you're a comer, I'll let you have it for thirty." Or they would expound on rules of comedy, everybody pontificating something opposite: "Never talk to one

person in the audience or you'll lose the whole group"—
"Always talk to one person, make him your audience."
"Come on with music"—"Never come on with music." "You
got to get 'em in the first ten minutes"—"It's the last ten
minutes that sock it home." All of it was a lot of hot air sitting
over a cup of coffee.

But at least I was smarter about comedy managers, aware
now that there were lots of Harry Brents, lots of sleazo,
cheezo managers. Every office held nine. They came in pods.
Some slept in the office; some had no office at all and worked
out of phone booths. By agreement with the other nomadic
managers, one would have rights to a certain booth in the
Brill Building from, say, two to three, and could sit there, the
door open, studying horse race handicap sheets and receiving
phone calls. Many of them were specialists, men who handled
only circus acts or variety acts or strippers. If possible, all
these penny ante managers were more ragtag than theatrical
agents, maybe because they were dealing with a lower stratum
of society.

The comics I met in those offices were, like me, on the
bottom of the cage. To be an actor, you had to be a little bit
intelligent, had to have been exposed to a couple of plays or a
movie or even read a book. To be a comic, you needed nothing. You could be a funny derelict and you were a comic, and
that was my level—all of us sad sacks together, aspiring to be
admired and loved and famous like the Bob Hopes and Milton
Berles—and stealing their jokes for our sorry little acts. I was
right there with them, desperate and wild with frustration,
fighting for the same seven jobs in Queens. Nothing else
mattered to any of us except that breakthrough job we could
not get in show business.

At the B & G I used to see Dom DeLuise, desperately
driven, always hysterical. He went a year and a half without
even the smell of a performing job. Once he spotted in *Actors
Cues* a casting call ad for the new musical *Wish You Were Here.*

They were looking for handsome men who would look virile in bathing suits.

Dom, who has always been chubby with a cherubic face, rented an 1890s striped tank suit, hoping he would make the producers laugh and he would be hired. Wearing his striped suit, he got in line with the other actors and was immediately turned down. He went back to the end of the line, came through again, and was escorted bodily from the theater. In a frenzy of desperation, he sneaked back in, went up to a stage box, and made a flying leap to the stage, where he landed on his stomach and was knocked cold, so they carried him out of the theater and deposited him in the alley. I'm sure he dusted himself off and two days later forgot the humiliation and did something equally insane to get noticed. We are all lobotomy victims in this business.

At the time I knew him, Dom was a movie usher, selling Thom McAn shoes in a store and checking coats during *Guys and Dolls*. He took Milton Berle's coat, and Berle gave him a dollar. Absolutely thrilling! Ruth Buzzi, trying to be a dramatic actress, stayed alive cleaning apartments. She would ride the subways with her spaghetti mop and bucket, dressed as the character she later used on *Laugh-In*—the hairnet, the baggy sweater, rolled stockings, flat shoes. That made everything endurable. She was not a cleaning lady. She was an actress pretending to be a cleaning lady.

During the winter of 1959 I actually had a temp job I liked at Claire Mallison & Associates, who were photographers' representatives and ran a studio. I was the fashion coordinator for the Modess Because . . . ad campaign and the photographer was Cecil Beaton.

Fashion coordinator had nothing to do with fashion. The fabulous designer dresses had already been chosen and bought in size fourteen to fit one of the wives of Johnson &

Johnson, who manufactured Modess. My job was to make the dresses fit the size-six models. I took huge tucks, using clips and pins—so I was constantly down on my knees, short and chunky, my mouth full of pins, my stockings making bunches at the knees when I stood up. I pinned and ironed and steamed and ran and got shoes dyed and fetched coffee and was a glorified gofer—but loving it because I felt very show business—and there was Cecil Beaton.

He was elegant, elegant, elegant—imposing, gray-haired. He was tall and portly, but somehow because of his clothes and manner, thin-looking. He did not wear a morning coat— but should have. He was very, very grand, very much the genius, very aware of how a person of his stature should act. I never saw him relax, but he had tremendous charm and tremendous affectation. Very Cyril Ritchard: "Oh, Priscilla, my darling. Never more beautiful! Oh, the shoulders of a queen." He had a violinist on the set to create a mood and lunch was sent in from The Colony and there was champagne, and Diana Vreeland and her entourage would pop in from *Vogue* to say hello.

This was the first time I encountered the jet set—wealthy, slim women coming and going in black, a waft of perfume preceding them, diamond pins worn in unusual places like the crook of the arm, masses of pearls, amusing jewelry: "It's really too much, isn't it—but it's such *fun!*" I also learned British understatement. I heard Diana Vreeland saying to Cecil Beaton, "Did you hear what happened to Pookie? She married an earl, but he went through all her money and then left her and the twins were born dead and she was hit by a taxi, which of course had no insurance, and she is now paralyzed from the waist down."

Cecil Beaton raised an eyebrow, clicked his tongue. "Pity."

I worked for Claire Mallison off and on for six months and was there for all of Beaton's performances. Maybe it was one of his affectations, but he never seemed to know how to work a camera. His assistant, Charles Biasiny, under the black cloth behind the camera, made an approximate setup and then Beaton would perfect the lighting and hypnotize the model and say, "Splendid! Hit the button, Charles!" I realized that Beaton's genius lay in the lighting, the atmosphere, the posing, and making the model feel like Eliza Doolittle going to the ball. His pictures were magic.

I never opened my mouth and Cecil Beaton, in all that time while we worked and worked and worked, never said a word to me. Then, the day he was leaving and saying his good-byes, he looked at me and said, "Lose ten pounds and streak your hair."

In the spring of 1959 I met a person who revolutionized my life, and began a relationship that created a major shift in my understanding and approach to comedy. At that time I had evolved from believing I could do anything, to finding out I could do very little. I knew my act was terrible. Instinctively, I scorned hunks and chunks and shtick, but anything beyond that seemed inaccessible—especially since I had no confidence at all in my own everyday humor. I admired the new, acted comedy of Mike Nichols and Elaine May, who did comic dialogues of classic human moments like a space scientist telephoning his mother. I thought it clever and classy and way above my abilities. I thought I had no options more elevated than Robert Orben gags, than "Wild About Harry," than saying, "Remember the picnics, Harry? I can see you now, standing on the hilltop, the wind blowing your hair, and you too proud to chase it. And you'd look down at me and laugh. Your teeth all white. All shiny. All uppers."

But then that spring I met Treva Silverman. She was tiny and blond with a roundish face and a small Marilyn Monroe voice which would break startlingly into a big laugh. Very intense, supersensitive, a bundle of tears, she was clearly a thoroughbred. Desperately trying to be a comedy writer, she was constantly sending in newsbreak fillers for the ends of columns in *The New Yorker*—the newspaper errors accompanied by a wisecracking line. She supported herself by playing the piano and singing in cocktail bars in New Jersey and in East Side bars which were basically hooker places. When they regularly closed down and reopened under a new name, Treva would always be amazed. Like me, she was naive and would say, "What! There were prostitutes there? But I borrowed her lipstick!"

Unlike me, Treva kept to her high standards. At work she refused to compromise and play popular songs, so when people asked, "Do you know 'Ebb Tide'?" she would say "No," and do some obscure Rodgers and Hart song like "Suppertime." Also, unlike me, she was courageous. She had broken away from the safety of her home and its room and board and was living in a minute first-floor studio apartment way east on Eightieth Street. When I had free time, I went there, and as usual, feeling like the second banana, I brought sandwiches in my purse or containers of coffee to be absolutely sure of my welcome.

I can remember hurrying in the door and through the hallway kitchen, already talking about the manager I had just come from or the performer who did not deserve her success because Treva and I were more talented . . . and in the same breath saying, "I just want to use your phone for a minute," and I would plunk down dimes and call fifteen managers and agents before finally flopping onto the bed, which masqueraded as a daytime couch. On the wall above my head was an extravagantly romantic poster of *Gone With the Wind*—Rhett carrying Scarlett through the flames of Atlanta—and pinned on another wall were the long folios of movie programs for the Thalia Theater, an art movie house. At the rear wall was a window overlooking the bleakest, most rundown basement

garden I had ever seen. On the opposite side wall was a
bulletin board filled with *New Yorker* cartoons and, beneath it,
a brick and board bookshelf choked with programs of Broadway shows. Among these artifacts of Treva's ambitions, I felt
absolutely at ease.

Suddenly in my life there was a girl with my background
and my obsession, a dream sister who had graduated from
Bennington College, done her thesis on James Joyce's *Ulysses,*
and known since day one that she belonged in show business.
We were two salmon swimming upstream together. We did
not know why we were struggling so compulsively against the
current, but we had to do it. Unlike me, Treva had no self-
doubts, no contingency plans, and I warmed myself in front of
her positive energy, her wonderful confidence that she was an
artist and success was coming to her and, because I was her
friend, it would come to me too. Between us, business was
first. Before breakfast we would be on the phone. "Listen, are
you up? I just thought of an interesting line: 'They fired the
wine taster for drinking on the job.' Tell me what you think."

During our girl-to-girl sessions at Treva's apartment, she
would also flop on the couch and one of us would drape our
legs over the arm of her little easy chair and we would talk in a
way wonderful to me and brand-new. We were both accus-
tomed to men being the funny ones while we sat quiet. But
here was a girl who understood my private humor and could
be funny right back in the next millisecond. We would think of
"concepts"—if you like a man, how could you get him to take
you out on a date? We would rummage back and forth between our minds, laughing, looking for "the line," and when
one of us found it, she jumped up with excitement, saying,
"I've got it! You call the guy and tell him, 'My parents bought
tickets to *My Fair Lady* and it turns out it's their wedding
anniversary and they're being given a party, so out of the blue
I've got two tickets for *My Fair Lady.*' And he says, 'When are
the tickets for?' And you say, 'When can you make it?' "

At last I had a person in my life who understood what it was like for me to be female in the fifties. Sprawled on the couch against the pillows, we talked a lot about men and how much trouble we had finding the right one and how far we were from the stereotype they expected. We both had been taught at home that a girl always asks the man about his hobbies, always comes out in her apron and says, "Did you have a hard day at the office, dear?" But for Treva and me that was impossible, and we discussed the trouble men had dealing with a girl who was obsessed with her work and was funny and quick and maybe, God forbid, a mental equal. We agreed femininity and humor were not supposed to go together and men were thrown off balance by us, were afraid of us, and we had to hold back, be careful not to banter with them, not to top them. We believed, too, that men were jealous because our highs came so much from our work, and they were resentful that our intensity of feeling did not go to them. Treva wanted to be Elaine May. She was the best role model we had —an assertive woman with a marvelous, fast mind and, at the same time, good-looking and feminine. We did not know of any other woman like that.

Treva's boyfriend was Johnny Meyer, a rich kid who was going to be both Ira and George Gershwin combined. His mother and father had always said, "My boy's a genius," but it was the old story: somebody with money who could afford to sit unsullied above the fray while he waited to become the Gershwins—which never happened.

Treva and Johnny did not doubt that they were brilliant and, intoxicatingly, did not question my talent. They introduced me into their group. The core included boys named Rod Warren and Michael McWhinney plus others who came and went—all college-educated kids who had read the reading lists and approached everything in terms of humor. We would eat dinner at cheap Italian and Chinese restaurants, places where we could sit a long time and talk because talk was the main thing—interrupting each other to verbally rewrite the line and then somebody else would rewrite the rewrite until we found the definitive line—all of us laughing and jubilant.

In the same way that tennis players rally, nobody keeping score, we were playing comedy as a game, nobody competing to be the funniest, everybody excited to take it higher and higher until we were drunk with exhilaration. We had a crush on the Algonquin Round Table and decided they became famous because they called each other by their last names, saying, "Well, Benchley said to Thurber" or "Woollcott said to Parker." We thought we should start doing that so we would become famous, but could never understand how everybody at the Algonquin was always overheard. Treva suggested we hire somebody to overhear us and go around saying, "Did you hear what Silverman said to Molinsky?" But I must admit, that did not have quite the same ring.

We really were a family for each other, the family we all desperately needed. Everybody, even I, though I did not know it, was setting out to do a heartbreakingly, painfully difficult thing—expose ourselves through our deepest thoughts and most precious insights—going out on a limb by voicing them aloud through our work. Our parents could not understand our thoughts, but our friends could and thought they were wonderful and were telling us, "You said the funniest thing last night." We deeply needed that because our parents were still saying, "Be sure to wear your boots because it's raining out."

In the group I was a tiny bit to one side because I was the only one who wanted to be a performer. The rest were writers, determined to be the comic brains of the next generation of nightclub revues and musical comedies. They did not think a stand-up comedian was funny doing setup, punch line, setup, punch line. They were exposing me to the idea that comedy was certainly a craft and maybe an art. They were students of comedy, sneaking into musicals after the first act and later picking apart every line and move. Treva, using a clunky old Wollensak reel-to-reel recorder, taped everything interesting on TV and radio and then played it back, analyzing, "See, there are too many words in that sentence. It didn't go fast enough. The rhythm was off. That word stuck out too much and you don't hear the end of the sentence. That pause was too long . . ."

I was learning what was good funny compared to bad funny, clever laughs compared to easy laughs, comedy based on true insights into human behavior compared to hackneyed mother-in-law gags. I was being taught taste—but almost too much taste. I was, in fact, being corrupted upward into a humor so precious, so insular, it was above my natural, broader strata. These friends were beginner humorists still without their personal, original brand of humor, still unable to create original characters and funny situations in their own heads. So they were cutting their comedy teeth on satire, writing put-downs of other people's creative commercials, TV shows, ads, movies, plays. Many of their subjects—the new design of the Bloomingdale's shopping bag, Zeckendorf's plans to build a tower on the West Side—were so rarefied and parochial that only New York dogs could hear them. Treva did a satiric sketch about a couple who were watching a foreign movie and could not decide whether they had seen it before—and concluded they had not, because the headboard on the bed was different.

These writers' ultimate goal was to write a musical comedy, but their immediate ambition was to get a piece into a Julius Monk revue at the Upstairs at the Downstairs, an exotic little boîte in the old Wanamaker mansion on East Fifty-sixth Street. Julius Monk was the improbable king of the revue world. His career reached back to producing and directing cabarets in Paris and London and for fourteen years he had been at the Ruban Bleu in New York, where he launched

Imogene Coca and Jonathan Winters. Now at the Upstairs he had switched to a new kind of revue in which the performers were interchangeable, most of them out of the same WASP cookie mold, and directed to blend without individual personality. The material was the star, not the performer.

A tall, lean man, impeccably tailored like an English lord and gloriously affected, Julius Monk was the original Man in the Hathaway Shirt in the ads, wearing the black eye patch. His mixture of fake British and native North Carolina accents was so BBC that even the English could not understand him and the joke went around that the cast of one of his revues decided to give him consonants for Christmas. When there was a fire in his apartment, he stopped the firemen at the door and made them take off their boots, saying, "Gentlemen, please hold your water. Fire or not, I have white carpets."

I went to parties with my new friends, intoxicated to be with peers I admired and who thought I was funny and belonged in show business. To them I was the young comedian who could perform their works in front of an audience in a nightclub. These kids in their early twenties, walking around with a bunch of songs under their arms looking for somebody to showcase them, did not care that my singing voice had a three-note range and sounded like a blend of Raymond Massey and Margaret Mead.

I began replacing the Harry Brent routines with cute revue songs and sketches. Rod Warren, who became an important Hollywood writer-producer, doing special material for the Oscar ceremonies, gave me a talk song called "Photoplay": *"Now what's this Frank Sinatra,/who's this Molly Bee?/And who are they to Shirley MacLaine/or Hecuba or me?"* A young composer named Ronnie Axe, who later committed suicide, wrote for me "I'll Never Forget What's His Name": "I'll always remember—the color of his hair./It was dark. Or it was fair./I could swear that he had hair." Treva was helping me— gave me one line I still use: "If God wanted me to cook, my hands would be aluminum." Johnny Meyer wrote, "I'm in Love with Mr. Clean," and I went up to his apartment and the composer himself worked on the song with me.

But, unsure, unfocused, reaching out wildly, I was also busily stealing new stand-up gags wherever I could find them. I was friendly with Herb Hardick—who now does a million voice-overs for TV ads—and he and his girl invited me to a club to hear the act he was doing with Paul Mazursky, who is today a major film director. They called themselves Igor and H, and did a takeoff on an outer space movie—staring upward and saying, "Well, John, there they go and Earth is safe once more. I wonder what they were after, don't you, John? John! JOHN!" The next day that bit slid right into my act. There is no shame when you are desperate.

It was a bewildering, confusing, schizophrenic time for me. On one hand I was immersed in an ultrasophisticated *New Yorker* world with my writer friends and, on the other hand, clinging to street-smart Nick Clemente, who was contemptuous of these boys in trench coats, thought they were precious and phonies. Living in two worlds, I kept Nicky separate from the revue crowd because, in their turn, they would have laughed at him and I would have been embarrassed.

I was also leaving the revue world to type at my office temp jobs and to wait in the anterooms of flyspeck managers, among the lineup of hunks and chunks comedians, the younger ones dreaming of stardom in the Copacabana, the older ones just hoping for a weekend in Jersey. All I wanted was to get an act together that would give me a living, make fifty dollars a week, so I could stabilize my life, raise my head, look around, and decide what I *really* wanted to do.

I had not *totally* given up on acting. While telling everybody I was a comedian, whenever there was a new theatrical agent who did not know me, I would secretly hit his office, hoping still to be Kim Stanley without going into comedy. I auditioned for the role of Emily in *Our Town* and the director told me I was too old for the part. That was a major shock. I was twenty-six and too old for Emily, too old to play a fifteen-year-old! Nobody had ever said those words to me—"too old"—and they were really a wet blanket of reality. I was out of business as an ingenue—and therefore as a woman. My mother, pushing marriage, was right—the meter was running!

My mother had pounded into me the idea that youth was a crucial commodity, and if I did not move in those few years, I would probably stay on the shelf forever. In an argument, as her ultimate crusher, she would say, ". . . and you're not getting any younger!" So my advancing age welded me even tighter to comedy, which is one of the few fields where age and sex do not matter. Nobody ever said I was too old to play the Silver Slipper. I think the final push into comedy came from the *Our Town* director, because after that I gradually stopped going to theater agents. A door that was never open began to close.

One of the last theatrical agents I called on was Tony Rivers in a walk-up office on Seventh Avenue. He was an American Indian, big, handsome, with wonderful black hair, a sweet, sweet man. Ordinarily, he would have taken no notice of me, but that day I caught him in his outer office and he said, "I can't speak to anybody today. I just put my poodle to sleep." Suddenly, he began to cry and it was awful to see this big, imposing man so upset in front of a stranger and I began crying—and we cried together—and that formed a strange kind of friendship. When I came back the next day, he wanted to send me to a major cattle call, but looked at me and said, "I can't send you out as Joan Molinsky. You've got to change your name."

Under Treva's influence I had stopped worrying about my name and was scornful of the kids around me constantly agonizing, "Should I be Crystal Vanity? Is that too much? Maybe it should be Crystal Vanderbilt—that would give me a little class." In Tony Rivers's office something went click in my head and I said, "Okay, I'll be Joan Rivers." He was very quiet for a moment and then said, "Okay." It was as simple as that. I never thought about it again.

Having a stage name made it easier to perform in those raunchy nightclubs. Joan Molinsky was not up there onstage —*I* was not doing the comedy—a totally different person was getting hurt. Joan Rivers was like a party dress I put on, so in those early days she was only the tiniest part of me and Joan Molinsky was still frightened and confused and bewildered in her life. I was not good enough to get work on the high level that my revue friends were urging. Only the bottom-rung agents would see me and they only offered jobs in small seedy joints that made the Silver Slipper seem like The Stork Club. Every third week or so some agent or manager would say, "Go down to the Port Authority and take the bus to Perth Amboy" —or Malvern, Long Island. Or go to Brooklyn and play spots called the Club Safari, the Swiss Terrace, the Monkey Club— where I would do an esoteric takeoff on a Civil War movie: "Mr. President, Abe, on behalf of all of us, we ask you, no, we beg you, not to give that speech at Gettysburg . . . Mr. President . . . it's too hip." Around me was a show of sexy dancers and dog acts, a tap dancer doing a salute to Rodgers and Hammerstein, a gross emcee saying, "Every time I kiss my wife she says, 'Cut that out.' So the other night I went to touch her breast and she said, 'Cut that out.' Did you ever see one of these?" And he pulled out a rubber breast.

I was always frightened that this sleaze would rub off on me, imprint itself on me permanently as my parents had predicted. I knew I should not be there with what my mother called "that element," and my mother's side of me was almost angry with my father's side of me, really frightened that I could, like my father, simultaneously laugh at those people yet go out for coffee with them and fit right in, making friends with the stripper whose husband ran the lights, and perhaps, someday, become them.

But without any other options, I could only persist, take that risk, continue creeping onstage, very tentative, with a lot of "So hello" and "uhs," a lot of stammering and an air of apology and terrible Robert Orben jokes to cover bombing: "Don't laugh, it'll interrupt my rhythm"—"I feel like I'm Rembrandt and I just finished painting you." I was still scared to touch the microphone and stood anchored, absolutely rigid, unable to move my head because my voice would fade. I would be hired for Friday and Saturday nights and never make it past Friday, always arriving back home by Saturday and always crying—told by those rough audiences that I was not funny, not talented, perhaps not even human. My whole professional life was fired and cry, fired and cry, fired, cry, fired, cry, fired, cry.

I played a place called Bill's Castle up in Connecticut where the boss told me, "Go out between shows and talk to people—and don't forget to keep your swizzle sticks." That meant push drinks, order Scotch and soda—but, winky, winky, always get ginger ale—and later cash in your swizzle sticks for dimes. I started my act. "Tonight I want to show that in a marriage there are strange things that happen when both partners drink. The scene is a bar. 'Hello, George, has my husband been in . . . He's drunk again . . . He has? . . . An hour ago? . . . Was I with him?' "

While I talked, the audience talked. I sang, "I'm in love with Mr. Clean, no hips could be thinner, no head more Yul Brynner"—and three drunk couples, to be funny, got up to dance. Suddenly over the PA system the boss's voice screamed, "Get her off! Get her off!"

I had been taken up there by an actual agent, Gary Nardino, who went on to be president of the television branch of Paramount Pictures and gave us *Laverne and Shirley*, *Mork and Mindy*, and *Happy Days*. At that time he was a young secretary in the William Morris Agency, trying to get ahead by handling me—his one big error in judgment. Well, Gary was a great big guy and he had a huge fight with the boss—Bill, I guess—in the parking lot, fists going pow, pow, pow. I was hoping Gary would not get hurt because he was my agent and Treva would kill me because he was her agent, too—so I would lose a friend *and* an agent. Slightly rumpled, but triumphant, he came to the car with seventy-five dollars in his hand, God bless him.

I was willing to do almost anything to be on a stage and get money—and, in fact, did it. One day I was in some dingy office and the sad-eyed agent asked me, "What size are you?"

I said I was size six, but could be any size he wanted. Why?

Well, a magician named Kuda Bux, The Man with the X-ray Eyes, needed an assistant for a show in Sainte Anne de Beaupré, Canada, leaving in two days. The costume was size ten and if I could wear it, I had the job. I said, "Fine. I'm size ten sideways." The job was Wednesday through Saturday and I would get forty dollars plus expenses.

I met Kuda Bux in Grand Central Station to take the overnight coach to Canada. He had the strangest eyes I've ever seen—except for The Captain of The Captain & Tenille. Very black, huge pupils. He had been in *Life* magazine, driving a car through traffic with his eyes bandaged, and it was easy to believe he could see through things. Within his profession, he was much admired—"a genius with silks," I was told.

Kuda Bux had a friend with him, Omar, who was always on *The Ed Sullivan Show* spinning plates on billiard cues. Walking across the floor of Grand Central between them was one of the big embarrassments of my life. I am five feet two and I was the tall one. Their shirt collars were grimy. Their camel's hair coats had grease spots. Their turbans did not look clean. Kuda Bux had yellow fingernails. It was really the underbelly of show business. I kept praying, "Please don't let anybody see me here. Please, God."

I sat up all night on the train across from two Indians who had not showered. I told myself, *This is not happening to me. This is absolutely not happening to me,* and then I would rescue myself with fantasy, imagining I was Audrey Hepburn in *Love in the Afternoon.*

Sainte Anne de Beaupré turned out to be a charming town on a lake in the Laurentian Mountains. The hotel was pretty with a small show room where Kuda Bux rehearsed me. Mainly I handed him silks or took them away and pointed and went, "Tah dah." I was part of two tricks. I was sawed in half and I stood in a box with my head out, looking comfy while he stuck swords through the box. It was not hard. It was not *that* magic.

In my room, I tried on the size-ten costume. It was one of those terrible Indian jobs with big fat pantaloons—the Indian bloomer girl look. A bare midriff was topped by a wonderful brassiere with lots of beads and pearls and gold coins and big, fatsy sleeves, gauzy, so you could see my chubby arms. On my feet were Aladdin-and-the-Magic-Lamp shoes, gold, with toes that turned up. Lord knows how many girls had worn that costume over the years—all size ten.

Kuda Bux did his preparations in secret, so I was banned from the stage and dressing room. At the last minute I walked through the lobby, my coat over my horrendous costume, but with my gold Aladdin shoes showing, size 8½, which meant plenty of room in the back for the heel to grow. I kept them on my feet by gripping with my toes. I kept the pantaloons from falling down around my ankles by rolling them three times at the waist and sticking out my stomach.

I played the Wednesday night performance straight— pointing, fetching, bandaging his eyes, handing out the putty, serenely letting myself be sawed and stabbed. Everything went fine—except for a drunk Eskimo girl, who stood up and began to scream, "Why does everybody hate Eskimos!"

The next morning in the hotel people were saying to me, "Boy, is Kuda Bux good. I sure enjoyed your act. Shame about the Eskimo." I found myself saying, "I don't really do this for a living. I'm really an actress and comedian. Just a temporary thing."

On Thursday night I was *really* overcome by the schlockiness of it all—Kuda Bux in his dingy turban and colorful ruffled shirt, major cuff links, tuxedo jacket threadbare at the elbows, black street shoes, and myself dying of mortification in that yellow-and-gold harem getup. I felt so thick, so fat, so clumsy, so ugly. I looked as though there were two complete people in my thighs. I looked like two potato sacks with heads. When I came onstage, my hips were still arriving five minutes later. I was a sight gag! It was the fulfillment of every nightmare I had ever had.

My reaction was typical: *They won't like me because I'm ugly. Make them like me for another reason. Make them laugh with me, before they laugh at me. Then we'll all be friendly, then they'll know I don't think I look terrific—and I'll be home free.*

When the swords went through the box, I made faces, winced, crossed my eyes, called out, "Oooo, watch it, Kuda Bux. Ouch, Kudy, don't do that! Oooo, that was a cold one! Oh! Oh!" I got some laughs. The second show I did it even more—"Kuda Bux, be careful. Mon Dieu, close call." When he sawed me in half, I added a voice from inside the box. "Oh, oh, Kuda Bux, be careful with that saw. Ahhhhhh! Only fooling! Voilà!"

He did not need that. The next morning he fired me. He said, "Joan, you're not funny, you're not professional, and, what's more, you're not a size ten."

Years later Kuda Bux came to see me someplace where I was performing. I made a big fuss over him—"How wonderful to see you." He brought with him a manila envelope full of his clippings and they were twenty years old. Early Ed Sullivan. Early Steve Allen. Every clipping was yellow. It was an old man sitting there and the eight by ten glossy was of a young Indian. I invited him on the Mike Douglas show when I was hosting and he did his act. After all, he had paid me for the entire week—and maybe I should not have slept fully clothed in the hotel room next to his. Maybe he really did not have X-ray eyes.

But in all those terrible experiences in 1958 and 1959, I was putting in time on stages, paying my dues and not completely stupid. In the course of all that bombing in cheezed-out clubs, I gradually saw my mistakes and tried not to repeat them—it is the bad that teaches you, makes you think; good takes care of itself and only gets better. I kept dropping pieces from the act and putting in other bits and, gradually, by the spring of 1959, began to like my material and feel I was performing it well. I had a little more courage onstage, coming on a tiny bit faster, finding a stronger voice, and if something was not working, getting out of it immediately. I understood, too, that I was not meant to wear gowns. I was meant to wear my little black dress, my little string of pearls, and my little circle pin. I was becoming just a wee bit more myself. But unfortunately, my cutesy adorable act was not being done in front of cutesy adorable audiences. I was trying to make "Mr. Clean" work between trained seals and an over-age tango team.

However, no matter how many times I bombed and cried, I could not wait to get to the next job. Hope always lived in the next show. And once in a while, coming onstage, radiating my eagerness to please, I *would* connect and people would listen and laugh. Then, after the next firings, I did not cry quite so hard, because I knew there were audiences, if I could just find them, who could understand and accept and love me. And I kept reassuring myself, "I know *Treva* thinks I'm funny. I *know* Rod Warren does. And remember those people six shows back in Jersey City? They really liked me in that little bar. If I can get stronger material, I know I can reach people again. I know it. I *know* it."

Treva Silverman came up with the idea of a two person revue with her boyfriend, Johnny Meyer—me singing, he playing the piano. I clutched at the idea. I could escape from my limbo state, strung out between stand-up comic and chic entertainer. This was the answer—go all the way with my wonderful revue friends. We ended up in the office of an agent named Ira Ring—a small man, bald except for a fringe of hair around the back of his head, and dressed in a dark, very shiny mohair suit—a typical Catskills agent. Most of them were sleazy and liars, never enthusiastic, always pretending they were doing you a huge favor—which they were, because they controlled the jobs at the mountain resorts.

An agent like Ira Ring would guarantee the Fairview Hotel three shows a week, Wednesday, Friday, and Saturday, and would send up whomever he wanted, sometimes trading off with other agents: "All my magicians are working; I'll trade you my girl singer and I'm telling you she's a steal." The hotel would pay Ira Ring, say, a thousand dollars for the summer to supply weekend acts, and he could slice up that pie any way he wanted. The less he paid the acts, the more he could keep himself. But Mr. Schwartz of Schwartz's Bungalows wanted good talent for his thousand dollars—and if the acts were bad, Ira Ring would not get the account next summer. So all the Ira Rings were trying to cheat the acts but get the best ones they could for as little money as possible.

Johnny and I auditioned in his office and Ira Ring took us, I think, for our freshness—two young kids putting on the show in the barn. But the first thing he asked was, "Have you got a car?" Well, as a matter of fact, I did. My Aunt Alice had given an exhausted 1950 Buick to my cousin Allan, who kept it in Vermont for skiing, and, when it became too rusty and horrible for him, he passed it on to me. It was one of those huge grotesques with tail fins and a bulbous front with a big rusty grille and gross headlights like bulging pop eyes. The body was rotting away with scabs of rust around the edges of the fenders and the headlights. The upholstery was so destroyed, I had to buy a little rattan seat to sit on. Originally it had been white, but the color was now grunge—"Last seen driving a grunge-colored car."

It also had natural air-conditioning. On the passenger side of the front seat, the floor had rusted away entirely and there was a huge hole which I covered with a Rubbermaid mat. Whenever the mat fell through, I would buy a new one, otherwise all kinds of schmutz and dirt and phew came in from below and insulation material blew up and covered the passenger with little fine pieces of fuzz. People were always asking Nick Clemente if he owned a dog. Also the hole was dangerous. The same hypnotic impulse that tempts you to jump in front of a train made people want to touch the road whizzing beneath their feet. Sometimes, for laughs, when we stopped for a light, people would put their feet through the hole and stand on the ground.

But I was very grateful for that car. It meant I was no longer a prisoner in Larchmont—like an old person. In New York, I was liberated from the frantic race to make the 11:25 train—and missing it and waiting for the 1:25—or missing that and sitting till 3:25, surrounded by drunks and bag ladies and forced to phone my mother, who was waiting up, and tell her I would be late. And that car assured my career as a Catskill comic. It was as good as talent. If the act had a car, the agent excused a lot of things, because you could take other acts with you and he kept the transportation money paid by the hotels. The agent would say, "On your way to Schwartz's Bungalows would you mind dropping off Fifi and her talking parrot at Cass's Cabins?" You would say, "Absolutely no problem," but Cass's Cabins would turn out to be forty miles the other way.

Ira Ring sent us to the Swan Lake Hotel. There were hundreds of places for everybody—Grossinger's or The Concord or Kutsher's for the rich—and Cass's Cabins for ladies who worked in bakeries or at sewing machines and for the factory workers who sent their families up and followed them on weekends. Most places were kosher and orthodox—which meant you never got a good dessert.

For three performances Johnny and I were to be paid six dollars and two free rooms with food. Nicky and Treva came with us and we hid them in our rooms, feeding them crackers, Rice Krispies, half a sandwich, a lamb chop in a napkin stolen from our meals. When we arrived at the hotel, the emcee came running toward us and said, "I'll trade you two swimming pool jokes for a good flat tire joke." Somebody had had a blowout. We just stared at him. Then Ira Ring turned up with his entire family for a nice weekend—paid for, I am sure, with what he chiseled from us.

On the stage of the Swan Lake Hotel recreation hall, the two of us—Johnny, beaming charm and good intentions, wearing white ducks and blue blazer, I in my sun dress, both with cute straw boaters—hurled ourselves into takeoffs of obscure foreign films and itsy, bitsy songs:

When the soldiers join the sailors and they lick the
  Jap,
When the hero's in a frame-up but he beats the rap,
When the maiden greets the villain with a well-timed
  slap,

All you want to do is clap.

Applause, applause, there's nothing like applause.

But this audience was not taking the hint. In front of us
was a field of blank faces, empty of any emotion beyond boredom and mystification. The energy we blasted outward died
and disappeared at the footlights, sucked away into the nothingness, nobody moving, everyone dazed by the tedium. But
they were polite, perhaps because they had children of their
own and thought it was nice that these two youngsters were
doing whatever it was they were doing up there. Only occasionally, in the oppressive silence, did the pale disk of a face
tilt downward to check a watch and guess when this interminable thing might be over.

Suddenly, the door at the rear burst open and the owner
rushed down the aisle with his arms up, shouting, "Excuse
me! Excuse me! Johansson has won the fight. Ingemar Johansson is the new heavyweight champion."

"Mr. Clean" froze on my lips. Johnny and I sat mystified,
mouths open, trying to imagine who this Johansson might be.
Out in the audience, the dulled faces flashed into life, erupting into smiles and laughter and cheers. Pleasure bubbled in
the room—for two minutes. Then, like a record running
down, the happy chatter trailed off, the delight drained away,
and the faces turned politely back toward us, the smiles sub-
siding into apathy and resignation.

I could not go on, could no longer impose my crazy
ambition on these innocent, decent people. I whispered to
Johnny, "Let's give them a sing-along. Let's do 'Bicycle Built
for Two.' " Johnny's face flushed. The Juilliard student hissed
back, "I don't do sing-alongs." Flashing a smile toward the
audience, I whispered, "We're bombing. We should do whatever entertains a Jew on vacation." Gershwin folded his hands
and put them in his lap. He knew *he* was not the problem with
the act because when he played and sang in living rooms,

everybody went, "Wonderful, wonderful." And the material could not be the problem because it was *his* material. So there was only one other element, which was sitting on a stool in a sun dress. He hissed, "You don't even have enough voice for a sing-along." I bowed to the audience, thanked them for coming, and left the stage, releasing us all from purgatory. The next two nights Johnny and I were put in the cocktail lounge and told to do the best we could, which was not very well, particularly because we were no longer speaking.

Back in New York Ira Ring gave us our six dollars—and took out sixty cents commission. Then he told us we were not for him—"You're not a Ira Ring act." Years later, the first time I played Las Vegas, I bumped into Ira Ring in the lobby of the Riviera Hotel. He threw his arms around me and told his wife, "I found her."

Now I was as baffled as that poor audience at the Swan Lake Hotel. My one-liner material—"Harry, Harry"—had been bombing. I had tried to move into revue comedy—but the sophisticated audiences for that material were in nightclubs far above my reach. My revue friends—especially Treva —would have scorned me if I returned to "Harry, Harry," so I split the difference, mingled some one-liner routines with my chichi Johnny Meyer material, and went back to my sleazy circuit of bomb, bomb, bomb, connect, bomb, bomb. I even made it to the Catskills a few times alone, thanks to the talent of my car.

But Treva kept pushing and insisted I go to Greenwich Village and audition at a club I had thought was stratospheres above me—One Fifth Avenue, a small, intimate boîte catering to the swank uptown trade.

The first time I auditioned, the manager ate lunch and talked on the phone the entire time. I felt like a friend of mine who had a singing puppet and auditioned for *The Tonight Show*.

When the puppet began to sing, the talent coordinator said, "Keep going; I'll be right back; I know the song"—and left the room.

It was not till my third audition at One Fifth Avenue that I was accepted and then only for the amateur night held every Monday, their device for filling the club on the slowest evening of the week. The prize was a one-week booking and the winner was chosen by the volume of applause, so each contestant packed the house with friends. I paid for a table that included Rod Warren, Michael McWhinney, Nick Clemente, Johnny Meyer, who was a friend again for Treva's sake, and Treva, who brought along to hear me the momentary king of off Broadway stage revues, Ben Bagley, a boy wonder who turned out to be a dud rocket.

There was no stage, only a small area in front of two grand pianos, a few feet from the audience. I stood there in my black gown, feeling terrific, like Cinderella arriving at the ball, and I sensed something strange and new, a connection, a two-way tone of intimacy with this gathering of strangers. Out in the tiny room were four mirrored columns and as I began my act—singing, "Look at me, what do you see? A reasonably mature girl, a knowing self-assured girl . . ."—there I was reflected in each column, glowing in the spotlight and moving and performing and my pearls were sparkling at my neck— and I looked the way I always looked in my dreams.

Everywhere among the columns, even repeated in the mirrors, were tables of happy, sparkling, laughing faces. For the first time in my life everything in my act was working. For the first time I experienced the intoxication of being in charge of an audience, of playing a roomful of people like an instrument, of sensing that every person was riveted, was catching every nuance, laughing the right amount at the right places, quiet when they should have been quiet.

I felt myself opening and expanding, every fear dropping away. I felt able to be silly, fool around, cross my eyes, make a

second gesture and get a second laugh, which let me do variations and invent and go even further—and they followed me
to that new level—and I was free and soaring. It was everything I thought comedy was going to be and should be. I did
not care that I was chubby and getting older. They loved me
because I was funny and adorable onstage. I was back again in
my little kitty cat hat, being accepted for what I was pretending to be.

At the end of the show the contestants were lined up and
the audience voted with applause. I did not win. Treva and
Johnny were too hungry to scream and Ben Bagley had only
one lung—and the next day used it to telephone Charlotte
Rae and tell her I was stealing her diet routine. That night's
winner was a singer whose father was in the flag business and
had brought down from the factory a four-table claque and
you would have thought he was Frank Sinatra.

But the owner came over to me, saying he was definitely
going to book me—and among my all-important revue
friends I had new credibility, even stature. I was sure now that
my act had jelled, that I was on my way, that I had found the
formula—performing Treva and Johnny's songs forever to
adoring college graduates. It was a miracle that I got home to
Larchmont that night. I was flying. I did not need my car.

8

MY PARENTS HAD never seen me like that—floating, radiant, excited, convinced that I had scored a major hit, that magic had finally struck. They wanted to believe in me, wanted me to succeed, so they must have allowed themselves, suddenly, a little hope, because my father suggested, "Why don't you try it at the club?"

My parents had been members of the Riviera Shore Club in New Rochelle for years—not the best beach club, but one my parents could afford. The Molinskys always pretended we had a cabana, but we did not, we had a locker. The clubhouse had been one of the great mansions on Long Island Sound and was managed by a man named Bill Scott who decorated a lot of rooms in gold with flocked wallpaper, transforming it into High Bronx with lots of tassels and lots of upwardly mobile families with sons who were going to be doctors. If there was anything *not* in that club, it was someone earning less than sixty thousand dollars a year and a gentile. We belonged to it so Joan and Barbara could get a tan and a young man.

My father was suggesting that I be the professional entertainer for one of the regular Saturday dinner shows. I was very touched. It was a charming, warm, fatherly gesture, though I am sure he also wanted to show me off to their friends, prove to them that, "See, our daughter really is doing all right." I told him, "Sure. I'll take a shot."

He made the arrangements with Bill Scott, who booked me the Saturday after Labor Day, the last show of the summer. Totie Fields, a real professional, had performed there that summer and been loved and Bill Scott probably thought, *Female comic. Okay.* Also, after Labor Day, before closing for the winter, his entertainment budget was used up.

I was confident, and eager to justify my parents' faith—and to show how wrong they had been in the past—so for the occasion I rehearsed a cutesy new song:

> Get married, Shirley, get married!
> Your girlfriends got married in style.
> They stood at the altar like Rocks of Gibraltar.
> But you! You'll be wheeled down the aisle.

To further embellish the occasion and remove all chance of failure, I went to Ohrbach's and spent my office temp money on a pink-and-white sun dress, an imitation Anne Fogarty. I was ready!

On the day of my show, in the late afternoon, I rode to the club with my parents and they parked in the lot in front of the club—and I did feel my glamour dimmed a bit when the star of the evening got out of the car with her mother and father. In the lobby of the club a poster was on an easel:

TONIGHT
THE RIVIERA SHORE CLUB'S
OWN
Joan Rivers*

Daughter of Dr. and Mrs. M.C. Molinsky—club members

I could not help noticing who got the capital letters and who did not.

I ate dinner with my parents—greaso chicken with carrots and peas—and while the dessert, sherbet, was being served, Bill Scott came on the makeshift stage and introduced me, and then the daughter of Dr. and Mrs. Molinsky, club members, stood up at her parents' table and made her way past all the other tables—"Excuse me; excuse me; hello, Mrs. Fineman"—past all the people who had watched her grow up and lumber around the pool, watched her nose peel, watched her stand at the snack bar and wolf down three hamburgers— past all the women who had listened to my mother lamenting my alleged career, all the men who had heard my father sighing, "What can we do?" As I wended my way, the public address system was going, "Dr. Pinsky, please move your car. Dr. Pinsky, please move your car." I sensed again that the audience was not being set up for magic.

On the little, low stage, the ambience on a scale of one to ten, was minus ten. Bright, bright sun poured in through a long wall of glass, giving the room the glare and temperature of Arizona in a heat wave. Waiters serving sherbet were moving noisily among the huge round tables, where half of the 300 people were forced to turn uncomfortably toward me. I knew that after sunning themselves, they were tired and hot and sunburned and had just dressed to the teeth in tiny cabanas and lockers—lots of heavyset women in low-cut cocktail dresses, lots of old skin tanned and covered with makeup, lots of satins and brocades in the summer sun. Nobody there had said, "Okay, let's buy some tickets to see Joan Rivers." They were there to decide how good I was.

I started the act—Rod Warren had driven out and was playing piano for me. At first there was a hush. Then there was a lot of, "Oh, it's Joan Molinsky. You know, Dr. Molinsky's daughter. No, not Barbara. Joan. Locker forty-eight just down the line from us." That took two minutes and then came the awful moment when people had to decide between Joan Molinsky and the sherbet. The choice was, "Clink, clink, clink, clink," and, "Waiter, a little more coffee here."

The next thing after clink, clink was murmur, murmur, murmur: "How long do you think she's going to go on?" "Will you sit still, please; have a little courtesy—it's Betty and Meyer's girl." "Yes, but shouldn't we leave now and avoid the traffic?" Something was very wrong from One Fifth Avenue. This was not the same response, "Mr. Clean" did not have the same burnish. They saw no humor in Charlotte Rae's diet routine when I said, "One morning . . . at breakfast . . . Mother very tactfully, so as not to hurt my feelings, leaned across the table and said very gently, *'Hey, Fatso, stop stuffing your mush.'* " When "Get Married, Shirley, Get Married" struck no chords, I told them, "It's been a pleasure to entertain you," and beat it off and hid inside the kitchen door, shaking, my dress wet with sweat and sticking to me.

I wanted a giant eraser so I could go back in there and erase everything. I wanted to say to everybody, "Announcement, announcement. Let's make a pact. This never happened. Okay?" and go from table to table and all touch hands. "Never happened. Never saw it." "Thank you." "Next table." Then I wanted it to be a movie running in reverse, everybody walking out backward, getting in their cars, and going back to the Bronx. Then I would burn the film.

What did happen was that Bill Scott saw my parents dying of embarrassment and led them out through my escape route. Coming through the kitchen, was my father, confused and shocked, looking as though somebody had sat on him. With one outstretched hand he was trying to steady my mother, dressed in very high heeled satin shoes, a lace Bergdorf Goodman dress, wearing the good pearls and clutching her little Judith Leiber bag. The reigning Queen of the Shore Club, who spoke only to the six women who understood the necessity of service plates, was tottering, half blind because she refused to wear glasses, across the slatted wooden platforms on the kitchen floor and pushing past Puerto Rican dishwashers stripped to the waist, sweating, cigarettes in their mouths, cursing in Spanish. On her face was the look that must have been on somebody's face at the first sight of Hiroshima.

As it turned out, we could have walked right through the whole stupid club. We came out the side door, but then had to go around front and wait for our car in the middle of all those people who had just talked through me and watched me die. Mostly they looked away and said nothing. A few women came over to my mother and pressed her hand and said, "Betty, I'll speak to you tomorrow."

In the car going home I sat again in the backseat. From the front seat there was no "Hey, a bad audience," or "What do they know!" or "We thought you were very good." There was silence. In my family outward appearances were important above all else and I had publicly embarrassed them. Women my mother had scorned would be saying, "She thinks she's Mrs. Important. But did you see the daughter two weeks ago?" And now my parents believed everything about One Fifth Avenue was a lie and henceforth nothing I said would be believed.

Slumped as low as I could get, I was contemplating suicide, trying to decide which method would be the least painful —maybe baby aspirin. I finally settled on eating—"Did you hear about Joan Molinsky? She bombed at the Shore Club and two nights later stuffed herself till she burst."

At home I went upstairs and changed into blue-and-white-checked Bermuda shorts and a cotton top. My room faced toward the rear garden and the window was open. I heard my mother and father come out and sit in the two metal peacock chairs on the flagstone terrace. My mother was saying, "She has no talent. What can we do? There's no talent there."

My father answered, "I wasn't exactly laughing my hips off."

My mother said, "It's gone on long enough. We've got to do something about it."

My father said, "In my opinion, it was a memorable performance in reverse."

"She is throwing her life away," my mother said.

My father said, "The people expected more, even from an amateur."

I went crazy. I ran down the stairs and out the back door. In the darkness, half crouched, leaning forward, the fury humming inside me—I screamed at them, "I don't *care* what you say! You don't *know!* I *do* have talent! You are *wrong!* I did *well* at One Fifth Avenue! I *can* do well!"

Their voices were parental—soothing and condescending. "Now, Joan, we love you and don't want to see you hurt. If it was a stranger, we wouldn't care."

I remember my whole body straining, clenched, frantic, and my fingernails digging into my palms and hurting. "You're wrong! You're wrong! You're wrong!"

Now their voices were hardening—reason edged with exasperation. "How much longer can you have failure? It's been a year and a half. If something was going to happen, it would have happened by now. It's enough now. You've got to give up."

My father said, "Look what you're associating with. A bunch of derelicts and fairies."

"Don't talk about my friends like that. They're terrific. They're talented. It's only *you* that says I'm ruining my life. What do you know!" Yelling, crying, I beat myself on my hip with my fist. "You've *never* understood!"

My mother stood up. "Come inside. People will hear us. We'll talk about this inside."

We went indoors and immediately my mother hurried through the living room and dining room, closing the windows. I ran after her, screaming, "It's *my* life. It's *my* choice how I live it," and between windows my mother would turn and say, "Just stop it! For God's sake, stop it! I can't deal with you."

In the front hall my father was saying, "Let her go to hell."

"Leave me alone," I screamed. "You don't know what the hell you're talking about."

"Don't say *hell* to your parents," my mother answered. "Don't ever swear at us again."

That sent me completely out of control. "Goddamn it, I'll swear all I please! Don't tell me! I'm not a baby! I can say what I want!"

"Don't talk to your mother like that," my father yelled from the hall. "You got no respect. You're turning into a tramp like your friends—just like I said you'd be."

I turned on my father. "I am *not* a tramp! You're talking nonsense!" I began stamping my foot. "Hear me! I'm going to do what I want!" Stamp. "I'm going to do what I want, do you hear?" Stamp. "I'm going to do what I want!" Stamp.

My father said to my mother, "She's an idiot!"

My mother stood very straight, very stiff. Her voice was controlled and firm as stone as she went into her refrain. "Joan, if you're going to live in our house, you're going to live by our rules."

"In that case, I won't live in the house! You can't tell me what to do. I'm too old. I've been married and divorced."

Now my father was bright red. He shouted, "You want to leave? Leave! Who wants you! It's our house, just get out!"

I yelled, "You got it," and was through the door, into the driveway.

I got into my car and waited. Soon my mother would come to the door and call out, "Don't go. Let's talk for a minute." Nobody came. I warmed up the car. Nobody came. I drove out of the yard *very* slowly. Still nobody came.

I told myself, *Now you've done it.* The two me's, like Doctor Dolittle's Pushmi Pullyu, were literally at a fork in the road. Joan Molinsky, aching with fear and guilt and regret, wanted to take the path that wound through Larchmont for an hour and ended back at the safe harbor of the house. Joan Rivers, burning with rage and vengefulness and wounded pride, wanted to head for New York and her own world and her friends who said, "Yeah, yeah. Talented, talented."

In an awful languor of indecision, I drove at random through Larchmont, several times passing the house, my strength drained out of me, my arms heavy, the steering wheel heavy, every motion a supreme effort. I kept telling myself to go home just long enough to pack some clothes—but then imagined a knock on my door which would be my mother, very casual, with toothpaste and toothbrush in her hand as though on her way to use my bathroom and not coming in for a talk. I could hear her voice saying, "Calm down and we'll talk about it tomorrow. Get a part-time job. Something a little more solid. Maybe work on your career till January and then go back to school. You like the theater. Get an M.A. in theater; then you could teach drama, have something to fall back on."

Then, meandering through the silent streets, rage poured in again—rage at myself for *wanting* my mother's knock on the door, for wanting the one word of sympathy from my mother that would let me keep the comfort of my room, keep the warmth of family around me, keep the option to change my mind and go back to Lord & Taylor—keep the option of a comfortable marriage. Leaving Larchmont cut off any chance of meeting Doctor Right, meant committing myself to living and breathing solely my scrounging show business world, working among trashy comics and feeling common and low and everything I had not planned to be.

Then in the next second I would decide, "I'll go home at 11:00. Maybe they're right. Maybe I don't have it. Maybe nothing is open to me because I have no talent that will open doors," and instantly, in a rush, the fury and hurt and frustration would pile in again and I thought, *Screw them! I'll show them! They'll see. I'm not going back!* I told myself over and over that I *had* to get away from my parents, had to keep my self-respect, had to survive, and almost cried out aloud, "Why can't they believe in me! Why do they have to hit me when I'm down!"

All this time I kept looping automatically toward New York. I knew if I went back home what the surrender terms would be—live a respectable, middle-class life and get a respectable job—and the very core of me recoiled, while simultaneously in my head were the words, "I'll go back at 12:00. I don't *have* to cut the cord and cross my name out of the Bible and go out into the unknown."

By now I was entering New York and understood at last that I could not return to Larchmont until I had had some success. In the same way that I could not face the Riviera Club members again, I could not face my parents because this time they had actually witnessed my humiliation and they had not been on my side. They now believed what their friends believed—that I was ridiculous and wrong and a loser. Living at home would be facing that club audience over and over, day after day. I felt that something central had snapped, that every tie that mattered, that had created me, that bound me to myself, had been cut. I was set adrift from the place and possessions that defined me and was a brand-new person. I knew that I would never again be Dr. and Mrs. Molinsky's daughter, Joan, who is performing. I knew that never again, both literally and figuratively, would I ever sit in the backseat. My sense of loss was overpowering.

Finally, at 1:00 A.M., I was in New York—with no bed waiting for me. Aunt Alice would send me home and Treva was in Europe, so I drove to what seemed like the one safe place to park in New York City: right in front of the YWCA where there were plenty of lights and policemen. I ran inside and telephoned Nicky at home in Brooklyn—woke up his parents—and he promised to come immediately. Poor Nicky.

Between his acting classes and taking care of me, he had no time for a job. I was still his job.

Locking myself inside my grunge-colored car, I sat behind the steering wheel with tears streaming down my face and feeling like a champion chump. Within the security of Larchmont, it was easy to say, "I'm very talented." But now Miss Big Mouth, Miss Talent, Miss I Can Make It, had put her hand into the fire. Every bit of sense and logic was on my parents' side. On my side there was only hope and a night at One Fifth Avenue.

While I cried, another part of me added up my assets— which did not take long. I had my rusty old Buick, about a dollar in change, a little Peck & Peck crew neck sweater that happened to be in the backseat, and, of course, my Bermuda shorts, which would not be the height of chic on a temporary job Monday morning. But I absolutely knew I could survive, knew somewhere inside myself that if you want something badly enough, you do not worry about hardship.

In an hour, Nicky arrived. My Jimmy Stewart was here, putting his arm around me, saying, "Good for you for leaving. Fine! Relax. Don't worry. Everything is okay." Eventually, I dozed, and Nick, solid, handsome, stalwart, stood guard outside, leaning against the hood, protecting his girl. After a while a punk came along who knew Nicky—one of the many punks who kept asking Nick's father for an introduction to the Mafia dons.

Knowing that the family considered Nick, the actor, a worthless bum, the punk was very happy to find him pimping a hooker in a car. Nicky was finally making good. The punk kept congratulating Nick: "I didn't know. Your father didn't tell me."

I learned later from Barbara that while this was happening, my heartbroken parents were at a movie, hoping for distraction. They did not get it. The movie was about a Mississippi girl who came to New York to become an actress and ended up a prostitute.

The next morning, Nick gave me all the money he had—which was about a dollar—and drove the Buick home to Brooklyn without a driver's license. I went into the YWCA ladies' room and gave myself the first of many French baths. I filled a washbowl, got lots of paper towels, wet them, went into the toilet booth, and sort of stripped and washed around, doing one section at a time. When I ran out of towels, I came out and got some more, and when nobody was looking, I put one foot at a time into the wash basin and washed it, while the water ran back down my leg.

It was very embarrassing, because everybody who came in sort of glanced at the panties, shorts, shirt, and sweater draped over the radiator and the door to the toilet booth and right away they knew what I was doing. I would smile and say, "I spilled coffee all over myself."

Next, feeling not dirty, not clean, just grubby, I telephoned home. I only wanted to let my mother know I was all right, but maybe I wanted her to come on the line and cry, so I could go home. Fate let Barbara pick up the phone and I asked her to bring me a suitcase of clothes. She said, "Okay," very cold. It was enemy camp time. She told me, "Mother and Dad are terribly upset. Do you know what you're doing to them? If I were you, I'd get on the next train and get back here fast."

I thought, *Well, screw you,* and said, "I'm not coming back. Just bring me my clothes."

"Where are you living?"

"I'm not going to tell you." I could be very dramatic too. "I'll meet you in Grand Central."

I am sure my mother helped pack my suitcase, saying to Barbara, "She's probably at Treva's or Rod's. Okay, let her live a week without us. But when you get there, tell her she's killing us." Which is what Barbara did later that morning when we met at Grand Central, started right in with, "Mother's not feeling well." That became the leitmotiv: "Mother is ill. You've made Mother sick." And it worked. I worried, *Maybe it's true.* But being manipulated that way made me even more furious and determined.

I took the suitcase back to my ladies' room in the Y, changed my clothes, persuaded the woman at the reception desk to keep my suitcase, and went off to Brown's Office Temporaries. That day she sent me out to a doctor who worked with lawyers suing insurance companies. No matter what the accident, every patient suffered from whiplash and headache. Missed a step into an elevator? Whiplash and headache. Tripped on a carpet and fell downstairs? Whiplash and headache. And the doctor kept a perfectly straight face, never broke, never winked at me.

I am sure he hired me out of pity. Even to myself, I looked drained and worn out, exhaustion lines deep around my mouth and eyes. The tension and unhappiness felt concentrated in a knot at the back of my head, and every hour I disappeared into his bathroom and napped in the toilet booth for ten minutes. At lunchtime I slept with my head on the desk. Those reports I typed must have been absolutely unusable. I could not spell, and they looked as though somebody had spattered them with Liquid Paper.

That evening I waited in the YWCA for Nick to arrive with the car—my room for the night. He came sauntering down the sidewalk, beaming. "Where's the car?" I asked, worried, edgy, not beaming.

"Tonight," he said, "you sleep in a bed." He had dipped into his one source of cash to rent me a room for a week at the Y. His friend, Sal, had a sister, Janice, studying typing in high school and every time Sal or Nick needed money, they took this poor kid's typewriter and pawned it. She would come home to do homework and it was gone and hysteria would sweep the family. Whenever Nick went there to dinner, Sal's father would look at Nicky and shake his head.

The typewriter brought thirty-five dollars—so I figured I could live on five dollars a day plus the income from my stamp business. At large offices where I typed, I slipped eight-cent stamps into my purse and resold them to deserving friends for five cents. On a good day, I made seventy-five cents.

The Y was heaven on that Monday night—a clean little cubicle with my own iron bed, wooden chair, and bureau. By Saturday night the Y was hell for this Jewish Princess. It was depressing and institutional, smelling of disinfectant to my delicate nose. There were the three nice German students who had just arrived for a few days, but mostly there were semipermanent girls who could not quite fly—something was wrong with those engines. I never saw any *Cosmopolitan* gals piling into the Y with their arms filled with Bonwit boxes. The residents' arms were not full of anything. Those arms drooped at their sides.

By Saturday I was sitting in Grand Central Station, once again sobbing, once again with Nicky's arm around me, once again with his soothing voice saying, "Just don't worry. I'll get you a good place." He would do anything for love. If I had said, "Nicky, please go out and murder Harry Brent and Ira Ring," he would have said, "Just don't worry about it," and they would have been dead. No quest was inconceivable for Nick.

He went into the Roosevelt Hotel, carrying my suitcase, and checked himself in under an assumed name, giving as a business reference Nick Gandy at Revlon, a friend of mine who would cover for us if the hotel phoned him. Then Nicky retrieved me from Grand Central and we settled into a great room, ordered a roast beef dinner from room service, and had a wonderful evening watching television. In the morning I took the elevator that bypassed the lobby and check-out desk and delivered me into an underground passageway that led to Grand Central, where I nervously waited for Nicky. A few minutes later he followed me, carrying the suitcase. I did not mind beating the Roosevelt, but we did tip the room service waiter and the maid. There was morality in there somewhere.

It worked so nicely, we kept on. The Roosevelt was always my favorite, but we were very partial to the Taft, an excellent hotel, so big you could just disappear. We felt the Edison was a little sleazy and never gave it any of our free business. Compared to a lot of other performers—who did not have Nicky—I was very lucky. A comedian named Howard Storm told me that once he could not pay his hotel bill in Miami, so they kept his suitcase and let him take one piece of clothing. He put on his tuxedo over his bathing suit in case he got a club date. He made his rounds at night and slept during the day on the beach in his bathing suit, using the tuxedo for a pillow. He did not get the club date, but he got the greatest tan of his life. Flip Wilson, when he first arrived in New York, slept in pay toilets. Barbra Streisand had a ring of keys and divided her nights between a cousin's apartment, a sofa in the office of a public relations man, and a cot in the apartment of Peter Daniels, her pianist.

My daytime routine went on as usual, checking Brown's, making the rounds of comedy agents and managers. I would telephone Larchmont, and if my mother answered, hang up. If it was my sister, I asked if there were any messages. I was still giving managers and agents the Larchmont number, because it was a little hard to tell their secretaries, "Tonight you can reach me at the Roosevelt, but I'll be under the name of Nick Costa—and tomorrow you can get me at the Taft, ask for Tony Collasimo."

I kept on seeing my sister Barbara—meeting for coffee, occasionally sharing temporary jobs—because I wanted news from home. But what I got was, "Mother is ill. Daddy felt lousy the other day. Mother and Daddy were both very upset last night. You're killing Mother." Once she told me, "Some horrible girl called you—said she was an exotic dancer who worked with you at the Show Bar. Mother was so upset, she went to bed. We think it's her heart." That's what I got from Barbara—Jewish guilt messages. A guilt-o-gram. She would arrive carrying a guilt-o-gram.

I did not believe Barbara, but did believe her and would think, *My God, I wonder if Mother really is sick and she's going to die and I'm not there and I've done this to her.* I would go to Nicky and cry and he would tell me what I wanted to hear: "It's just their way of getting to you"—which was true. They would have done anything to haul me home. In their minds a girl stayed under her parents' supervision as long as she was single, and my mother told me again and again, "You will leave this house only as a bride." I kept saying, "I already did," but she would push right on, drilling into me the belief that only trampy single girls move into their own apartments.

But the truth was that the company of their children and the control of their children was their only real bond, the only part of their lives they could discuss and share and my mother's major reason for living. Ultimately, when Barbara and I were totally gone, my father disappeared into his religion, spending most of his time at the temple. My mother hated the temple, had few friends, no compelling interests, and was left with nothing in her life but her house, and there was no longer a reason for that.

After ten days of hotel hopping I was hit by Yom Kippur, the Day of Atonement, when God and you look back over your past year and you atone for your sins—the day when every Jew is introspective and prays for forgiveness—and was I in need of absolution! For the first time in my life I was away from

home on this holy, nearly 6,000-year-old night when all over
the world, every Jew, rich or poor, crowds into a temple.
Every Manhattan temple was jammed, so I ended up in an
obscure synagogue in the Bronx where I told them I was from
out of town and they took me in.

It was a humble temple, deeply Orthodox, the service
entirely in Hebrew, the men in black hats and yarmulkes and
prayer shawls. For me it was like returning to the seventeenth
century. I was segregated upstairs in the balcony with the
women and girls in hats and babushkas, all of them touching
and smiling with bright eyes and reaching past others to grip a
hand or to wave—a vast family reuniting on this profoundly
important, deeply thoughtful night. I sat alone with a hankie
on my head and tears on my face. Somebody passed me a
Hebrew prayer book I could not read. I was a stranger.

The service began—very theatrical, musically magnifi-
cent, incredibly moving, the taproot of everything I longed to
believe. I had been taught since childhood that your family is
your secure foundation, the one place where you can always
return and count on unconditional love—and perhaps because, in fact, there was never unqualified love in my house,
conditions attached to everything, my roots never feeling
solid, the idealized idea of *family* was enormous in my emotions. And to be away from my family on Yom Kippur was the
sin of sins.

The reader intoned:

> O Lord our God, help us to see ourselves as Thou
> seest us. Make us conscious of our sins and failings;
> cause us to turn from our evil ways. Give us strength
> to make amends for our wrongdoing and grant us
> pardon for our sins.

I was flayed by guilt, accusations out of control in my
head: *How could you have done this to your family—sucked them into
your unhappiness—tortured them. You are self-centered, a spoiled brat*

who broke away in the meanest way. What if your parents died this year?

I knew my mother, who never wept, would be crying somewhere in temple—crying like me because we were split on Yom Kippur, and not split because of something wonderful so she could say, "My daughter is in Greece, studying." Yom Kippur was the one precious night of the year when we existed as a family, when we all came hurrying home, all got dressed up and looked wonderful, and all four of us walked into temple together, appearing to the world happy and united. It was our one night of solidarity. Then at sundown we would return to our home with our guests, return to a table set with crystal and Meissen china, return to antique Georgian wine coolers filled with masses of gladiolas and peonies, to a fire burning in the fireplace, to extra servants and my mother so gracious. But on this night I would be sneaking into some hotel room with a boy my mother hated.

To me, personally, in my head, God that night was deciding what I deserved in the coming year, and, as always, I prayed and prayed, *Please forgive me, please put me down for A + on next year's blank pages.* At the end of the service, everybody turned to one another, smiling and touching, wishing each other happiness in the coming year. When they turned to me, here was somebody they did not know and I felt like an interloper, felt alone and lost. I did not have a person to hold hands with tightly while I made my prayer, *Please, God . . .*

For days afterward, draped in guilt, I was on the brink of going home. Maybe, with all three of us suffering, I could make them understand, make them want for me what I wanted. Maybe it was only pride that was stopping me—the sin of pride—and it was not too late to show some class. Then, at one of those meetings with Barbara in Grand Central Sta-

tion, she handed me a letter from my father. I sat alone in the
waiting room and read it.

Dear Joan,

Your welfare has always been and always will remain a concern to us. What has actually happened?
Take time out and reflect—take stock of yourself!

You interested yourself in acting, though you got
little if any encouragement from us. We still went
along with you—for a while, hoping you would mature mentally and stabilize yourself. Instead, what a
price it all adds up to. You ran away from home in a
wild rage; you have been vile, abusive, and insulting
to your mother; you've broken with the family;
you've cast all moral principles to the wind; all this in
exchange for a despicable bunch of failures, ne'er-
do-wells, parasites, procurers, mistresses, fairies,
and possible dope peddlers!

Even a minimum of intelligence would suggest
that surrounding oneself with such low-lifes could
lead only to degradation, frustration, and ultimate
despondency. The crowd you are consorting with
cannot bring you anything but evil results. Surely
you are not so senseless as not to see the handwrit-
ing on the wall! Come to your senses! You can still
strive for stage success without surrendering your
moral principles, decency, and self-respect. Think it
over carefully and you are bound to understand the
errors of your ways.

With a feeling of grievous disappointment, we still
wish you lots of luck and good sense—

Daddy

P.S. You're welcome to come home at any time!

The anger and hurt started tears in my eyes. He *really* believed all that. I read the letter again: "It's disgusting what you're doing with your life"—"The crowd you are consorting with cannot bring you anything but evil results." He was disgusted by everything I held sacred, disgusted by my dream, disgusted by me. Instead of saying, "Come back. Come back," he was calling me a tramp who was never going to make it. Inwardly I raged at him, *How dare you think that little of me! How dare you insult my intelligence. How dare you—who should know me the best—totally misjudge me! "Degradation and craziness and pimps and drug peddlers and prostitution!" That's what you think of me! Well, that's really wonderful!*

Now it was settled. I would never go back until I could walk in a big winner, my arms full of flowers. "Evil results!" he had said—when I was working all day and sneaking into hotels at night—a very simple existence. That night, worn out by work, by hurt, by nervous strain, by anger, by everything, I sat with Nicky in Grand Central crying again. He had planned to hit the Hotel New Yorker down at Thirty-fourth Street—virgin territory—but I was sobbing, "I can't walk another block. I'm exhausted. I'm finished." Telling me, "Don't worry," he registered at the Biltmore, right there by the station, where we had been twice before. I was so depressed, so used up, so sick of my gypsy life, we stayed two days.

The next evening, when I came back, the key would not work. I had been locked out. With my heart pounding and my stomach raw with fright, I called Nicky at home. He ran immediately to Sal's house where Janice was typing. He pulled the typewriter out from under her fingers, rushed to a pawnshop, and got the money. He raced into town and indignantly paid the hotel, very angry, saying, "I will never stay here again, and I'll make sure nobody from Revlon stays here, either!" Then we stayed two more days to show them—and sneaked out.

That was the last straw. It may seem young and adventurous and romantic, calling room service, putting on television, slipping out after a nice breakfast, going off to the temporary job—"Meet me at six. Where are we staying tonight?" But, in fact, it was horrendous. Without a nest to come home to, without order in my life, without any anchor—I felt nervous, crazy, irritable, disconnected, floating—a bag lady in a Saks dress. I was literally carrying all my belongings with me, except what I left in public lockers. The most minor bits of life became complex tasks—if I washed out my underwear, it had to be dry the next morning or I put it on wet. And the tension was constant. Will Nicky make it out of the hotel with the bag? What if they recognize us and come knocking on the door? What if we go to jail?

Sitting in the waiting room of Grand Central—other derelicts around us settling in for the night—I broke down for the four hundredth time and told Nick, "I just *can't* anymore." Nick said, "Don't worry. You've got to have your own place." He checked me into a women's residence hotel called The Midston House. My temporary job money had not come through yet, so he pawned his watch to pay the deposit for a week. By that time Janice's typewriter was chained to her desk. The kid was failing the course. She had been the only sophomore in typing one who was passing in handwritten assignments.

9

LIFE TOOK ON some shape, a pattern. I had my tiny home at The Midston House, a women's residence hotel, a Y with ruffles. No men were allowed above the ground floor, but the lobby was a place where Nicky and I could sit and keep warm. It had a 1930s look—an old-fashioned marble floor with big rugs and a few heavy sofas and heavy wing chairs among the thick columns and even heavier velvet draperies at the windows—a silent, somber, sober lobby for somber, sober people. At the far end was a grand marble staircase with a brass-topped iron railing. My room on the second floor was the smallest in the place, but there was a private bath, a little bedside table with a soft light, a rug on the floor, a small blue velveteen easy chair, and lots of free stationery for scribbling jokes—and I now had a permanent phone number and somebody to take messages.

The other place besides the Midston lobby where Nicky and I could keep warm was his new job as night receptionist at Channel 13, sitting at the front desk and directing people where to go for *The Ted Steele Show* and the shows of Mike Wallace, David Susskind, Alexander King, and Wendy Barrie. That reception room became a magnet for Nicky's beginner actor friends, almost a nightly party. It was my sanctuary. I still saw Treva and the revue crowd, but only occasionally. Treva did not protect me and that was then my primary need and what Nicky offered in abundance. So I put myself into that side of my life, choosing my twenty-four-hour source of companionship and humor, reassurance and safety.

Also, I found glamour at Channel 13. When you are

trying to break into show business, just hanging around it is heaven. Wendy Barrie or Faye Emerson would sweep past with the secretary, the entourage, the fur coat and perfume, the excitement of show business that was actually happening. I tapped into that positive energy.

I always tried to get to Nicky by 5:45 and grab the phone on his desk. With luck, I would get four agents before six o'clock, which was forty cents saved. That was what the next three months were all about: counting pennies. The Midston House cost thirty-five dollars a week and I was averaging four office temp jobs a week for about thirty-eight dollars, which left me three big dollars to throw around. I was finding out the facts of life fast. After a phone call I quickly dialed the operator and said, "My call didn't go through and I didn't get my dime back." She would go click, click, click for me—and sometimes the dime would come back.

I could never afford a decent meal. Orange Julius was a way of life and I ate lots of date-and-nut-bread sandwiches at Chock Full O'Nuts, lots of $1.49 steak house dinners. At Howard Johnson's I could fill up on a frankfurter and a soda, and I practically lived on bran and corn muffins for twenty-five cents—cutting the top off and putting the pat of butter inside. Whenever Nicky and I ran out of money, we went late at night to the Ham & Eggs on Broadway, where his actor friend, Sal, was the chef in the window with a white hat. We would order toast and Sal would slip in some scrambled eggs. During those indigent months, I sat on so many counter stools that still, today, when I eat, I'm afraid to lean back.

I felt constantly grubby. I was still living out of that one suitcase, mixing and matching, over and over, three skirts, two tops, and a couple of sweaters—never shabby, but never bandbox, spanking clean, never the way my mother taught me to be, never up to those standards of style, propriety, etiquette, decorum, she ingrained in me—that level of elegance where you put down the place mat, use the pretty glass even when alone in the house—and a gentleman *always* uses the sugar tongs. It was an irrevocable part of me that gracious living gives life a form, makes life an art, lets you enjoy it— that life can either be a picture or it can be ugly.

The picture began turning ugly for me in the second month when the scrounging stopped being a campy lark we would someday laugh about. I was going from the ugly Midston House to the ugly stool for my cheap breakfast, to the ugly office temp job, to an ugly Grand Central Station phone booth, where somebody would stand outside tapping on the glass with a coin even though I called out, "Just a minute, I'm waiting for a phone call," and they were still angry, banging on the glass. Everything was becoming gray and there was nothing pretty anywhere and it was getting me crazy.

A big, bright spot in my life—which made it almost worse by contrast—was Myron Orlofsky, the only remnant of my Larchmont past. I had met him the previous summer at a fund-raising cocktail party for young singles at the Jewish Guild for the Blind—where I was not exactly *hunting*, just window shopping. There was Myron, the man I never thought I would find, absolutely adorable, dark-haired, short, a graduate of Harvard Law School, preppy as hell, rich and Jewish, terribly bright and terribly involved, doing urban renewal in White Plains before that cause was fashionable.

On top of all the perfection, he had a wild, nonsensical, almost limerick kind of wit, always there with a quick remark. He introduced himself to my mother as Dr. Orlofsky, a veterinarian, and talked to her about his patients, telling her he was terribly upset because he'd had a cow with a hysterical pregnancy and didn't know how to break the news to the farmer. She liked him, even though he called her Bea right away, which she never allowed anybody to do, and would say, "Bea, time for a waltz," and off they'd go, whirling around the living room. Myron was show biz struck and had backed an off Broadway play and he loved what I was doing—always made me feel I was right, always introduced me, "She's in show business."

In these Midston House days Nick Clemente was the core of the strength that enabled me to cope with the reality of my predicament. Myron Orlofsky was my escape, my relief from reality. With him I was still the rich doctor's daughter from Larchmont, the young, aspiring comedian, doing well, not a care in the world, lark, lark, lark. To preserve that fiction, I kept him away from The Midston House and met him at the restaurant when we went out with his Harvard Law School friends, or met him at an art gallery on those magic Saturdays we went laughing up and down Madison Avenue, in and out of galleries, everything glamorous and fabulous as we added to his major collection of modern art.

He was always in on the latest fashion—early Warhols and Rauschenbergs—and owned three-dimensional art. At the Martha Jackson Gallery he bought a green canvas which was a backdrop for a real pile of coal with a shovel stuck into it. It was delivered to his parents' house in White Plains and the artist personally arranged the stack of coal. The maid came in that afternoon and cleaned the room—shoveled up the coal and dumped it in the basement.

But underneath Myron's wit and good looks and major wealth was a deep current of unhappiness. He wanted a relationship, a home, children, and that could not be. Though he was seeing a psychiatrist four times a week and much later did have a family—he was at that time impotent, really asexual. But that was okay with me. After David Fitelson I was fed up with love—though David remained a presence in my mind and my feelings and I always asked Allan Thenen about him and was always glad to hear he was still single. I guess I was keeping the link tenuously alive—and also nourishing the fantasy that one day, when I was a star, I would walk into the

Fitelson house as a guest—"Hello, David. It's been a while." But in the meantime, I think if Myron had asked me, I would have chosen escape and married the money and the good times and the backing for my career.

Then one Saturday we sat in a private room viewing a painting, sipping wine, eating cheese, and they said, "Mr. Orlofsky, Sonja Henie wanted this, but we saved it for you; it's ten thousand dollars." And he said, "I like it. Send it." Next, after dropping by the Museum of Modern Art, we went to dinner at Le Chambord and in his pocket were tickets for a play.

So, after casually spending ten thousand dollars right in front of me, Myron sat across from me at one of the most expensive French restaurants in New York, telling me how wonderful I was, how funny and talented with a glittering future. While he talked, I was remembering the stories I had heard about backers—a millionaire who had backed Jerry Lewis to get him started, somebody who helped Carol Burnett, somebody who sponsored Florence Henderson—and I looked up and there was my backer right in front of me, buttering a roll. I said, "Listen, Myron, how would you like to back this Little Miss Bundle of Talent here? If you give me ten thousand dollars, you can have fifty percent of my income for the rest of my life." I was absolutely serious.

He laughed and made a joke and kept on talking and laughing, but I could see in his eyes that I had done what is unforgivable to the rich—made him wonder whether I was his friend because I wanted something. And on my side of the table I could feel my skin hot and tight from the hurt. Myron had done the worst damage possible—become yet another important person from my respectable past who did not think I was talented, who did not think I was a good bet to succeed, who did not think the product of my entire life was worth what he had casually spent on one painting. I thought, *Love me, love my talent.* I did not see Myron again for eight or nine years.

Part of my daily ritual was still reading *Actors Cues* and suddenly I was swept by a blazing revelation, a rapturous moment of truth. There before my eyes was an advertisement for a boy and girl comedy team. Of course! Boy-girl. This was the solution—my way into the business. Mike and Elaine! How totally stupid I had been. It was a comedy team they were after. Everything was finally within my grasp.

Well, I had the girl half. I was fifty percent there. And here was my Mike Nichols drinking coffee in the other side of the booth. Sure, he was Italian and dark, but that was not the point. Nicky was an excellent actor and comedy is really performing. Also, he had a great natural sense of humor. At dinner, I was the one laughing, not he. I thought, *No problem.* Nicky said, "Are you crazy?" But I kept telling him, "You can do it. You can do it," and, unfortunately, after a while he believed me.

I hired Ronnie Brown from the B & G to be my pianist and answered the ad in *Actors Cues.* The place was the Adventurer Motel in Atlantic City, one of those deals where, for expenses, they let you audition onstage for nothing and then maybe they will book you—one of the standard scams to get free acts. They gave me a date only three days away.

We rehearsed our act at Variety Arts Studios on West Forty-sixth Street. I *loved* Variety Arts. It was total show business. When I stepped into the dinky little elevator, maybe I would literally bump into Ethel Merman or Nancy Walker or Robert Goulet—or there would be Julie Andrews and we would all say hello. On the way up, when the elevator door opened, I saw girls in leotards doing stretching exercises or six people with scripts walking up and down, memorizing before a reading—and I felt part of all that. I, too, was rehearsing something. I belonged. Nobody was saying to me, "You can't" or "You shouldn't."

When I got off at my floor, I could hear the sounds from the rehearsal rooms—a piano with a drummer, somebody singing, music from a tape recorder, dancers tap dancing in unison. In the hall was a pay phone with hundreds of numbers scrawled every which way on the plaster wall—like insect tracks—a whole life in show business—every agent's number, every big casting director, Brooks Costumes, NBC, CBS, ABC, Capezio, some hot dates, all the delicatessens in the neighborhood. For a dollar you rented a little room with a wooden floor sanded down regularly, a piano tuned every night, a couple of chairs, a dusty, streaky mirror, an exercise barre—and a whole lot of cigarette butts and not quite empty coffee containers. It was heaven.

In the rehearsal room we practiced the whole act. Nicky had seen Shecky Greene on television pump the mike stand up and down like a toilet plunger and say, "Are you sure that it was Kleenex you threw down here, lady?" Then he put the mike in his ear and called Tokyo. Stupid, but funny—when Shecky did it. Nicky wanted to open the act alone doing that. Then I would come out and do Rod Warren's "Photoplay." After Nicky and I did some he-she jokes from Robert Orben books, I would go into my movie takeoffs with blackouts and, for a closer, we would sing together "There's No Business Like Show Business." Nicky was very confident, kept saying things like, "I'll go out and I'll warm them up and when you're needed, I'll say, 'Oh, by the way, Joan Rivers is here.'" He kept telling me, "Don't worry." I worried a little, but I believed in miracles.

That rehearsal was the first time I had the pleasure of Ronnie's fiancée, Lenore. Ronnie was chubby, looked like a cute little Buddha in glasses. Lenore was skinny as a pencil, never said much, and was deeply in love. The two of them, no matter where, if you sat them down, they necked. It became a joke. If they sat, they kissed.

We drove down to Atlantic City in my car, Ronnie and Lenore necking all the way in the backseat. The Adventurer was a big motel with an area in the dining room where they had taken up the carpeting, put in a drum set, and called it a stage. You knew right away the place was a make-out joint for cheaters. The only reason anybody ever ate there was because, between shtups, the girl said, "I'm hungry."

The room was very dark and the stage was lit by just one spotlight—plus a window at the back, opening toward the turnpike. You could hear the cars going *whoosh, whoosh,* and the panes rattled when the big semitrailers roared by. The dressing room was the toilet and we made our entrance at the far end of the room from the kitchen, which was also the location of the light box—an on-off switch—which Nicky would have to turn for my movie blackouts.

As we had planned, Nicky, full of confidence, set out first from the kitchen and I could hear him bumping into tables in the dark. I heard him begin, "Good evening, ladies and gentlemen . . ." and three breaths later Mr. Don't-Worry-I'll-Call-You-When-I've-Got-Them-Warmed-Up was saying frantically, "Want to meet my partner, Joan Rivers? Where is she? She'll be here any second." I was struggling through those tables in the dark, which kills your entrance a little bit because everybody has heard you saying "Excuse me, pardon me, pardon me, excuse me, terribly sorry, excuse me, thank you, sorry," and by the time you reach the stage you are hoarse.

Well, of course, they were not ready for "Photoplay." Probably they had already heard Robert Orben. While I did the drunken wife routine into the silent room, Nicky rushed back through the tables to the kitchen to work the light switch for the blackouts. In the kind of quiet I imagine in the arctic—except in the arctic there's no *whoosh, whoosh* through a window—I did the first movie takeoff. No blackout. Dimly I could hear loud voices in the kitchen and thumping. I did the second movie . . . and the third. Still no blackouts. Worried and mad, I thought, *Where's Nick? Goddamn him, he's wrecking the act.* Then I heard, getting louder, "Excuse me, sorry, pardon me, sorry." Onstage Nicky was gasping for breath and therefore not in good voice for "There's No Business Like Show Business." And out in the room there was no sing-along. It is hard for people to sing when they are making out under a table.

We literally ran out of that club. In the car I said, "What happened?" Nicky said, "I had a fight with the owner." I said, "But you got the expense check?" He said "No."

Then I went crazy. "What do you mean you didn't get the check?"

He said, "No, the fight was about you." Gradually, in disconnected pieces, the story came out. It seemed that the owner had walked up to Nicky at the light switch and said, "She stinks. Tell her to work blue." Well, you don't say that about Nicky's girl and Nicky yelled at him, "She doesn't work blue." For some reason, that did not satisfy this large man. He answered that if we wanted our money, I had better get dirty. Nicky, inspired, came up with a line he had heard used by the producer of *The Wendy Barrie Show*—he said menacingly, "I'm going to turn this place into a garage." Apparently words failed the owner, because he hit Nicky in the jaw and walked away.

I was outraged—by Nicky. I screamed that he should have promised I would work blue—anything to get the check —and I rose onto my mother's high horse and lectured him, "We don't use our fists. We're not animals. We don't fight. It's so distasteful. This is not a James Cagney movie."

Nicky got mad and yelled, "I can't believe it. I was defending you. I'm not going to eat dirt for you anymore. I'm always eating dirt for you." By then I was crying. I had desperately wanted our boy-girl act to work. I had dreamed of saying, "Hey, Mom and Dad, the joke's on you. It's Mike and Elaine at the Copa and Joan and Nick at the Latin Casino." Now Nicky was saying, "I'm an actor, Joan, not a comedian." I wasn't arguing with him—and I could not ask Ronnie and Lenore's opinion because they were necking.

It was November of 1959 and cold and awful. Channel 13 was not thrilled about walking into their little lobby and always finding at least three creatures there with the guy behind the desk. Nicky was fired. Now, neither one of us had any income and I was freezing to death. I asked Barbara to bring me my winter coat, but the message came back from my parents, "You can't have it." They were going to freeze me into coming home. Naturally, I became twice as stubborn—if they were going to play hardball, so was I.

I went to Peck & Peck, which was not my mother's favorite store and where her account might not be in arrears, and they actually let Joan Molinsky charge a winter coat on her mother's account—did not even call the credit manager. Wearing it, I hit Fifth Avenue running. I figured I would pay my mother back someday, which I did. So now I was a little warmer when I started out each morning from The Midston House. On the days I did not have an office temp job, I walked briskly to the West Side, then headed uptown, renewed by the cold in my face, in one hand my manila envelope full of pictures and résumés, in my head the certainty that this would be the day of my breakthrough.

Also in my head, screening on the back of my eyeballs, was a movie starring Joan Molinsky, about a starving young actress making a movie called *The Joan Molinsky Story*—so a camera followed me all day and, since it was filming the first third of the movie, the struggling years, I had to look plucky and determined.

Proceeding north, I called on managers and agents, arriv-

When I make jokes and tell stories about being fat, people often think it is just my neurotic imagination. Well, *(above)* on the right, with her mother and sister during a vacation trip to Williamsburg, Virginia, is the thirteen-year-old fat pig, wishing she could teach her arms and hips to inhale and hold their breath. *(Right)* Of course front and center is an earlier version of the same lovely body planning to be Snow White in the Camp Kinni Kinnic play. The girl seated rear, left, got the role because of parental pull.

My sister, Barbara *(above)*, at about twenty, who grew up beautiful and smart and got a law degree at Columbia. We had utterly separate lives—different friends, different goals, different ideals. The only thing we shared was a bathroom.

I adored my Aunt Alice, my mother's widowed older sister, who was my fairy godmother and role model. An art gallery owner/interior decorator, she had an independent, self-supporting life doing work she loved, and was the only one in the family who encouraged me to be a performer.

Bruno of Hollywood

In 1949 my mother got her dream house in socially impeccable Larchmont, a suburb of New York. For the whole family it represented what my mother called "background." I clung to the security and status, the reassurance the house gave me, and lived at home till I was thirty-one.

In the sophomore class picture at Adelphi Academy I sat where I belonged—in the lower right-hand corner, the last and least. I was the class doer, but lonely, with no idea how to be popular.

At Barnard College from 1953 to 1954 I exercised my show-business fantasy to the fullest, performing in all the plays, immersing myself in the tiny theater world it shared with Columbia. Here I am at the cast party *(above)* after *Othello,* in which I played Emilia.

A year out of college, Mrs. James Sanger *(right),* like her mother, is marrying for peace and security, not love, and thinking, "Am I insane?" The marriage lasted six months.

This is a mother in 1957, standing with a daughter she does not understand. Though the daughter was given the best of everything, and taught the finest values, the ungrateful girl wants to throw away her life and be an actress.

Clearly ready to be a Hollywood Deb Star—and wearing the brass necklace given to me by the cast of the Connecticut College freshman play which I directed—I posed for the first 8x10 glossy that I took on the rounds to agents.

My first composite was the serious face of a Theater Person, ready to play Anna Christie or Mother Courage or Saint Joan. It says, "Heavy drama and do not send her up for anything but classical drama."

JOAN MOLINSKY

Franklin Photos

© *Charles Biasiny-Rivera, 1986*

In my first professional role, Off-Off-Off Broadway, I played a lesbian in my little black dress and pearls so this Jewish girl from Larchmont would look good if a talent scout came around. It was brilliant costuming, since this horrific play, called *Seawood,* was set in a ramshackle beach house. At twenty-five I figured the eyeglasses would age me and the handkerchief would show that I was a lesbian with class—and maybe give me a touch of Tennessee Williams.

© *Charles Biasiny-Rivera, 1986*

In my part as a lesbian, the object of my desire was a dark-haired high school girl with a big nose, a New York accent, and the same obsessive ambition that burned within me. Her name then was Barbara (three a's, count 'em, three) Streisand. We both knew the play was a joke, but were thrilled to be in it, thrilled to be able to tell agents, "I'm currently performing Off-Broadway in *Seawood*."

ing full of cheer, bringing the cup of coffee for the secretary, doing the fun things to make her laugh. But I was not a fresh face anymore. They knew I did not have a good act and I am sure after I left the office most of them were saying, "Poor thing." Only when I hit the street after my last calls did I let myself realize it was another day of futility.

But immediately I would escape from real life back into my playacting, this time adding another layer of fantasy to the movie. I was only posing as an actress in a movie and in reality carried major secrets in the heel of my shoe, unsuspected by the stream of people passing me on the sidewalk. They thought I was just some loser girl lumbering down Seventh Avenue with crackers in her pocket saved from lunch.

I did not dare have one quiet minute when I might think, when I might see that absolutely nothing was working out, see that I was a moron whose instincts had been wrong since I was three years old, see that THE DREAM was *wrong,* which would mean I was just another girl sitting in The Midston House getting older. I could not endure the reality that I might end up Joan Molinsky, an unattractive, nondescript little Jewish girl, run-of-the-mill, who might just as well have stayed in Brooklyn and married the druggist and had a normal life. I had come from normal life, from real life, and nobody there had been happy. I knew I *had* to be special, had to have a life different from anything I had ever known, and if I ended up ordinary Joan Molinsky, I would always be unhappy and make my husband and children unhappy.

I was so afraid of these thoughts, I never shared them, not even with Nicky. To him I whimpered about my career: "Is this the way it's always going to be? By now something should be happening. Every door is closed. Every other girl is prettier and sings better." I knew that those were fears Nicky could erase. Almost by voicing them to Nicky they lost their edge and he could become my parent saying, "Don't be silly, there is nothing to be frightened of in the dark." There were many times, after wailing to him half the night, when I fell asleep on Nicky's shoulder.

But there came an evening at the end of November when we were sitting in our regular spot in the lobby of The Midston House. That day had been particularly horrendous. At my temp job I had been alone in a windowless room with fluorescent light, no phone, no radio, filing thousands of names alphabetically—is Poa ahead of Pao? At lunch I ran out to see an agent, who said, "Look, honey, it's stupid for you to come around so often. We'll call you if we have anything." A permanent brush-off! On the way back I heard that somebody was auditioning for a revue at four, but the office would not let me leave until Myrtle came back from her coffee break and Myrtle was late, so the audition was over when I arrived. On the way home, with not twenty-five cents in my pocket, I met Linda Lavin, full of good news about herself and saying, as she always did, "I was just at an audition where they were looking for a chunky streaked blonde with brown roots and a New York accent . . . I thought of you but figured you wouldn't be interested."

On the sofa in the Midston lobby with Nicky, it was not young love, holding hands on a summer evening. It was sitting, cold and hungry, with a guy who was also broke, and figuring whether or not we could afford a hot dog at Howard Johnson's. What was even worse, the guy sitting next to me did not seem to mind being broke.

I began wallowing in self-pity—dramatic on top of dramatic—saying, "Everybody is moving ahead of me. When something good happens, it doesn't matter. One Fifth Avenue meant nothing. It was air, smoke. What does any of it matter now? I'm sitting here without a cent."

Nicky went right into his backstage pep talk: "Listen, a star isn't born overnight. Do you think Judy Garland had it easy? You're jealous of Linda Lavin? That stupid face? Did you see her legs? So what if those girls are working for Julius Monk. Can you tell me one of their names?"

I said, "Oh, some of them are good."

"Joan, nobody is going to become a star out of a Julius Monk revue. Sure you're broke, but what does money really mean! Nothing!"

He said the last thing to the wrong person. I knew what money meant. It meant *everything*—freedom, power, happiness—everything—a good dinner that night in a nice restaurant. I had been taught that from the beginning and learned it and knew it.

Suddenly, I could not stand this Pollyanna sitting there so happy when I was so miserable. I said, "Don't you understand we're in a rotten place in our lives? When you're cold and hungry and tired and you have no job and can't afford dinner, it's not fun and wonderful to be sitting in The Midston House. Don't tell me this is fine. It's horrible. And if this is going to be my life, I'm going to do something, Goddamn it. I'm going to get a steady job."

I waited for him to say, "But then you won't be able to make your rounds. *I'll* get the job."

He said, "Everything's going to be okay. Things will get better."

I was too tired and angry at the world to be tolerant. I did not want Mr. Happiness telling me life was adorable. I wanted him as upset and miserable as I was. I gave him one more chance to agree with me, to shake himself into action. I said, "I'll get a nighttime job so I can make rounds in the day. That's what I'll do—a night job."

Nicky laughed. "Maybe that's a good idea."

That was not enough. I was going to wipe those rays of sunshine off his face. I went the limit. I said, "I've got a better idea. I don't need a steady job. I'll turn a trick or two. I can be a hooker, make myself fifty dollars in one night instead of eight days behind a stupid typewriter." That got him.

Nicky, his forehead scrunching up, said, "What?" For an Italian boy from Brooklyn to have his girl become a hooker was a fate more hideous than death. "Don't talk that way," he said, taking me seriously as always. "You *can't* be a hooker. I won't allow it! I won't even think it!"

"Hear me," I said, even more dramatic. "I don't have to go on grubbing like this." And perversely poking the wound, I repeated, "Fifty dollars a night."

Nicky turned nasty, which for him was like Jesus slapping a leper. He said, "You couldn't get two dollars."

"What?" I said.

Nick went on, "Well, maybe you could get five dollars, but only under the boardwalk at Coney Island at night."

"Well, it's my life," I announced, delivering my third act curtain line. "If I want to be a hooker, I'll *be* a hooker!"

Nicky stood up, dug his last $1.50 in change out of his pocket, and flung it at me, saying, "Okay, fix yourself up so you can get work." He stormed out of the hotel.

I sat for a moment, drained and purged, went upstairs to my room, took a bath, and relaxed with a book, figuring I could make up with Nicky tomorrow. Another day would bring a new dawn.

I learned later that Nicky, now with no carfare in his pocket, ran uptown to borrow subway money from Sal in the white hat in the window of Ham & Eggs. Nicky arrived sweaty and pale, having just lost his great love to the streets. Sal said, "What's happened?"

Nicky blurted out, "Joan's gonna be a hooker!"

"My God," said Sal, another Italian boy. "That slime."

Sal took him home, where Janice was pounding away on her typewriter which was still chained to the desk. In Sal's room, under posters of Rudolph Valentino and Marlon Brando, Nicky told him the whole story, ending with, "Look, she's crazy. She ran away from home and slept in her car to stay in show business. She'd do anything!"

Sal, believing, commiserating, whipping up Nicky's frenzy, kept muttering, "Yeah, yeah, that slime." At that point, Guido arrived, a dees-dem-and-does Italian friend of Sal's, a big guy with a skinny tie and carrying a bottle. He and Sal began drinking and when Guido heard the story, he agreed, "Sure, she'll do that. It's always the Jews."

Now Nicky began talking about the movie *Waterloo Bridge* with Vivien Leigh, a nice girl turned whore, never out of her slip, which made Sal say, "Nicky, if you love her, you got to call her family."

"Good idea," Nicky said. He went to the phone and telephoned Barbara in Larchmont. He said, "You got to do me a favor, you got to go down to The Midston House tonight and get your sister because she's gonna get into a lot of trouble."

"What do you mean, trouble?" Barbara asked.

Nicky said, "Your sister wants to become a prostitute. She wants to become a goddamn tramp. Go get her before it's too late."

Suddenly, on an extension phone, my mother screamed, "What do you mean, *too late!* It's already happened! And you did it to her!"

"No, it's your *fault,*" Nicky screamed. *"You're* the one who wouldn't give her the winter coat."

Sal decided they were abusing his friend Nicky, so he grabbed the phone and yelled, "Listen, you fuckers . . ." When Sal hung up, he said, "Nicky, you shouldn't-a called."

Nicky said, "I don't care. I wash my hands of her. I close the iron door. I have never heard of this Joan Rivers Molinsky. It's all over, and good riddance to bad rubbish. I'll never hear her voice again." But after a half hour, he decided he had better warn me. He phoned me at The Midston House where I was relaxing in my jammies after my bath and he said, "I think maybe I made a mistake."

"What did you do?"

"I called your family and told them you were going to become a prostitute and they'd better go get you."

"Aaaaahhh!" Crying and screaming, I told him, "You come here right now and straighten out this mess. I'll die before I go back home. I'm going to jump out the window." Never mind that I was only on the second floor.

Nicky hung up the phone and said, "I gotta go back. She's gonna jump."

Guido stood up and said, "You don't go alone." He knew a big black guy who had a car. Now my neurosis had become completely contagious. Nine people were racing to save me. There was: (1) a car running every light and containing Nicky, Sal, Guido with his bottle, and a big black guy, (2) another car from Larchmont filled with my mother, father, and Barbara, and (3) a chauffeur-driven limousine from uptown carrying my Aunt Alice and Aunt Fanny—"Happy" Fanny Fields in the choker and pearls—summoned to the rescue by my mother.

The cars emptied onto the sidewalk pretty much simultaneously, my mother, Aunt Alice, and Aunt Fanny all in mink coats. Aunt Fanny, crying out, "Better dead!" rushed to my mother. My father stalked directly inside to the hotel desk, got the number of my room, and headed up the marble stairs. The clerk called out, "This is a ladies' residence. No gentlemen allowed above the first floor." My father shouted, "I'm a doctor," and kept going. Guido and Sal and the black guy stayed leaning against their car while Nicky, who was hysterical, went to Barbara and said, "If you don't take her home, she will become a tramp."

My mother wheeled on Nicky as though she was going to hit him and yelled, "You're the bum! I know your type."

The black guy, now into the spirit of things, hulked up to my mother and shouted, "Who you calling a bum?"

"Who are you?" my mother demanded.

The black guy, grabbing Nicky's arm, yelled, "I'm his brother."

My father knocked on my door. I put on my bathrobe and opened the door—and knew I was in major, major trouble. He said, "You're going home right now." I said, "No, I am not." He said, "Yes, you are," and grabbed my arm and began pulling me out of the room. I hung on to the doorknob, screaming, "No! No! No!" My bathrobe ripped, so he threw my coat over my shoulders and began yanking me down the marble stairs while I hung on to the brass banister, rail by rail by rail. A man was wrenching at a hefty twenty-six-year-old woman and the two of them were screaming, "You're coming home!" "I'm *not* coming home!" "Oh, yes, you are!"

Suddenly, in the middle of the stairs—while I clung to the railing, hysterical and crying and panting—he stopped and bent his head down next to mine and said evenly, "You have two choices. You can come home quietly to Larchmont. Or I will have you committed to Bellevue *tonight!* I can call two friends right now and they'll sign the papers. No problem. I'll have you certified tonight. Which is it, Larchmont or Bellevue?"

All along my father was convinced I would end up a whore and now it had happened. Why would the Italian lover lie? And the only reason his daughter would turn to prostitution would be insanity. I knew he meant it—and that he could do it.

I had lost. There was no weapon. Even if I ran away again and still tried to live on my own, when two doctors said I was committable, they would come and find me and put me away. I turned and went back to my room and while I dressed and packed, I trembled with fear—shrinking into myself, hands wet, heart beating a mile a minute. If I stayed in show business, maybe he and my mother might decide to put me away anyhow—and then I really would go insane.

When I was a child, we went on an awful family trip to Williamsburg, Virginia. As usual, with no money even to go to the movies, we took a walk and came up against the state asylum. I remember being frantically scared, crazed to be anywhere near mental illness. Anybody beyond control, unpredictable, always panics me, and I knew that if I was put into an asylum, locked in with the insane, I would absolutely kill myself—and my father had hit that terror.

When I came back downstairs to the lobby, I descended into something close to a madhouse. Sal and Guido were drunk and my mother was screaming at them, "My God, what have you done to my daughter?" and Aunt Fanny was poking at them with her cane and Aunt Alice was calling, "Fanny, your heart, be careful." The black guy was shouting, "Don't worry, I'll call some friends," and my mother was yelling at Nicky, "It's your fault!" Sal was shouting, "Don't yell at my buddy. Who do you think you are, so fine in your fancy coat." It was a class war. Three Jewish ladies, none over five feet tall, in mink coats and Delman shoes, were screaming and swinging Hermès pocketbooks at three rough Italian boys. I ran to Nicky, weeping with rage. "How could you do this? How *could* you do this?" He lifted his arm, I guess to comfort me, but I ducked away from it. "I wasn't going to hit you," he said, his face grief-stricken. Aunt Fanny screamed, "My God, he hit her."

Then Aunt Alice took over. "Stop it! All of you stop it!" She told my parents to go home and let me spend the night with her and we would work it out. The Italian tong and the black guy went into the little bar off the lobby and ordered rye and ginger ales. When I got out onto the sidewalk with Alice, a touch of sanity returned. The fight was over and Nicky had been through enough and I did not want to break up with him. I went into the bar and said to Nicky, "Will you come home with me and my aunt? I want to talk to you."

Nicky said to the other three, "I'll see you guys later."

Guido said, "You're not going. She's not Italian."

Nicky stood up, saying, "Guido, leave me alone. It's my life."

Guido stood up. He said, "You don't go with her," and grabbed Nicky by the coat.

"This is my *life!*" Nicky yelled and squirmed out of the coat and ran to me, while Guido stood there, still holding the coat like a rag in his hand. Guido never spoke to Nicky again. Nicky had sold out their race.

We went to Aunt Alice's apartment on Park Avenue. Nicky and I sat on her Chippendale sofa under her Vlaminck, surrounded by her wonderful English antiques, and I told Alice the whole stupid story and said I was making my own living and should be left alone and everybody was assuming the worst. The usual song.

She kept saying, "Calm down. Calm down." She said that the time had come to go home and I could not go on like this. She said, "Look at yourself."

I kept telling her that I could not go home on their terms, which meant giving up show business.

She said if they could accept my being in show business, I should be able to stop causing them such heartbreak and be kinder to them. "Go gracefully," she said. Also, there was the threat of being committed. Finally, she telephoned my parents and a truce was negotiated.

The next morning, after my father had left for the office, I drove home. I was tremendously relieved that the grungy living was finished, glad to go into my bedroom and find that my mother had put out pretty towels. But I was returning defeated. My father had won and I was ever afterward frightened, because he had a weapon now. He could go one step beyond being a parent and be a policeman. No matter how old I was—if I was forty—my father could pick up the phone and call two doctor friends and say, "Will you help us? Betty and I think Joan is in a very bad way."

I knew that I would henceforth avoid my father, only speaking to him when it was absolutely necessary. He had never been able to have me as his little angel and now he had totally lost me. I am sure that it caused him a great deal of pain, because he must have felt he had really tried. But he was dealing with somebody he hardly knew. And how could he be loving when from childhood he had never been taught what it is to love—when his wife did not love him and his children did not love him? I am sure that half his anger at me in The Midston House was actually at my mother, because I was her favorite. What happened there was never mended, never forgotten, never mentioned—except on the very rare occasions when my mother saw Nicky. She always asked, "How's your brother?"

10

WHAT MAKES A comedian finally jell? What must happen before a comic can hit? What creates a comedy act? When Jack Rollins kept saying to me, "You're not ready," what did he mean?

I know the answer to that now. The act evolves out of yourself—but not intellectually. It gathers emotionally inside you, in a strange way a by-product of struggle, of a willingness to do anything, try anything, expose yourself to anything— staying in motion because sooner or later those ripples will cause change. This is paying your dues, appearing again and again and again on every sort of stage in front of every kind of audience, until you gradually, gradually acquire technique and a stage identity, which is not you, but has your passion, your hurts, your angers, your particular humor. This is a birth process and it can be very painful. Mine began in December of 1959.

My real entrance into show business coincided with my return home from The Midston House. Until then my talent had been so raw, so submerged under amateurism, so unreinforced by technique that it was virtually invisible onstage. But now, during 1960, like a fetus, I began to take on a tiny, tiny bit of identity as a performer and one could see the threads of minuscule fingers, see the misty shape of the skull, the blurry outline of scrunched-up legs. But there was still in my mind the lingering confusion whether that organism was an actress or a comedian. I still imagined that some discerning hand might suddenly elevate me out of shameful comedy into a theater career. So part of me was holding back, waiting for the hand to appear and solve my indecision. And it did, sort of.

It belonged to José Quintero, a major Broadway director who is still America's foremost interpreter of Eugene O'Neill. Nicky and I did a scene together in front of Quintero's acting class, which Nicky had joined, and afterward, Quintero talked to me privately for an hour, saying, "Who are you? Where have you been? You must study with me and stay in the theater." Here was a power able to project me into a play, able to be a mentor, and he was saying "Yes!" I stalled and finally said "No."

Then, out of hundreds and hundreds of kids, Nicky and I were included as actors in *Talent '60*, a showcase produced for unknown performers by John Effrat, a tall, tweedy, craggy-faced man who had been a Broadway stage manager and was now head of the Actors' Fund, the theater world's charity for ill, poor, and elderly performers. The Fund still raises money through collections in theaters at Christmas time, using it to help needy cases and run the actors' retirement home in New Jersey—which was the prototype for the home in Neil Simon's *The Sunshine Boys*. The Fund also, through Actors' Equity, administers the Conrad Cantzen shoe fund. A journeyman actor named Cantzen, munching along in smaller parts, saved his money and left his entire estate to provide free shoes to needy actors. He believed producers paid smaller salaries to actors who were "down at the heels." And twice a year I lined right up for that chit that got me a pair of A. S. Beck shoes. Then, for a while, when I crossed my leg in somebody's office, something nice was peeking out.

John Effrat also understood the huge problem of young performers finding showcases. Each year, wangling donated facilities, he produced three afternoon shows: straight dramatic, musical comedy, concert operatic. Admission was by invitation, and every agent, manager, critic, and talent scout came. On those afternoons there was no point calling any office on Broadway.

For *Talent '60* Nicky and I did a scene from Paddy Chayefsky's *The Goddess*—basically a boy making out with a girl in a car while she talks nonstop about going to Hollywood and being a movie star—a crazy, neurotic girl's monologue that was perfect for me. The showcase was at the Majestic Theater and onstage, as we finished our scene, there was the magic moment that only comes with drama—an instant of absolute quiet, a beat of silence—which means you have moved an entire audience—and then *tremendous* applause.

In Douglas Watt's review of *Talent '60* in the *New York Post,* I was one of the few mentioned by name—"Joan Rivers was appealing." My mother showed the review to Aunt Fanny, who sniffed and said, "There hasn't been a critic worth reading since George Bernard Shaw."

Some extremely important part of me knew that José Quintero and *Talent '60* had come too late, knew that veering off into comedy had been right for me, because in those crummy clubs I could be comfortable and endure the rejection. Junky comedy was not the core of my being, but acting, the tenderest center of THE DREAM, meant offering to an audience the essence of me that mattered most in the world. If a theater full of people rejected my acting, that would be unbearable, that would be two-thousand-baby-aspirin time.

Talent '60 did one thing for me—it brought back into my life Irvin Arthur, the first comedy agent I had approached, the man who had originally sent me to Jack Rollins. Irvin now became a continuing and important person in my life. A short, dark-haired man who had originally wanted to be an actor, he had been wounded in the Korean War and walked with a limp. He became one of the few honest agents and was then book-

ing the most prestigious intimate supper clubs—The Blue
Angel in New York, the Hungry i in San Francisco, Mr. Kelly's
in Chicago, the Interlude in Los Angeles, the Crystal Palace in
St. Louis. Like Jack Rollins, he had a shrewd eye for young
talent and was a hustler who battled to book young performers—including Mike Nichols and Elaine May, Barbra Streisand, Woody Allen, Bill Cosby, and Jerry Herman, at that time
playing cocktail music.

Though this circuit of cabarets was way above me, Irvin
Arthur had always been nice to me and I called him and asked
if he'd seen *Talent '60*. Yes, he had. Could I show him my act?
He was very sweet and said yes. I was thrilled, absolutely
thrilled. For the audition I took a precious dollar and rented a
rehearsal room at Variety Arts. Irvin brought a friend with
him, but I was crazy with nerves and hardly noticed.

With my eyes fixed about two feet above Irvin's head, I
did my act, which was still an amateurish descendant of the
Harry Brent act—routines stolen from television, songs from
my revue friends, one-line jokes scrounged from anywhere—
whatever I thought might be funny or cute. The movie takeoff
on *Golden Boy* seemed to get the biggest laugh. At the end
there was a little silence. Irvin's face was unreadable. Then he
looked embarrassed. Then he kind of chuckled and said,
"That was terrific. The only trouble is, you just did his act."
Irvin gestured toward his friend.

I felt the blush, hot as a heat rash, spread over my entire
body. I thought I was going to crumble to a cinder right in
front of them. The friend was Dick Gautier, then a comedy
star, and the movie takeoffs were his. I had copied them down
during an *Ed Sullivan Show* and done them so many times, they
had become mine. That happens. Totie Fields once borrowed
a few jokes from a routine on sourdough bread by a comic
named Pete Barbutti. Two years later she told him, "Stop
doing my sourdough routine."

I stood there in front of Gautier, feeling like an idiot and babbling, "I'm so sorry. I'm so sorry. I didn't realize it." Groveling.

Dick just said, "I'd appreciate it if you didn't do it anymore. You should buy your own act."

Irvin Arthur said, "You're a funny girl, you should write material yourself."

I just stared at them. I had no money to buy anything. And when people suggested finding my comedy in myself, I could not imagine what that was, could not see myself sitting alone with a pencil composing routines. And because I never heard my private sense of humor echoed on any stage, it was obviously not what audiences wanted to hear. Moreover, not one friend, when we were sitting around a table and everybody laughing, ever said, "Hey, you ought to write that down." It did not occur to any of us then that you could say something in conversation and then use it onstage.

When Irvin and Dick left, I could hear them laughing all the way down the hall, crying with laughter. Hysterical—that poor, dopey girl.

The next day Irvin called me up and asked, "How would you like a job?" My heart leapt; he had forgiven me. Visions of smart little supper clubs danced in my head.

"Oh, my God, would I!"

"Can you type?" Irvin asked.

That was how I became his secretary in the converted apartment he shared with four other agents distributed through the dining room, living room, and bedrooms. There was Lenny Jacobson, who booked the Catskills, and his partner, Gene Mann; Ray Heatherton, a vocal coach and Joey Heatherton's father; and Marty Erlichman, who was going around asking everybody whether he should manage Barbra Streisand.

I was Little Miss Efficient, a former college girl who could answer phones, get messages straight, open mail, type miserably—and be frantically jealous of all his women clients who were working, even a sexy black singer like Nancy Wilson. Irvin would say, "Make sure you send Nancy Wilson's pictures out to the Hungry i," and I wouldn't do it.

Irvin often worked with Jack Rollins and when Jack telephoned, I'd be full of pep: "Hi, Mr. Rollins. The act's coming along quite nicely now, Mr. Rollins. I just put in a thing on orangutans. I think it's working really well, really well. I can't wait for you to see it. I'll put you through to Mr. Arthur now. Best to that nice secretary of yours. Happy Valentine's Day." He was always darling: "Glad to hear it, Joaneleh." How that man must have dreaded calling the office!

When the unknown performers came in—the underbellies like me—I was very nice and tried to make them laugh. When an agent said, "Please tell so and so I don't want to see them anymore," I would make up lies to spare their feelings. "Mr. Jacobson is getting a divorce and he doesn't want to audition anybody for a year." "Mr. Arthur's wife is having a major operation, so don't come back for a few months. He's terribly upset."

Sometimes Milt Kamen in his big coat would come up to get out of the rain. He had started out as a French horn player in a symphony orchestra, but became a comic because, he told me, "At nine o'clock in the morning, when eighty musicians pick up their instruments and the first thing you start to rehearse is Wagner—you better love music a lot."

Milt was now white-hot in the business, the bright, new funny man appearing at the Bon Soir and The Blue Angel, the most prestigious, glamorous cabaret in New York. When you starred there, you had arrived, so I was inordinately flattered that he would bring me coffee and, if Irvin wasn't there, sit and talk. He was a sweet, sweet man whose humor was wonderfully benign. He had a line about being intimidated by people with French accents who sound so sophisticated, so elegant. He said, "Believe me, you wake them up in the middle of the night and they talk the same as you and me."

Milt became an avuncular teacher, discussing comedy with me the way an adult talks to a child with respect. He told me one piece of technique which I have made my own: When you begin losing an audience, do not get loud; get quiet, make them find you and come back to you. To give me an object lesson about comedy, he talked about Mort Sahl's career and why it cooled off so drastically. When Milt was working his first club date at the Purple Onion in San Francisco, Mort Sahl was across the street at the Hungry i, followed about by an entourage, everybody agreeing with him, talking like him— short, staccato. Milt hung around, but could not get with the group. "Sahl was shorthand," Milt explained. "I was longhand."

But Milt came to some personal conclusions about him. Onstage Sahl cast himself as the great liberal gadfly, born to devastate the Establishment; that was his persona and the world believed it. But Milt thought Sahl was just a nihilist who cared passionately about nothing except himself. Free of real convictions, he could say anything and was dazzling. The persona worked onstage because Sahl did feel genuine indignation, but it was the anger, Milt believed, of a man counterattacking, a man who felt threatened by the Establishment. When Sahl became *immensely* popular, the Establishment became fans and he lost his enemies, lost his fire, lost his authenticity onstage. Without a central core of convictions and anger, his act became only the cold sparks of a brilliant mind.

So Milt was another person telling me that comedy has to come from your center, from who you really are—but this was still a concept too large, too all-encompassing, too frightening for me to grasp and make my own.

There was an afternoon when Milt, his umbrella dribbling a puddle on the floor, sat by my desk—Milt Kamen, the subject of articles in *Time* and *Newsweek*, lines waiting to see

him at The Blue Angel, a regular on the Jack Paar show—
white white-hot. Talking about comedy as we always did, he
said, "One day they're going to realize I'm not funny."

Well, that scared the hell out of me. You think everybody
else is secure—that Mommy and Daddy are not scared. Then
the day comes when the mother says, "You look in the closet,
not me," and you realize you were correct to be frightened.
Milt Kamen was on quicksand, too, and it would never be any
different for me. That's the comedian's psyche. That's where I
am right now.

Since I could not get Jack Rollins to help me develop my
act, I had to find a stand-in for him and what I found was a
huge six-foot gay man wearing a multiflora muumuu. His
name was Bob Waxman and he was a pianist-composer who
wanted to be Oscar Hammerstein.

Bob had also produced a successful revue for a Greenwich Village coffeehouse called Phase 2. At that time, revue
fever was permeating New York nightclubs—lots and lots of
groups called Four in the Front or Four on a Stool, lots and
lots of tuxedos and black dresses with pearls, lots and lots of
cutesy songs. My friends Rod Warren and Treva Silverman
were born for the craze, and Treva had now done a revue for a
Time-Life sales meeting. The vogue for revues penetrated
even to the recesses of Irvin Arthur's office and the creative
consciousness of Lenny Jacobson, who rented the living
room. He decided Jews in the Catskills were ready for chic,
itty-bitty songs and chatter. It was ideas like that which separated Lenny from Flo Ziegfeld.

Lenny Jacobson hired Bob Waxman and they packaged
me and three other hopeful kids into a little revue called Four
for the Season. We came out on the stages of Fleischmann's
and Kutsher's, chirping, "Hello, hello, hello," and my big
song began, "Every bee can make a beeline, every cat can

make a feline, but a man's best line may fail." All through the show room you could hear murmurs of "Vas is das?" As they watched the boys, the whispers changed to "feigela, feigela." We lasted two weeks.

Bob Waxman asked me if I would work up an act with him and he became my wonderful midwife-Jewish mother. Together we assembled my first act that was designed and written and did not contain anything stolen from television. Because of Bob's background, it was a one-person revue and we called it "The Diary of Joan Rivers" because onstage with me was a huge red cardboard diary. I opened each sketch or song by turning a page and revealing a lead-in line painted in big letters: "Dear diary, today I almost got married . . ." which allowed me to go into a piece called "Bride at the Airport," based on material from a young writer named David Cox, which I then embellished. It was the first solid spoken routine that, almost by accident, followed Jack Rollins's advice and tapped into who I was—a sassy, unmarried girl dying to get married. It was based on a newspaper item I saw about a girl who had gotten on an airplane in full wedding dress because she was late to the wedding. It still holds up well:

> Hi, darling, this is Joanie . . . Your fiancée. Joanie Rivers . . . Rivers. R-I-V-E-R-S. Yeah, right. So how are you? . . . Well, actually not so good. See, my plane was late taking off. We didn't leave New York until eleven . . . I know our wedding is in an hour . . . I can't get a cab . . . I know Chicago is full of cabs . . . I'm not in Chicago. I'm in Denver . . . *Denver* . . . How am I going to get married in an hour? Well, the baggage clerk is kind of cute. Only kidding. Only kidding . . .

I begged Lenny Jacobson, begged Irvin, "Please get me a booking for my act." They said, "We've seen your act." I insisted. "It's all different." Finally, they booked me into the Cherry Grove Hotel on Fire Island.

Driving to Fire Island in the Buick, I swung by Larchmont with Bob Waxman to pick up some clothes and Bob came into the house with me. My mother took one look at Bob standing there—Orson Welles in a full muumuu—and she said to me, "Joan, may I see you alone in the kitchen?" My father went upstairs and lay down on the bed, probably with an ice pack on his head. In the kitchen my mother said, "Why did you bring him here? I don't want that kind of person knowing where we live. Meet them on the outside. What if the neighbors see him? How am I going to explain a six-foot man in a dress!"

I told her Bob Waxman was absolutely wonderful and nice and went slamming out, saying, "Come on, Bob, let's go. Everything's fine, let's just go. Careful, don't trip on your hem." I was furious, partly at their rudeness to Bob, partly because they had broken the truce we made when I moved back home. They were not leaving me alone in my show business life. After that, I split away the performer part of me, the major part, even more systematically. I began spending frequent nights in New York, staying with friends or using the key Aunt Alice had given me and flopping on her sofa. That made my mother even more furious at Alice, who condoned everything I did and encouraged me, saying, "If you want to do it, go ahead, Joansie." Alice was my fairy godmother.

Even though my mother's side of me was still connected umbilically to house and family, I came home mainly to sleep and was just a body in the bed. After my mother died, I found a little saying she had copied out of a book: "These are my daughters, I suppose. But where have the children gone?"

That weekend, doing "The Diary of Joan Rivers" on Fire Island, I finally found the audience that would keep me alive in show business until I could, so to speak, go it alone. Basically, it was people who were smart, realistic, literate, up-to-date, with a taste for the camp and the outrageous—and the best of those, I learned at Cherry Grove, were the gays.

There has been nothing nicer than 500 gay faces looking up at me onstage. Gay audiences have been the most loving, the most generous, the most forgiving, the most loyal. Their humor is everybody's humor, but to the nth degree, spicier, more paprika in it, the highest camp. They love to see the uptight, conservative, straight ethic put down. Gays are like many comedians—born into trouble, outcasts, living in trouble, not accepted. When you are an outsider, hungry for recognition, you can be noticed by being outrageous and the more you ridicule your pain, the less it hurts—and that is why I love gays, they will go far, far out with me into silliness.

The Cherry Grove job was, I think, twenty-five dollars for the weekend, two shows a night, Friday, Saturday, and Sunday, which barely covered our rooms and food. In front of that audience my cute little act, tailored by a gay, was everything it was supposed to be and the show-stopping hit of the evening, for obvious reasons, was my old song, "I'll never forget what's his name, I'll never forget how he kissed, whatever his name was."

On Friday the hotel booker, Jack Lundy, paid me nineteen dollars and said he did not have the other six dollars right then.

"What ferry are you taking?" he asked. I told him the 6:00 A.M. on Monday. He said, "I'll pay you at the ferry."

On Monday at 5:30 A.M., while Bob Waxman stayed on another day, I paced the dock, knuckles white as I watched the crowd board the ferry back to the mainland. I was going to miss it, but I *had* to have that money. There was only a dollar in my purse and an unknown amount of gas in the car for the drive back to New York—and eventually I would have to pay Bob as my accompanist. I let that ferry go and waited, pacing the wooden pier, churning with anger and anxiety, knowing I was a total fool. Nobody gets up at 6:00 A.M. to give somebody six dollars. I went back to the hotel, but Jack Lundy had magically vanished. After I had done four packed shows at his hotel, he had stiffed me for a lousy six dollars.

Today, because of the Jack Lundys of this world, I will not get on a plane for a concert date unless half the money is in the bank, and I will not go onstage for the second performance until there is a certified check for the balance. Most experienced performers do that. We have all been burned by owners. Sarah Bernhardt insisted on being paid in gold coins before each show.

It becomes a sort of game, the owners trying to get the most out of the performers for the least amount of money, and the performers trying to anticipate the penny ante ways they will be cheated. At one place my contract specified a private bathroom, but did not say towels, so there I am in a fabulous bathroom drying myself with paper towels. In Denver in a restored theater, the dressing room had a broken-down couch, broken chairs, a mirror nailed to the wall, and a kitchen table in front of it. Comes the accounting, the owner had deducted two hundred fifty dollars rental for dressing room furniture. The rider on my contract is now up to eighteen pages.

Beginners are constantly being used and abused. Desperately eager to be noticed, they are the perfect, defenseless victims. The biggest scam ever pulled on me was that summer of 1960. An agent called up and offered me fifteen dollars to emcee a Catholic church bazaar in Queens, Long Island— draw raffle tickets out of the bowl, do my act, etc. I said yes, thrilled to do it. The agent came with me—which was unusual —and at the stage door of the school auditorium, we were met by ladies with corsages and acetate dresses and blue hairdos.

They kept saying to the agent, "Where is she? Where is she?" And he said, "Don't worry, she'll be along."

I could hear a little band playing out front and feel a humming excitement and electricity in the air. As I was about to walk onstage, the agent said, "Good luck—and one more thing. When you get out there, tell them your name is Rosalind Russell."

I said, "Excuse me?"

He said, "When you get out there, just say your name is Rosalind Russell. I'll explain it to you later." He pushed me onstage.

The room was jammed with kids and parents and priests and nuns, crowds of people standing along the walls where banners read, WELCOME ROSALIND RUSSELL TO ST. IGNATIUS. YOU'RE OUR WOMAN OF THE YEAR. WE LOVE YOU, ROZ. And here I was, this short chunko standing there. I went to the microphone and said, "Hi, my name is Rosalind Russell also. I'm the other one. Isn't it a coincidence? I get this all the time."

They did not take it well. The place went crazy! A wave of hate rose over the footlights—yelling, stamping on the floor. Have you ever seen screaming priests? Nuns shaking their fists?

I tried to sing "I'll Never Forget What's His Name," but there was so much noise, my accompanist could not even hear my cue. Pretty soon I said, "I'm terribly sorry. Good night." And got off. The agent, who did not want to be lynched, had disappeared. I felt *terrible*. I had ruined their night. Can you imagine the anticipation, thinking that Rosalind Russell at her height as an actress is going to show up in Queens to close your bazaar? For fifteen dollars? Think of all the ladies figuring they were going home with a Polaroid shot of themselves with Rosalind Russell.

I called the agent up the next day and said, "How could you do that?" He said a lot of performers make a buck doing it. "How would you like to be Marilyn Monroe on Tuesday?"

Having more or less found my audience on Fire Island, I
next found my turf—Greenwich Village. Dave Gordon, an
unreconstructed preppy in a crew cut and colored Brooks
Brothers vest, had opened the Phase 2. He gave it a logo—
"cafe theater"—booked in entertainment and unwittingly pi-
oneered what became known as the Greenwich Village coffeehouse movement. Pretty soon the Café Wha?, The Bitter End,
Café Bizarre, the Gaslight—all began to book acts. Suddenly,
there were respectable places with sophisticated but unde-
manding audiences who were delighted to drink cappuccino,
eat pastries, and watch young, apprentice performers do
something sweet or amusing or funky. But Dave had no passion for what was happening on his stage. His passion was
waitresses. Later he told me he'd opened the Phase 2 as a
great way to meet girls.

The young performers he was auditioning and booking
were desperate for a manager and he could have gathered in a
major stable. One day he auditioned Bobby Zimmerman—
who became Bob Dylan. In Dave's opinion, Bobby was "this
scruffy, turkey-necked kid in a peaked hat, with a squeaky,
lousy voice, and a crazy harmonica thing, and he played depressing songs I did not recognize as prime material—one of
the worst who ever came through." After ten minutes Dave
told Bobby, "I literally do not have any more time for you."
Dave regarded me as "a clumsy, clumpy girl who hadn't made
it as an actress and probably wouldn't make it as a comic
either."

But Bob Waxman, on the strength of his previous revue
for Dave, was able to persuade him to book "The Diary of
Joan Rivers" for two weeks after Labor Day. For the first time
in my life, after those years and years of longing and fantasizing, I at last felt I was truly in show business. I adored arriving
and getting a cup of coffee and going into the little outdoor

café in rear garden, where sometimes I would see Mel Brooks courting Anne Bancroft. Inside in the show room, which held about sixty people, there was a tiny stage with a piano on it and you made your exits and entrances from the cellar.

I got by at the Phase 2 on what Jack Rollins called my "likability"—a tremendous eagerness to please combined with hopefulness—the quality which makes puppies charming. But I also received my first bad notice. *Off Broadway Reviews* said:

> There are two main things amiss with Miss Rivers's approach: her material is tired and her delivery is frenetic. The several songs she offers are very local, bounded by the range of the NYC subways. The Bronx, the suburbs, Coney Island, have been done, and Miss Rivers has nothing fresh to offer on these topics. Then, having gotten her material, she strains hard to put it over, as if her bright energy could somehow embellish the skeletal comedy. But her frantic and strained efforts are only nerve-racking and do not disguise, but rather point up, the material's essential aridity.

I felt then—and now—not only destroyed and outraged but also discovered. This person had seen the real nothing beneath the shallow veneer and now in print he was telling everybody—all of whom would see the review. That is the way of this world. *The New York Times* might say, "If you have a choice between seeing the second coming of Jesus Christ or Joan Rivers, go see Joan Rivers," but nobody will catch that issue. If a once-a-week, giveaway blue sheet in Jersey says it does not like Joan Rivers, seventy friends will call up and say, "Oh, my God, Joan, you poor thing."

Our deal at the Phase 2 was the same as all the acts. We worked for free, but a hat was passed after the performance and then in the basement Bob Waxman would dump the money into the lap of his muumuu and while he counted it, we would go, "Ahhhh." It was *very* exciting. You had performed and here was the physical cash—tangible, cause and effect— and that money paid for the sandwich on the way home—a simple cycle.

Today I have no sense of being paid. I almost never touch the actual money. There are only checks and drafts transferred by computer between banks. I do not *truly* believe the money exists. As far as I know, it is only a lot of talk. When I perform at small clubs in Los Angeles to develop new material, we insist on being paid in cash because maybe those places will not be open a week later. The owner hands the money to me and zip, it goes right into my purse—and no, I will not give it to my husband when I get home. This is physical money. They say, "You can't do that." I answer, "Too bad, too bad. Nobody's getting any of it . . . except the IRS and me."

Despite Dave Gordon's opinion of me, whatever I was doing onstage at the Phase 2 was right, because we were held over a third week. I thought this was fabulous, wonderful, marvelous—and that is the show business mentality: a twenty-seven-year-old woman was crazed with joy because she was held over at a place where they paid her out of a hat. Then one night Bob Waxman and I were down in the cellar counting out the take from the hat—almost fifteen dollars a show—and Don Gregory appeared, Dave Gordon's partner, a great big guy, an ex-marine who did not like me. He said, "Dave and I talked it over and we decided that from now on, we get a third of the hat." It was Mafia tactics. He wanted a piece of the hat!

I told him, "Make your money on the cappuccino. The hat's ours."

He said, "It's our club. You can go fuck yourself, we'll do what we want."

Well, I went crazy. First, they were changing the rules and that always gets me. Second, that four-letter word was not to be used in front of me. I went berserk. I screamed, "It's not *fair*," and went for him—punching him in the stomach—whap, bang, whap—and this big guy was backing away and doubling over and I was beating the hell out of him.

Nick Clemente, upstairs waiting for me, ran down the stairs, brandishing an umbrella—my Italian D'Artagnan with his rapier. He bellowed at Gregory, "Did you hit this girl?"

Gregory's face was a study in shock and amazement. "Shit, no," he said. "She hit *me!*"

Through the Phase 2 I reached the status of a new face on the scene, somebody to be considered. Bob Shanks, the talent coordinator for the Jack Paar show, had seen me in *Talent '60* and then brought Paar's producer, Paul Keyes, down to the Phase 2. Later, Bob Shanks called me and said, "Come up to my office and let's talk."

When I hung up the phone, I stood quietly for a moment savoring a rush of triumph. This was it—my vindication, the breakthrough I had known would come if I kept working, the proof that I could entertain, that I was funny. In a few weeks' time I could be a household name, fantasy and life coming together. Jack Paar had that power.

Making my breakthrough on that show would be perfect because it was my parents' favorite show. Like most of the country, they watched Paar every night and knew he was a wonderful, warm, emotional guy and they wept with Jack, laughed with Jack, cared emotionally for Jack. And that was why the show was marvelous—because Paar was so unpredictable, so mercurial, so impulsive. At any moment he might break down and sob—or he would bring on some unexpected person, some chancy guest who might come alive and something amazing would happen. He opened up television to politicians, authors, columnists, theater and movie directors. Paar really built his success on eccentrics and raconteurs—on

Alexander King, Milt Kamen, Moss Hart, Jonathan Winters, Selma Diamond, Oscar Levant, Malcolm Muggeridge, Elsa Maxwell, Robert Morley.

Paar had people all over town looking for offbeat characters, for kooky girls like Dodi Goodman, so that on camera he could go, "Oh, she is too much," and look right at the audience and roll his eyes and say, "She's crazy." But sometimes the risks did not pay off and a far-out comedian from a Village dive would bomb and Paar would turn on Bob Shanks, saying, "Kid, don't book any more acts from places where water is sweating down the walls."

Of course, very quickly, my sense of triumph turned to panic—suppose Bob Shanks discovered that I was neither funny nor talented, suppose in his office I babbled like a fool until he looked at me and said, "You're not right for us," and then I would *not* be launched, would not be through that closed door. For three afternoons in Bob Shanks's office, my energy levitating me one inch off my chair, I was a motor mouth with the accelerator jammed to the floor. In my head revved the thoughts, *Keep going, make him realize how funny you are. This is your big break. Keep him laughing. Keep him interested. Get all that charm out now.* I tried to be funny about everything that had ever happened to me, all my adventures as a doctor's daughter and a single girl in a Jewish family and as an actress-comedian scuffing in the basement of show business. Bob Shanks, at the end of a long session of taking notes on this manic girl, finally said, "Joan, you can relax. We're going to use you. Calm down."

But that was asking my heart to stop pounding as though it might split open my chest and I wondered if he could hear it too. My big break was *happening!* I blushed with embarrassment because it was *so* wonderful to me and I was so close to tears. Now I might be a Paar regular and become known to all of America and producers would recognize me as the funny girl on the Paar show. And then my high drained away and I became very serious and we went to work, plotting which material, which lines.

Before the show, Bob Shanks stood with me in the Green Room like a coach, going over with me again the stories we had chosen, telling me, "Just be yourself—everyone's on your side—just talk to Jack—it's going to be fine." I paced the room, alternately clenching my fists tight and rubbing my hands—and constantly stopping by the table to gobble cheese and crackers. To give myself heart, I had written GOOD LUCK and BREAK A LEG on my knees under my dress—secret voices giving me encouragement.

I walked onto the show like gangbusters—Miss Fun! Here we go!—and on an impulse I asked Jack Paar if he wanted to see what was on my knees. I flipped up my dress and a cameraman rolled in for a closeup. I told Jack Paar my mother desperately wanted me to get married, so she painted the entire kitchen pink, because she had heard pink made you look young and terrific. She even bought a pink stove and pink refrigerator—which was true—but nothing happened for my sister and me. However, three maids ran off with A & P delivery boys.

I told him about sharing office temporary jobs with my sister and her being fired in the afternoon because I had made a mistake in the morning and I told him that to get extra money, I stole stamps at work and sold them to friends wholesale for five cents or at a bulk rate of six for a quarter. When I said I was dating a guy whose father was in the Mafia, Paar asked with wide-eyed, faked innocence, "Do you really think there is a Mafia?" I said, "Is there!" I told him there is a Mafia school where they teach them math—if Johnny has ten fingers and they cut off two, how many does he have left? I told him I'd worked in a Mafia nightclub where the cigarette girl sold bullets. I said, "I love going out with an Italian man because all Italians are so masculine. You've never seen a gay Italian because anytime they turn gay, they make them into nuns. That's why so many nuns have mustaches."

Jack Paar asked, "Do you realize Italian people are watching this show?"

The audience liked me and laughed. I came off floating with relief and Bob Shanks said, "Good job! Good shot! We'll have you on again." Paul Keyes, the producer, said, "Fine." Nick Clemente and Rod Warren were in the audience and they said, "Great, great." In the dressing room I could giggle and be happy and say hello and thank you to everybody because I had proven myself, shown I belonged. Then, by some fluke, I got in the same elevator as Jack Paar and felt so good, I had the courage to say, "Thank you very much, Mr. Paar, for giving me the opportunity to be on your show." He totally ignored me. The great man stared straight ahead. Six floors down, not a word, then walked out of the elevator.

So I told myself, *Well, okay, he's tired.* The next day Irvin Arthur was thrilled. Lenny Jacobson was thrilled, everybody was saying, "You've done it! You're going to be a regular!" I did not really trust that . . . and yet I did. If it had happened to Dodi Goodman, why not me?

But before I could let myself absolutely *believe*, I needed confirmation. I phoned Bob Shanks and asked for another booking on the show and he said, "Meet me in the Cromwell Drug Store downstairs." Over coffee he told me, "Jack didn't believe you." At the morning meeting they had the list of names of future guests and Paar took a pencil and drew a line through my name and said, "Never again. I don't believe one word she says. She's a liar."

Bob Shanks told him, "Jack, they're jokes."

Paar said, "We don't do jokes."

I kept a smile on my face, pressing my tongue against my

teeth so I would not cry. But the tears were right behind my eyes and my lips were trembling and I wanted to become as small as possible and disappear forever. I told him I understood and excused myself and went right to a phone booth and wept.

Of course, the biggest joke of all was on Jack Paar, who thought all his guests told the truth. His show was the first to create television people—somebody funny who is all personality and tells wonderful stories—but Paar was as naively eager as his audience to convince himself that it was not prepared material, that the stories they came up with—". . . and I saw a man eating a shoe on a subway"—were spontaneous and actually happened.

I was sorry for my family because of their disappointment for me and their disappointment in Jack Paar. My father, who had been ready to commit me to an insane asylum a few months earlier, said, "Well, Mr. Paar obviously doesn't understand." I was still his child and he was still my parent and he would fight me himself, but would defend me to the death against the world.

My father sat down and wrote Paar a letter, saying that even though she is a doctor's daughter and went to the finest schools, that really is the way she is living—my daughter is not a liar. He and my mother really believed that Jack Paar was their friend and once he understood that I had been telling the truth, everything would be repaired. It was so sweet. They never received an answer and they never watched Jack Paar again. He was dead in my household.

The double irony was that my theme on the Paar show— the tribulations of being Joan Molinsky—was exactly what Jack Rollins, Milt Kamen, and now Bob Shanks had all realized should be my comedy flesh and blood. But if I had any glimmerings of that in my own head, Jack Paar effectively put

them out. What I thought was funny about Joan Molinsky, the
great man did not think was funny. So besides teaching me
again to trust nothing, the show set me back years professionally, shoved me right back to my mediocre, irrelevant Phase 2
semirevue material, saying to piano accompaniment:

> It certainly was a wonderful evening, Milton . . .
> I don't know when I've enjoyed a movie more . . .
> It's a shame we couldn't sit together . . . Would
> you like to come upstairs for a cup of coffee . . .
> You have a headache . . . What do you think causes
> your headache? . . . the sound of my voice . . .
> I've been going with you for seven years . . .
> You've had a headache for seven years . . . I'm glad
> the truth is out . . . For seven years you've been
> saying you wanted to marry me and for seven years
> you've been taking Bufferin behind my back . . . I
> thought they were mints . . . I guess marrying me
> would be like marrying a migraine . . .

However, if Jack Paar did not like me, I was appreciated
in other quarters. The *Princeton Tiger* did an article on me—a
whole page on the new comedian, Joan Rivers. They took me
to the 21 Club for lunch and it was one of those afternoons
which kept me going for a long time. I told them that in the
Catskills I had done a takeoff on the New York City parks
commissioner, Robert Moses, and the audience hissed me for
being anti-Bible. I told them, "Princeton is too intellectual for
me. I hear the numbers on your elevator buttons are square
roots." They wrote, "She *is* going places"—and I got out of
21 with a pocketbook full of hard candy.

Linda Sue Rex in Akron, Ohio, saw the show and wrote,
asking permission to start the only official Joan Rivers Fan
Club and I granted permission by return mail. She went to
work immediately on *Joan's Journal-ette*, and I had to write
down notes about Joanie—favorite color (pink, of course),

favorite food (spaghetti, but I shouldn't), favorite movie star (Laurence Olivier).

She sent me 500 membership applications which, for a dollar, promised an autographed eight by ten glossy, a membership card, bulletins, contests, all club activities and privileges, and two *Joanie's Journals*—which contained greetings from President Rex, the "Ask Joan" page, and a letter from me that started, "Hello, Everybody." Alas, there were not many people clamoring to join.

But hold it, Jack Paar! Hold everything, fella! Linda Sue Rex in Ohio saw talent in me!

11

SOMEHOW, SOME WAY, every person in the arts has to find an accommodation with disappointment and embarrassment. They are the pollen in the air we breathe. If you must go into the arts, go into them for yourself alone. On some basic level you must enjoy the act of doing it—be willing to paint a picture and just hang it on your wall. If you want to be an actor, then learn to enjoy it in your bathroom. Otherwise, you are going to end up frustrated and unhappy. Recognition in the arts is luck and gravy.

The only way you can go into show business is to expect no reward at all—which, of course, is impossible. Everybody goes into this business for profit and recognition. The paradox is: If you are *not* in it for the rewards, they are more likely to come to you. If you are willing to do anything just to work —if you are obsessed—you will make your luck. Making your luck is Barbra Streisand auditioning to play the blond, gentile Trapp child, Lisl, in *The Sound of Music.* But out of that, the casting director said, "Go be a nightclub singer," and because she was a nightclub singer, somebody saw her who was looking for a kooky Jewish girl who could sing and play Miss Marmelstein in *I Can Get It for You Wholesale.*

Talent rises to the surface like the best of cream because there is so little of it. All the neurotics go into this business, the unhappy people, the misfits, and they say, "I'm going to be an actor; I'm going to be a comic." The ones with talent always make it, unless their neurosis is so great it stops them. Talent shines through.

But to maintain success, stamina is more important than

talent. You have to learn to be a marathon runner. Even in the fall of 1960, I knew instinctively that my insane drive was my most valuable asset. And, in a strange way, maybe that is why I always hugged the negative side of everything. If I ever believed something good was permanent, maybe I would relax. I am still that way today, running on fear.

The year that began at the end of 1960 was one of tremendous highs and lows—really a normal state of affairs in show business—and I think this was when I stopped crying quite so constantly. I began learning to deal with the despair which is epidemic at the bottom of the ladder—and also with success, which can set you up for even deeper depressions.

In mid-October, thanks to my friend John Effrat of the Actors' Fund and *Talent '60,* I finally had the experience of sustained success. He included me in a USO show called *Broadway USA,* which was a classy pastiche of hit comedy scenes and show stoppers from Broadway musicals. My big solo was "Island Magic" from *Trouble in Tahiti* by Leonard Bernstein. For three months we toured Army bases in Korea, Japan, and the Pacific Islands, performing before enthusiastic soldiers starved for entertainment. The only member without Broadway experience, I had trouble at first keeping up with the rest of the troupe, and was especially disgusted because this time I could not blame the audiences. Late one night I wrote in my diary, "Tonight I flubbed lines, lost laughs, had no control at all. I was so upset. I want each program to sparkle, to have the audience enjoy me, feel they know me personally, feel I am a friend to each one. And when something doesn't happen, when I don't catch on—even though I still look professional and adequate—I am sick. I want perfection—and all the time, or else I'm not satisfied. Damn! I want to be GREAT!" And I still feel that way, which shows how much I have grown.

Very quickly on the tour I began to blossom, becoming a stronger and stronger performer. It was the first time I had ever had friendly, forgiving audiences night after night. Bathed in their affection, I became better and brighter and tried harder and when I did something right, I got a reaction and knew to do that thing again. I was learning better timing, more stagecraft, and feeling a form within myself that maybe I could put onstage. In my diary I wrote, "I do realize now that I have worth and value as a person and must not sell myself short."

During those three months I bathed in the China Sea on Christmas Eve, watched the sunrise from the Tokyo Tower, ate with Kabuki actors and saw Mount Fuji topped by its clouds like a Japanese print, and went to an Episcopal service in Hiroshima and heard the priest say, "God is Ruv." On December 7 several of us got lost sightseeing in some little town and an old man, courteously, with his gnarled finger, drew a map for us in the white snow—helping Americans on Pearl Harbor Day. I thought, *A lot's happened, mister, in fifteen years.*

We went from island to island—to Guam, Okinawa, Hawaii, and Pearl Harbor with its thousands of graves marked UNKNOWN. We had New Year's Eve on Guam and built a fire on the beach under a full moon that gleamed on the huge green foliage growing right to the edge of the silvery beach. Along it, like ruined monuments, were Japanese bunkers left from World War II. I walked down the beach to a half-buried bunker and stood there in the night glow of the moon, surrounded by so much history and beauty. I thought, *Life is very good.*

Arriving back in New York, I felt for the first time like a professional. I had held my own among kids with Broadway experience and at the end we won an award for the best USO show of the year. I knew now, beyond any self-doubt, that given good material, I was able to entertain an audience. And secondly, something deep, deep inside me had gone *click,* and my resolve to be a performer had become truly irrevocable—written in concrete. The doubts, the depressions, the craziness continued, but underneath, at the central core, my conviction gave me a version of happiness. The uncertain, thrashing Lord & Taylor side of me was at least quiet. I *knew* that I would be a performer the rest of my life, no matter how or where—no matter how many blows on the head from baseball bats.

Armed with my new confidence and my credential—the tour—and some pathetic little Japanese cups as gifts to get me into offices, I made the rounds again right away, despite a terrible blizzard. After my last stop—Bob Shanks at the Paar show—I struggled through the snow to a rendezvous with Nick Clemente in a booth at Howard Johnson's.

It was a measure of my self-assurance, my sensation of success, that I had decided to break with Nicky. Instead of missing him in the Orient, I had enjoyed a sense of freedom, relished my independence, felt that I was moving ahead, while unambitious Nicky was not. And now, sure enough, after I had seen the world, here he was where I had left him three months ago, broke and nowhere and waiting for me. I had always needed him there for trouble—he was Trouble Police—but those scrounging days were done and it was wrong to let a man I would never marry devote his life to me. The bottom line truth was: I was still hoping for that man with drive and money who would take care of me.

In the Howard Johnson's booth Nicky sat across from me, smiling with excited eyes, while through the window behind him the torrent of snow descended on Broadway. He told me he had missed me every minute of every day and proudly handed across a coming-home present, a wristwatch he could not afford. I felt selfish and mean and wanted to retreat till I disappeared inside myself, but I plunged ahead, trying to carry him unhurt in soft cotton platitudes. I said I thought it would be better for the two of us if we did not spend so much time together. I said it was not fair of me to take up so much of his time and pointed out that in the year and a half he had known me, he had made no progress as an actor, did not make rounds, and rarely went to acting classes. As I talked, I thought that nobody else would ever care so much for me or think I was so wonderful. Typically, he admitted it was all true, but the good face I knew so well was disintegrating, even as he was saying, "Fine. Okay. Swell. Good luck to you, Joan."

After we parted, I walked across town to Grand Central absolutely devastated. I had given up an enormous chunk of my life and hurt somebody who loved me. Before getting on a train, I checked in by phone with my mother, who said Bob Shanks had been looking everywhere for me. I called him and he said to come right over and be ready to go on the Paar show that night. A guest had been grounded by the storm and Hugh Downs would be the host because Jack Paar was in Washington at the Kennedy Inaugural. I hung up thinking, *Isn't fate wonderful! Just when I am really ready to do well, a snowstorm brings me my big breakthrough. Kismet, Kismet, Kismet.*

Next I turned cold with panic. Once again my whole life, all my struggle and pain, would hang on a few minutes on television. I thought, *I can't go there by myself. I can't do it alone.* I *had* to have somebody standing next to me saying, "You're going to be fine. You're going to be wonderful. It's going to be great." I needed Nicky, the rock in my life. Without a second's hesitation, I picked up the phone and called him and said, "We'll talk some more about what we were talking about —but right now I need you. They just called me for the Paar show."

Of course, Nicky said that was great and he would come right away. And he said, "Don't worry, you're going to be fine."

I am *not* lucky. I am the type who would go to Lourdes and drown in the waters. There are people I can be funny with and there is Hugh Downs. On camera I talked to him about the USO tour, saying, "It was such a bad show, we played to 4F's." Downs said, "Then how could it have been a USO show?" I told him, "I want to be so thin I have to wear suspenders on my girdle," and he said, "You don't look as though you're wearing a girdle." All during the show the station kept switching to news coverage of a big plane crash that night in New York, so right after saying, "I'm not pretty . . . I once dated a guy whose tattoo turned its back," I would see the monitor screen filled with burning wreckage and weeping relatives.

This time Bob Shanks and Paul Keyes just told me, "Good night," no little hugs and promises to sneak me on again. It was the end. After months of cultivating Bob Shanks, I could never go back. I had made him a proclamation of parchment, written in big English script and outlined in red and gold and tricked out with stars and gold seals and a red velvet ribbon. It read: "Bob Shanks is the sweetest, kindest man in the world."

After the show, Aunt Fanny—"Happy" Fanny Fields— phoned my mother and said, "When is that girl going to stop? Bea, *when* is she going to stop?"

For the second time the ultimate opportunity, the moment on television that could have made me the new girl in town, was a flop. Then, almost like a chain reaction, everything else went bust and I discovered the performer's paradox: the greater the high of a success, the deeper the pit of frustration afterward. On the USO tour I had proved there was something inside me, proved I could entertain, proved I had a place in the business—and still nobody cared. In Larchmont I was still the daughter being asked what time I would get home. In New York on my rounds I was still the pitiful girl they had given up on. Nobody cared that I was terrific on Guam, that I had received a standing ovation in the Philippine Islands. It was the very old story—if you have not made it in New York, you have not made it—and New York is a killer city.

Right after the Paar show fiasco my sister Barbara came to me, miserable, and said, "I have something terrible to tell you." During the tour I had sent her my savings to deposit in the bank and Barbara confessed that she had borrowed my money and had her teeth capped. My cushion allowing me to concentrate on rounds that winter was gone. I was a beggar again at Brown Temporaries.

I became obsessed with money. People say it is not the key to happiness, but I have always figured if you have enough money you can have a key made. I was so poor now that I could not afford root canal work on four molars, so the dentist just yanked them out.

Then one morning I was driving my car to an office temporary job in Mamaroneck. I was late and, distracted by reaching over to open a package of cookies for breakfast, I hit a tree. I sat in the car and wept, wailing to myself, "Not fair! Not fair!"

I left the fender permanently crushed, and though that car was hideous and rotting—hitchhikers used to wave me past them—it was still everything to me, my metaphor for success. Almost every time I got into it, I prayed, "Dear God, let me for the rest of my life make ten thousand dollars a year so I can pay for my car. That's all I ask, God." Just supporting myself by performing has always been to me major success in show business.

While I was in the Orient, Irvin Arthur had closed his office and joined a huge agency, General Artists Corporation. I went to see him to deliver his stupid little Japanese teacup and asked if he could give me a job. He laughed and said, "They have professional typists here. What you used to cost me in Ko-Rec-Type alone was my difference between profit and loss." But he must have felt guilty because he said maybe I was ready now for a Sunday talent night at the Bon Soir—the sophisticated pinnacle of Greenwich Village clubs—in a basement. That became my one straw to cling to, so, of course, I began harassing the poor man.

Every few days, month after month, I telephoned and Irvin would say, "No, no, no, not this Sunday. Call me on Tuesday next week." And I would call on Tuesday and the secretary would say, "He can't talk to you now. Call back." So I would call back five times and finally, tears coming down my face in some phone booth, I would tell the secretary, "I am staying on the line till he comes. Why do you do this to me!"

Finally, when Irvin did pick up, he would say, "We'll probably put you on the week after next." So I would live for the week after next. When I phoned that week, he would say, "One second, don't go away"—*click*—and I would be on hold, standing there, plugging dimes into the phone—fifteen, twenty minutes' worth—until he came back to say, "Hi, Joanie, Mr. Arthur. Not this week. Keep in touch." I would start to say, "But, Mr. Arthur . . ." *Click.* It had cost me fifty cents to be rejected. I based one of my earliest jokes on that: "I'm so depressed—I called the suicide prevention center and they put me on hold."

That winter, in fact, suicide became one of my options, a way to strike back at all the people who did not appreciate me, a way to make them pay attention and be sorry. The obsession with career was turning to an obsession with failure. My parents' fears and accusations were again at full throttle—answered as usual by screamed denials and slammed doors. On one particular night my mother and father escaped from the house for the evening and I lay on my bed, wallowing in my helplessness and my rage at them for giving up on me, for being so certain that I had none of their values and was becoming a bohemian and a beatnik—the last stage before bag lady or whore. Instead of holding out a hand to me, they were confirming that I was a failure, pushing me down even deeper. *It's too much,* I kept thinking. *It's too much.*

I wanted to do something terrible to myself, expend my powerless rage on my body, so I went into the bathroom and with a pair of scissors crudely chopped off my hair. I found a bottle of baby aspirin and could not wait to take the whole bottle, could not wait for my parents to come home and find me unconscious. Then they would say, "We've got to leave her alone because we're destroying her. We're taking away her dream, and if there is no dream, she doesn't want to exist."

But I have never been able to swallow pills with water; I have to take them with food. So I ate all the aspirin along with a box of Oreo cookies and lay down on the bed with the empty bottle in my hand and shut my eyes and waited. And waited. And waited—feeling like an ass there with my hair cut off. Never try to kill yourself with chocolate, because after a while it makes you feel good again and I began thinking, *Oh, maybe things aren't so bad. Tomorrow I'll call Lenny Jacobson; maybe he'll get me a Catskills booking. Things could be worse. What am I going to do about my hair?* When my parents came home, I was in the bathroom with scissors, trying to even off my hair and pulling it to make it grow back a little faster on the left side.

Then, from my nadir of frustration, I was suddenly rocketed sky-high by another success, brought to me by the one man in New York impressed by my USO tour, its producer, John Effrat. He put me into *two* segments of his *Talent '61.* In the dramatic section I did a scene with Ruth Buzzi from *The Goddess* in which I found God. In the comedy segment I did a telephone sketch by my revue friend, Michael McWhinney. I was a woman in the telephone business office dealing with a man who wanted a plain black phone:

> Black is for a bygone era, Mr. Zigler. You are a person, and a person should have a rainbow in his life. Pick a phone from our garden of colors. This week's special is magenta magic.

In both shows the applause was tremendous and I could feel my heart lifting to meet it. But even as I stood there bowing on the stage of the Majestic Theater, satisfaction flowing through me, I understood that this was encouragement applause. When I bought my first *Actors Cues*, two years earlier, I thought that recognition, adulation, and money came inseparably in a little ball, but now I understood that the hurrahs at the Majestic were not bankable. Maybe part of becoming professional is to become cynical. As I bowed and bowed to the clapping, I thought, *If each of you would just throw up a dime, I could get my car out of the parking garage.*

Talent '61 got results. Fred Allen's former agent, Mark Leddy, who still had a little power, invited me up to his office and asked me if I could sing. I said, "Sure." He asked me to perform. Three feet from his desk, without accompaniment, I croaked out "Just in Time," which has a very small range. Leddy said, "Wonderful! I'm going to arrange an audition for you with Gower Champion. He's looking for a girl to replace Anna Maria Alberghetti in *Carnival.*"

I was absolutely beside myself with excitement, plunging immediately into fantasy, thinking, *How strange to have come full circle and be returning to making my career in theater and how dumb I was to have wasted so much time on stupid stand-up comedy.* I had not known that Mark Leddy was so old he did not have all his oars in the water and was so deaf he probably thought I was singing Mimi's song from *La Bohème.*

For this private audition I bought new Capezio shoes and a black-and-white-checked dress, had my hair done, hired a pianist for rehearsals and the audition. I must have laid out $200, which I did not have. Gower Champion had to get out of bed, get washed and shaved, get down to the theater by 10:00 A.M.—which to him was the middle of the night—just to see one girl. A union crew had to be called to open the theater for me. Mark Leddy must have carried on as though I was the second coming of Ethel Merman.

Gower Champion introduced himself. We both said, "Nice to know you." He walked back up the aisle and sat down, a dim figure three rows from the rear. I stood there alone, looking out over the orchestra pit, out over the field of plush seats and up toward the gold filigreed balconies blending back and back into the darkness. I was onstage—the chubby fifteen-year-old with the crush on Ray Bolger had been invited back—and I had the sensation that only the theater gives, the sense that I was suspended in time, my identity fluid, able to be anything I wished.

I took a long breath, geared myself for a miracle, nodded to my accompanist, and started to sing "Just in Time." After a minute the figure in the rear stood up and walked rapidly down toward me out of the dark. I thought, *Great, he wants to see me closer.* He stopped at the edge of the orchestra pit and said, "Hold it." I held it. He said through his teeth in the silence, "Why are you here? And, what's more important, why am *I* here?"

I felt absolutely ludicrous. I was surprised that I did not vaporize. I fled to the sanctuary of my ramshackle car in a parking lot on Tenth Avenue and sat still for a long time, gripping the steering wheel, fingers going numb, palms hurting, telling myself again and again, "Think of it as experience. Think of it as experience." A tension ache at the back of my neck traveled up and across my head and stabbed my right eye and I closed my eyes. "It was a long shot," I told myself. "I never thought it would happen. But go on believing. Don't care when it doesn't happen. Don't care. I can still make it. The whole business is luck. It's luck, it's luck, it's luck."

I was absorbing a sorry truth of show business—rejection is the norm and acceptance the oddity. I was learning to cut the tops off my highs and stay with the lows where the rejections and letdowns would be shallow. From that day on, depression became almost more comfortable than elation. My old friend misery was a warm, consoling coat, easily shrugged around my shoulders. But at the same time, the more I was frustrated, the harder I pushed toward that something wonderful I knew was waiting for me. I still have not reached it and do not even know what it will be—but it is there and it is absolutely stupendous.

That winter of 1961, with my life on hold waiting for Irvin and the Bon Soir, I focused an even greater concentration of frenzy on THE ACT. I knew my material was ordinary, but still thought the solution lay outside myself and I begged and cajoled young directors and lyricists to hear me and help me.

Unaware that a good comedy line is so rare, so golden, it is instantly snapped up for big money, I saved my office temp pennies and commissioned special material from young writers I knew at the B & G. When, sure enough, it was worthless, I had to pay anyway, pay for a sketch on the first woman U.S. president who is facing impeachment and saying, "Hurry up, I have only five minutes to get to Nick's Beauty Salon." One sketch I did add to THE ACT was a Peace Corps volunteer addressing the natives:

> You've all seen the bridge we just built. Fifty million dollars of American money have gone into that bridge, 3,476 tons of concrete and steel; it's 8,453

feet long. We put the bridge up for you. Now, *you* put the water under it for us.

I still thought of comedy lines as objects you pick up like shells on the beach and I went back to gathering them from other acts, from the Robert Orben joke book, even from my own head. I carried scraps of paper in my purse and like a ragpicker digging through garbage pails, I saved anything at all that seemed useful, scrawling it down, every which way, joke after joke—"I had a boyfriend named Irving Feather. Everything about him tickled me, especially his hands." It was so sad, this girl desperately scribbling whatever might make people laugh—flailing out, not knowing what direction to go, not having any taste or discrimination, not realizing you must make crucial choices in comedy, must constantly say, "This is funny, but it is not for me."

I would end up with sheafs of odd bits of paper scribbled with one-liners like bird tracks and I typed them up and repeated them aloud, over and over to myself, walking along the street, driving to Larchmont, memorizing, straining to make my little routines sound good:

> There were lots of older men at the hotel—with their daughters. I had a small room. So small I had a folding toothbrush . . . and the only thing I could drink was condensed milk. The food was awful. Flies used to come to the kitchen to commit suicide. Pygmies came from Africa to coat their darts.

But this material did not work for me because the lines had nothing to do with me and I did not believe in them. In my mouth they sounded stock and mechanical. But the next time I worked in some dump, I doggedly changed everything around and tried again.

In the spring two things happened: First, "Happy" Fanny Fields died. All my life my mother had been saying, "Be nice to Aunt Fanny. Be nice to Fanny, she loves us. You're in the will. I'm telling you. You're in the will." What did I get? Nothing. What did Bea get? A Kleenex doll. The last months of Fanny's life she was bedridden, surrounded by nurses, but with her car and chauffeur still waiting downstairs, just in case. She lay there making intricate dolls out of rolled and tucked Kleenex—Kleenex arms and Kleenex fingers. I remember a Hawaiian doll with a lei of tiny Kleenex rosettes and a southern belle with layers and layers of Kleenex crinolines. But no matter how you cut it, they were still Kleenex dolls. If Fanny had left me one, I would have blown my nose in it.

My mother and sister went to the funeral. I refused and the family was amazed, exclaiming, "You're not going to Fanny's funeral?" I could not be that hypocritical. I missed her the way a teenager misses a boil.

The second thing that happened was that finally, finally—after 675 hours on hold—I stood in a phone booth and heard Irvin Arthur say the Bon Soir wanted me for a talent night. My pulse should have shot up to 6,000. I should have wept with joy and relief. I was simply empty. I no longer dared let this be a high. Like all young performers, I was a mendicant, shuffling up to people with my tin cup, begging for a chance. By the time somebody finally dropped something into the cup, my emotions were used up by the pleading and suspense and frustration and humiliation.

The Bon Soir was on Eighth Street in the Village, entered by a downward flight of stairs into an elegant basement room, the stage along one wall, tables in the middle and, at the opposite wall, a bar always stacked with gays. People said the club was so Mafia controlled, the liquor license was issued in Palermo. Its boss was Phil Pagano, who was half drunk much of the time and once said to a singer when her accompanist did not show up, "What the hell did you people do before they had pianos?"

That night, the second I hit the stage, looking terribly young in the twelve-dollar dress with a white bib I had bought at a Grand Central Station shop, I could feel the lightness of the air, no heaviness, good air, crackly and electric. I looked at the chic uptown crowd, checked my gay allies at the bar, and went into my obscure, silly opening. I held up a piece of sheet music with a cover picture of a woman nobody had ever seen. I said I wanted to sing some old favorites, hits made famous by show business idols like the immortal Jane Green.

I got my laugh from the bar and plunged on:

> Oh, how quickly we forget. Jane Green was the first Method Israeli actress. I remember her legendary scene in William Shakespeare's *Romeo and Naomi*. She made a fantastic Romeo. But poor Jane did not have a happy life. She married a young man about town, Lamont Cranston, and he kept disappearing on her.

At a table right in front of the stage a woman yelled out, "Same with me, honey," and erupted into laughter, went crazy, rocking backward and forward, pounding the table, thumping the men beside her, filling the room with explosions of pleasure. It was Sylvia Syms, who had actually been married to the actor who played Lamont Cranston, The Shadow, on radio. From then on, whatever I said, Sylvia Syms giggled and chortled, screamed and roared, carrying the whole room with her. It was another magic night, One Fifth Avenue again, the love enveloping me, lifting me in its arms— a taste of the something wonderful that had been fading in front of me.

My parents did come, along with Aunt Alice, and afterward I went to their table and told them I was glad that they were there to see me do well. Then the owner, Phil Pagano, who never came over to anybody, came over and said to my parents, "See this little girl, she's a million dollars. You got a million dollars standing right here." My father, he told me later, was thinking in Yiddish, "From your mouth into God's ears."

Irvin Arthur was there and he came over and Pagano said, "I'll give her a week." And Irvin picked up my parents' check, which meant to them that something had gone right tonight and maybe their little fatso might be good for freebies. So I stood there beside my parents' table, everybody smiling at me, and I allowed the high to take me, sweep through me. The boss of the Bon Soir had agreed that I belonged in this business. And I so desperately wanted to believe, to let it happen, let the world be mine.

Of course, the next day the roller coaster took its dive down into frustration—which is why I have never again allowed myself to revel in anything more than the one day. The world was not mine and I was back again to waiting, back to being put on hold when I called Irvin Arthur about the promised week at the Bon Soir. I would also drop into the Bon Soir and say to Phil Pagano, "Remember me?" and I have a mental picture of him standing at the bar torturing me, saying, "I'm not sure I should or shouldn't put you in."

On one of those supplicant calls at the Bon Soir, Barbra Streisand was performing there in her first booking. The MC, Billy Daniels, a very chic black man, introduced her: "Tonight, ladies and gentlemen . . ." and Barbra appeared on the stage where I ached to be. She had been living with Barry Dennen—her Nick Clemente—a droll, gaunt-faced, struggling actor who later played Pontius Pilate in *Jesus Christ, Superstar.* It was Barry, hearing her sing along with his records, who first urged her to switch from acting to singing. After she tried out for *The Sound of Music,* she won a two-week booking at a talent night at The Lion on Ninth Street and it was there she changed the spelling of her name to Barbra.

Next she auditioned for Phil Pagano and he yelled from the rear, "Get that broad outta here," but was persuaded to hire her and she stayed eleven weeks at the Bon Soir. Terrified of the audiences, she needed to be almost physically pushed onto the stage, but Barry Dennen had an illustrator friend make a drawing of her looking a little like Audrey Hepburn in *Sabrina*, and somehow that gave her the confidence she needed. Self-conscious about her nose, she considered having it fixed, but Barry talked her out of that. Her act needed polishing, so Barry dragged a recorder to the Bon Soir and between shows they replayed her performance and criticized and improved.

Following that first booking at the Bon Soir, she left for the Circus Room in Detroit, asking, "Do you think they have toothpaste in Detroit?" When she returned from Detroit, Barbra moved out of Barry's apartment. Ages later he was waiting for a bus on Central Park West and her chauffeur-driven limousine stopped at the light. Like a Warner Brothers' movie, their eyes met. She mouthed hello and waved her poodle's paw.

That night at the Bon Soir, as Barbra's amazing voice stunned the room, I slunk quietly away up the stairs like a trespasser. If I had stayed to say hello, she would have asked me, "How are you? What's happening?" And I would have had to answer, "I'm a temporary receptionist at the Widdicomb Furniture Company." It was the horror of seeing your contemporaries getting through that door, of picking up the newspaper and seeing that a friend has a part in a Broadway show. When Barbra later became the hit of *I Can Get It for You Wholesale*, that was very hard to swallow because I was still driving into New York in my terrible car with no floor. I ached and was angry and jealous and did not understand and wondered what was missing in me and avoided her because now we had nothing in common.

Of course, I should have been saying, "I'm glad for her," and in one small pocket of myself, I was glad, because she was very talented and she did deserve it. But when I was typing and she was on the cover of *Time* magazine, I was not so altruistic that I could say, "Good for Babs." Good for Babs if she called me up and gave me a part in *Wholesale*. Otherwise, screw Babs.

By now I was calling Irvin Arthur about the Bon Soir every other day, driving him crazy. I knew the truth, that Irvin had no faith in my ability, and I simply had to wear him down. On July 1, I phoned and asked, "What's happening?" Irvin said, "Phil Pagano just called and he can use you starting tomorrow night." I was to be the opening act for a revue called "Greenwich Village, USA" and, once again, I was clearly a last-minute replacement, starting on the slowest weekend of the year, when every gay worth his salt was on Fire Island.

And once again I felt nothing. Perhaps if I could have taken the news home and exulted with my parents, I could have had the thrill, felt the unbelievability of hope realized, of having a true, professional booking for two weeks at a top, major-league club where Milt Kamen was pleased to work. But nowadays home was disagreeable, soured by the old atmosphere that they were right and I was the mixed-up one— which I guess I was, but harmless. Whenever I did find a place to perform, I would be asked about it the next morning at breakfast and I would say, "It went great. Everybody thinks I'm funny but you," turning them off like a little kid.

So I hardly mentioned the Bon Soir date. There was no way I could have made them realize what love from an audience was like, made them understand that those rare moments superseded every other piece of my life—my family, my most crushing rejections, really, my own welfare.

When I arrived at the Bon Soir for the show, I found my name—the eleventh-hour substitute—written in pencil on the show card in the front. So I started my act saying, "I don't think I'll be here long because my name is outside on the marquee in pencil." That is the whole thing about comedy—you can tell them before they tell you. The audience could never tell me I was fat if I had beaten them to it. They could not say I was single if I had already said it. And now I could tell them, "I know my name's out there in pencil—and that's funny, not sad."

All my friends came down—Treva Silverman, Rod Warren, Ruth Buzzi, Michael McWhinney. A lot of the managers I had been seeing came down and said nice things, but nobody said they wanted to manage me. Milt Kamen came with Jack Rollins, who said, "In three more years you'll be very big." It was like the warden giving me another term in the slammer. I asked him if he would manage me. He said "No."

But he was right not to want me. I know now that I was splat onstage, eighteen minutes of splat. I was all over the place. You cannot go from the "Peace Corps" to "Bride at the Airport" to a monologue I had written on a beatnik poet. You cannot go from revue humor to Jewish humor to gay humor. There was no focus, no theme. I was doing hunks that sort of worked, but had no consistent image of myself onstage—and never even thought about it. There was no core to me, nothing that made it all the same girl. I was only trying to be a funny girl—anything for a laugh, whether it fit the character or not. The minute there was no laugh, there was no me—and the audience knew it instantly.

I did all right at the Bon Soir. Not a triumph. I survived. Pagano liked me well enough and I was held over two extra weeks—my name in pencil the whole time. I was a lightweight, opening eighteen minutes in my little black dress with a white collar, still not touching the microphone, still standing there stock-still, scared to death I would be electrocuted, and too dumb to know I was a lightweight. I was very proud of working there. From then on people looked at me differently, and when I went to the Stage Delicatessen, I could sit with Milt Kamen and Orson Bean and know I had reached the Bon Soir plateau. I could say, right along with them, "Is this funny? 'We were so poor—my mother used to buy one shoe at a time.' "

12

IF 1961 BEGAN AS a pregnancy, it ended as a birth in, of all places, Chicago. The chain of events started, appropriately, at a spring medical convention in Atlantic City. My parents always took my sister and me along to meet cute, eligible doctors. Everything for me was career, but if I had found a nice doctor, it would not have been tragic. I could have had both love and show business.

Barbara and I had big badges with our names on them and walked around the convention hall from exhibit to exhibit to exhibit, where there were lots of single interns, lots of single residents, lots of single medical students, and lots of mothers with their daughters. It was like a marketplace. Barbara and I would say, "He's cute. He's going into the liver booth," and we would go to the liver booth, hoping he would see the badge and say, "Oh, you're Dr. Molinsky's daughter." Then I could answer, "Yes, are you a doctor?" You had to be careful and find out that fact right away, because you did not want to get a salesman—that would be a whole precious morning wasted.

I was chatting with a doctor beside some fresh pathology specimens and told him I was an actress. He said, "You should look up my brother; he's an agent at William Morris." So I called the brother, Bernie Sohn, and went up to his office and he became a part of my rounds. Bernie was chubby and short. They only hired short agents. The original William Morris was about five feet six and he wanted to be the tallest. I think that's why the other agencies sprang up—MCA and GAC—for all the agents over five feet six.

Bernie Sohn was the first actual agent at William Morris I was able to get in to see face to face. Until then I had only made it to the male secretaries, who were apprentice agents learning the job by osmosis and encouraged to find talent on their own.

In September Bernie called to say that the producer and director of Second City in Chicago were coming to New York to audition for a girl. "Come on over," he said, "and I'll get you in." I had only vaguely heard of Second City but knew that a Chicago company—including Barbara Harris and Alan Arkin—were in rehearsal for a Broadway opening. And I knew that Mike Nichols and Elaine May had come out of that same group from Chicago and also Shelley Berman, who was now so successful with his telephone monologues. In later years Second City, with its offshoots, became a cradle for comedy performers, helping to train John Belushi, David Steinberg, Valerie Harper, Alan Alda, Harold Ramis, John Candy, Paul Mazursky, Linda Lavin, Zohra Lampert, Paul Sand, Peter Boyle, Gilda Radner, and Dan Aykroyd.

Wanting my mother to see me in the classy setting of William Morris and figuring the audition would be a quick twenty minutes and then we would go to brunch at Schrafft's, I took her with me. We arrived at ten o'clock and I walked confidently up to the receptionist and gave my name. The girl looked at the long sheet of names and shook her head and said, "You're not on the list." I explained that Mr. Sohn had called me in. She telephoned Bernie. He was not there that day. I could feel the tension, the humiliation, flowing through my body. I kept protesting, "But I was told to come in." Finally, to shut me up, the girl said, "All right. Have a seat. We'll fit you in."

In an agony of embarrassment, I went back to my mother. At home I had always maintained the Miss Winner facade— "Everything's fine"—and now she was seeing the truth, seeing that at William Morris I was a nothing, an amateur, not to be taken seriously—all her judgments confirmed. I told her, "We have to wait a few minutes."

We sat there watching a parade of sleek ambitious girls pass ahead of me—seemingly every actress, every revue performer, every would-be actress, every model, every hopeful between the ages of eighteen and death. When I went to the receptionist and asked how much longer it would be, she snapped, "I told you. I'll fit you in when I can. Everybody has appointments."

By one o'clock my mother's stomach was playing tunes and I could not bear the embarrassment another minute. I knew I had no chance anyway and I said, "Come on, let's get out of here. To hell with this."

My mother, who had fought my career with every weapon, smiled and said, "Don't be silly. We've waited this long and I'm perfectly content to sit here." It was the first time she had ever witnessed the humiliation I had been enduring. Perhaps, finally experiencing a little of my pain, she felt motherly sympathy. And also, underneath her disapproval of my career, maybe she was a latent Mrs. Show Business, fascinated by this first taste of that world, the glamour of girls of every shape and size, pretty girls pulled together, girls she recognized from TV ads and soap operas, all in the slick setting of William Morris. Maybe, given the chance, she would have become a major stage mother; maybe part of her actually wanted this for me.

I kept asking the secretary, "How much longer?" And she kept repeating, "You didn't have an appointment. You're just going to have to wait." From time to time some lovely known girl would rush in, saying, "I've only got twenty minutes; I've got to get back to rehearsal," or "Nat Kalcheim said to sneak me in," and in they would go. Finally, after fifty-nine girls I was sent down the hall to a conference room where two men sat at the end of a large oval table. One was Bernie Sahlins, small, wiry, intellectual, in horn-rimmed glasses, the head of

Second City. The other was Paul Sills, the director, a big, bearlike man, blond, round face, pale blue eyes, sandy kind of kinky hair, preppy, good-looking in a genius way.

The first thing that happened, the phone rang and Sahlins took the call while I stood there like an idiot. Then, when Sahlins went on talking and laughing into the phone, Paul Sills said, "Improvise something."

Improvisation was so new, I was completely flummoxed. I could only say, "Improvisation? Don't you have a script?"

Sills said loftily, "We don't work with scripts. Just describe something—anything—whatever you think is happening in this room," utterly cavalier, utterly condescending, to this last, this least, this expendable girl.

My head swam with fury. I had no chance to get this job, had nothing to lose, and years of accumulated hurt exploded out of me and my voice trembled with rage. "In this room there is a cheap ugly little man sitting behind the telephone without the manners to get off and watch somebody who has been waiting five hours. And the other man, so superior, is saying, 'We don't have scripts.' Well, I am sorry! I didn't know you didn't use scripts. I guess I was too busy doing my rounds, trying to make a living as an actress, to know what you are doing in Chicago."

I went on and on, feeling light and alive with anger and recklessness, blasting them, explaining my feelings about waiting five hours in order to be humiliated, detailing my estimate of their disrespect and discourtesy and lack of sensitivity, particularly unforgivable in two people, theoretically artists, who were running a new form of collaborative theater —and who the hell did they think they were, so arrogant. I was insane now, screaming, "I don't care about you, don't care about your goddamned show. You can go to hell and Bernie Sohn can go to hell and William Morris can go to hell!" I grabbed a glass ashtray and flung it, skidding it along the table onto the floor. Then, suddenly, I was empty. I said tiredly, "That's what I think is happening in this room."

Bernie Sahlins, now off the phone, answered, "All right, calm down. Calm down. Have a seat. Tell us about yourself." Soon everything became friendly and they asked me about my background and why I wanted to act, and they told me about Second City. I left thinking, *They're crazy. They're nuts.*

The next day I received an incredulous call from Bernie Sohn. Second City had picked me! The instantaneous flash in my mind was not career or breakthrough, it was an image of that procession of sleek, thin, groomed, right-looking girls striding past me and my mother. And then I realized that, for once, being a stubby packet of fury had paid off. I had probably been chosen precisely because I stood out from the pack, both in looks and, God knows, in behavior. This was confirmed in one of the early rehearsals in Chicago when Paul Sills demanded, "What happened to that fire we saw at the audition?"

Second City treated me like an adult and simply said, "Here's a ticket to Chicago, here's the address of Second City, report backstage at 7:30 Tuesday night." Nicky put me on the overnight sit-up train on Monday—a girl burning with self-doubt and insane determination. Fortunately, he kept our farewell cheerful with lots of talk about writing and staying in touch, and I think we both knew I was at last going out on my own, my first true attempt at independence with no place for him.

I arrived in Chicago September 12 with fifty dollars, a contract for five months, an Equity card, my USO luggage, and the name of the North Lincoln Hotel, which was across from Second City on Wells Street and hardly anyone's first stop getting off the Twentieth Century Limited.

I found my way through the big, strange city to the hotel, checked in, called my mother to tell her my room number, put down the phone, and began to cry. I cried and cried and cried.

Only that night in Boston after the Show Bar had I ever cried like that—wracking, heaving, convulsive sobs that went on and on till they hurt, and still I could not stop.

At the time I thought they were mysterious hysterics for no reason. Now I understand that I was not ready to stand on my own two feet, not ready to leave the security of Larchmont and lose the rich-bitch facade I could hide behind after each failure. I was not ready to arrive in a strange city with nobody pampering me, nobody meeting me at the station, no pocket full of phone numbers. I was not ready to deal with loneliness, to be without Nick Clemente. I still needed my lucky person the same as Barbra Streisand had needed her little friend always there during *Seawood*, somebody who knew Barbra was the best, who knew it even more than Barbra did.

I was lying facedown, the wet pillow clammy against my hot cheeks, fear rancid in my stomach, as I went over and over in my head my appalling predicament. With improvisation only a word to me, I was a replacement in a professional, ongoing company which existed only to improvise. This was not the cozy USO tour—six friends onstage crossing their eyes at each other when the audience did not like them. There was no cocoon here. At last I had, so to speak, followed my trunk to the Westport summer theater. I had devoted my life to getting to this point—worn blinders to blank out every-thing but career—fought with my family for this moment, lived in my car and bathed at the Y to be here. After saying for three years, "I can do it! I can do it!" I could not deal with being accepted, with being told very coldly, "Okay, do it." I was panicking, feeling, "Wait a minute. This should not be happening. Something is wrong. They should be rejecting me."

At 7:30 I reported to Second City, going through the main room of tables where 150 people could sit and drink coffee and soft drinks and eat pastry, past a small stage against one wall and into a narrow changing room behind. I said,

"I'm the new girl," and was introduced to the other actors—Avery Schreiber, Bill Alton, Hamilton Camp, Tony Holland, and Del Close—everybody in their twenties except Bill Alton, who was maybe a little older. Nobody said, "Welcome to the cast." They just nodded hello and told me to watch the show.

It was divided into two parts. The first consisted of a series of scenes which were presented as spontaneous improvisations, but, in fact, had been developed and polished during rehearsals. Most of these scenes had originated in the second section of the show, which, introduced by Bill Alton, was truly the ad-lib section. He came out before the intermission and announced that those who wished to remain should call out topics for improvisations—like "rowboat" or "Greek vase" or "penny-wise and pound-foolish." Then, after the intermission, the cast came back and ad-libbed sketches on a rowboat, Greek vase, etc.

I joined the show the next night, going onstage very tentatively in a scene called "A Nation of Sheep," which was the title of a big book that year. Hamilton Camp gave a takeoff of a Hitler speech and I was in the five-person crowd that went *baa, baa, baa* at the end. Before the second, spontaneous part of the evening, the company went up some stairs and through a doorway broken into an empty house next door. In a gloomy room—one bulb, I think, and some broken furniture—they stood around and paired themselves off for the improvisations. I did not say a word to anybody. As though I was unimportant—invisible—nobody said a word to me, nobody looked at me. I just watched, all my terrors full upon me, feeling a loneliness and embarrassment which made me ache, made me want to race out of the room. I remember that, to keep myself there, I held onto an old bedstead.

Three nights later, before the show, Bill Alton asked me to be in a black-out scene he had been doing with Barbara Harris. I was so grateful, saying, "Oh, God, yes. Thank you." The piece was a husband packing his suitcase in a fury, and

Bill told me to keep saying, "No, George, don't," and make up promises: "No, George, don't. I'll cook steak every night. No, George, don't. I'll let your mother come live with us." Eventually when George put down his shirts and moved to kiss me, I should whine, "No, George, don't." Blackout.

I soon realized instinctively that these men would be perfectly content to let me fill in the secondary slots that needed a prop female, let me go on saying, "No, George, don't," while I slowly withered and eventually died. I could see that they regarded Second City as a male art form, that they did not want a girl pushing in and saying, "I can do that scene." A girl who preceded me into Second City, Mina Kolb, once said, "A man almost always instigated a scene, so you had to make your ideas seem like somebody else's. It was like playing with a kid."

I could also see that, as somebody's girlfriend, I could move immediately into the group in a very feminine way, soft in the middle distance. But I was not their typical Second City girl—compliant, very pretty, uninterested in being funny, uncompetitive. To them I was a New York stand-up comic who was not anybody's sex object.

Except when working, I was entirely alone, silent and anonymous, eating sandwiches and dry cereal in my hotel room with milk kept cool in water in the washbowl—while the rest of the group was a social community, doing things together on days off and gathering for coffee after the show. Their refusal to accept me as an equal was even harder because they were bright and educated—and I desperately needed a group, a family, needed love and approval and recognition, needed more than ever the emotional support that had never existed in Larchmont. I called home every day and pretended everything was great—and then I called Nick Clemente and cried.

But after a while I also noticed that there were some stars in the company and some not-stars. I noticed that certain people always improvised with the same partners and certain people were more friendly with the director, Paul Sills. I realized, *here we go again:* There was a pecking order and I was going to have to make my place in the pecking order. And I could see that the way to do that was in the ad-lib improvisations after the intermission.

I saw, too, that nobody, not even Bill Alton, was offering, "Hi, new girl. Let me help you into the improvs." I could not exactly blame them. They did not want to look bad with a floundering, untested person who was writing in her diary, "I can't stand the frustration of being nothing onstage. I just can't improvise. The producer, Bernie Sahlins, said I am playing for laughs—well, well, that's a surprise."

For two weeks I built my determination and struggled with the improvising in the afternoon rehearsals. Finally, I began to get the hang of it. One night, during the intermission, somebody in the audience called out, "farmer and a hooker" as an improv request. Upstairs in the dim room, my heart pounding, I marched up to Bill Alton and said, "Let's you be the farmer and I'll be the hooker." To my amazement, he smiled and said, "Okay, I'll be coming to your room."

Onstage, Bill spoke first, saying, hot and bothered, "I shouldn't be here. I'm a happily married man."

I answered, without thinking, my fear suddenly gone, "Everybody has problems, mister. I understand. A lot of my customers are married men."

"Yes," said Bill, handing the initiative back to me, "but I have two wonderful children."

"I have two also," I said. "Plus one on the way," patting my stomach. In pantomime, he showed me pictures of his children.

I had none, I told him, because my wallet had been stolen

—but I had a tattoo on my thigh. "Actually, I like the tattoo better," I said. "If I flex my muscle, I can make my kid dance."

On and on we went, gently jousting—my mind going *click, click, click*—like doing a puzzle in a flash, knowing instantly where to extend the line to the next dot. I was astonished, electrified, relieved—absolutely thrilled. So *this* was improvising, and it was inside me. It was, on an acting level, all the mind games I had ever played with my friends—doing top-it with Treva Silverman, building higher and higher on each other's lines. I was going to be *fine* in Second City!

Now Bill Alton was forcing the scene to some finish we had not yet imagined. He said, "Well, let's get started," and began unbuttoning his shirt.

I said, "Fine," and just stood there—which threw him another curve.

He said, "Aren't you going to get undressed? It's a hooker's job to get undressed."

Faster than thought, the ending popped out of my mouth. "I don't know what kind of women you deal with. I always stay dressed when I hook my rugs. Now, what do you want? A six by ten? An eight by eleven? We're having a special on throw rugs."

The lights, controlled backstage, blacked out. The audience booed delightedly. We had successfully led them down the garden path and I was pleased.

I began to feel at home in Chicago. I liked the city—the elegance of Michigan Avenue, the many parks, the Near North Side which was a clean Greenwich Village, the beauty and richness of the Lake Shore Drive area, the funky restaurants, and the pomp of the Drake Hotel and Ambassador East. I could not get over the idea of liquor being sold in drugstores. I realized that the people had the same sophistication as New Yorkers, but were a little self-conscious about not *being* New

Yorkers. They were always saying things like, "We have a symphony orchestra too."

One day in September Avery Schreiber telephoned and suggested I rent Barbara Harris's sunny one-room apartment a block and a half from the club. I did, and created my first, entirely personal nest where I could feel safe. I painted the walls white, the bathroom green, the tub pink, bought pretty curtains, a green bedspread, striped pillowcases, and plastic shower curtains with pink flowers—which was poetic justice. When I did the office temp job at the plastic curtain manufacturer, I kept saying to myself, "Ugh. Who would buy these ugly, cheap things?"

In a way the apartment was my main companion. I am a great putterer and filled hours cleaning, washing out clothes, doing my nails, writing letters, and, like Marion Davies, working on jigsaw puzzles—while singing along with my eight-dollar Admiral radio, bought in a Goodwill Industries store. I inherited Barbara Harris's window box with geraniums and her gray Siamese cat with wonderful blue eyes. I loved that cat. It would sleep on my stomach and purr and was happy to see me when I came home. Don't tell me it was not. It was a living thing that liked me.

The rehearsals began to go better and one evening Tony Holland asked me to dinner and we became friends. I think he realized I was not what the others thought—just a pushy New York comic. He once told a friend I was very sensitive and had taken the trouble to understand him with all his complexities and complications. And we had the same humor. The first time I went onstage for "A Nation of Sheep," I stumbled and nervously grabbed Tony's arm. He said, "Don't touch me. I'm a bleeder." I loved that.

For me, Tony was luck beyond luck. He was Second City's boy, the heavy talent, one of the originals who had known Paul Sills as a teenager and been with him at the University of Chicago when the whole idea of spontaneous theater was

taking root. He was the brilliant intellectual they all aspired to
be. Today his idea of fun is writing a play telling what happened after they cut down the trees in *The Cherry Orchard* and
he has never, ever owned a book that had an illustration in it.
He mentions names that make you ashamed to keep asking,
"Who is that?"—so you only ask every fourth time. I was in
shock that he wanted to be my friend. It was like Lenny and
George in *Of Mice and Men.* But paired with him I moved
rapidly to center stage in the group. He was like Louis XIV
coming down and saying, "You are now Madame de Mainte-
non."

Also, however, I was luck for Tony. Onstage we were a
perfect combination—opposites who worked like wildfire and
had virtual ESP. He was wiry with thinning red hair and very
intense—a sort of intellectual Ichabod Crane who spoke
slowly, deliberately. I was soft and mushy-looking, but fre-
netic onstage, chattering like a Gatling gun. Tony was the
mind and I, with my dumb, earthy remarks, was the body.

Lines rushed from my mouth as though some other person was in my head reading a script—and Tony would instantly know where I was headed and leapfrogged me to a new
plateau and I could follow him, going higher, our minds
meshing, resonating, linked by a wire of ESP. The experience
was more exciting than acting in a play because we were
creating this ourselves that second. And when we hit a perfect
moment, everybody felt it, and Tony and I and the audience
were like tuning forks vibrating in sync. I felt lit from within.
Totally intoxicating!

My act—the way I work today—originated in those Second City improvs. I learned to short-circuit thought and hitch
impulses directly to my tongue. I learned that whatever comes
out of my mouth suddenly, on its own, will be new and star-
tling to everybody, including me. I learned to have supersensitive antennae tuned to the audience and follow the laughter
wherever it leads, improvising deeper into spontaneous, lucky

premises, building them, honing them, no matter how outrageous.

That is why on virtually all my free nights I perform in
small clubs in Los Angeles where I feel free to cut loose, let
my mind go in any direction. I tape-record my shows and
write down the ad-libbed passages that worked and use them
again with new variations. If people keep laughing through a
dozen performances, I include the new lines in my basic act.
Most of my material, certainly the best of it, began that way,
blurted out full grown.

To keep up with Tony—and the intellectual Second City
audiences—I went to the public library and read right
through the Greek tragedies, Restoration comedies, Russian
novelists, English poets. At night in my little apartment I
reread *War and Peace, Hamlet, Love for Love, The Magic Mountain.*
When an improv was not working, Tony and I could switch it
into the style of Congreve or Euripides: "Behold the daughter
of Meyer who has crossed the brown and flattened waste
following Apollo to rejoice in the bosom of the City of the
Seconds." We got 'em with footwork.

Also, at Second City we worked with the reality of the
moment. In a play, if water starts dripping through the ceiling
and hitting you on the head, you continue with Bernard Shaw.
In real life you would stop what you are talking about and
discuss the water and deal with it, and at Second City, whatever your partner did, you used it, responded to it, as you
would in real life. That is one reason I talk to people in the
audience—so I can work off them as a piece of reality, use
them to trigger inspirations, make them into my Second City
partner, my Tony Holland.

I also learned the value of knowing your audience. I read
all the Chicago newspapers to learn the local references and
phrases which would get instant recognition and make those
smart, sophisticated people feel we were all on the inside
together. I have carried that on into my act today, trying for

jokes that will create the same images in every mind in the audience—taking off from universal clichés. That is why, for instance, my jokes about southern women work. There is the instant image of Scarlett O'Hara, hoop skirts, the slow, sugar helplessness that conceals a shrewd mind quick as a Venus's flytrap. I say:

> Southern women are so smart because they know how to play the game. They never cook, but they don't say, "I won't cook." They say, "I'd love to cook but I never know how to read a cookbook. The book said separate two eggs. I put one on the chair, one on the floor. Did I do wrong?"

But beyond everything else in importance, I finally in Chicago came to *believe*, totally—for the first time in my life— that my personal, private sense of humor, my view of the world, could make smart adults laugh. On that Second City stage I was applauded by college-educated, nongay audiences who truly thought I was funny and laughed *with* me—like the grown-ups on my father's fishing trip. Those improvs washed away the scars of the Paar show and the awful times in front of terrible audiences when a personal line, sneaked in, was honored like a memorial wreath—with a moment of silence.

In Chicago I felt a comedy ego beginning to grow, which gave me the courage to begin tentatively looking into myself for comedy. Though I did not take my first toddler steps as a comic for another year, I was really born as a comedian at Second City. I owe it my career. No Second City, no Joan Rivers.

Our audiences came repeatedly to see certain actors— like a court theater—so you developed a cult following. Every night I would dress at home for the show, putting on the Jax dress bought for me by the management—black silk, sleeveless, with a midcalf crinoline skirt. Then, all made up, I would walk to the club and it was nice to arrive a little late and hear people say, "There's the girl," as I walked through the lobby, eyes down, very modest.

The Second City actors were Chicago's darlings. In what was actually a small town, it was *the* revue, admired by the critics, interviewed on the radio shows. Anybody in the theater and the arts coming through Chicago was taken to Second City to see what the new group was doing. Melvyn Douglas, touring in *The Best Man,* was there one night—the grand, statesman actor, looking a hundred years old to us and probably only fifty. We met him afterward—and I reported to my diary: "Even though he accepted us as his equals, I still stammered and stuttered and felt my nose was shiny and that my brown roots showed, etc., etc., etc."

One night Tennessee Williams came to see us during the out-of-town tryout of *The Night of the Iguana.* All of us were brought out to Tennessee Williams's table to meet him and when I came, he stood up—this rather shy man with a great, flamboyant courtesy, a southern charm which is so wonderful, whether or not it is fake. He invited us to come watch rehearsals, which I did several times, mesmerized to see a big, lumbering play being redone—whole chunks pulled out, speeches rewritten, direction changed—until it became a hit on Broadway.

I had no concept till then of the incredible dedication of somebody like Tennessee Williams. I had always thought he sat down in his room and wrote *A Streetcar Named Desire* and brought it to somebody who said, "This is very good, I'll produce it." But here was this Pulitzer Prize winner, who had already given us Blanche DuBois, working like a beginner with his first play. After all the pretty parties, all the nice manners, all the big limousines that he pulled up in, there he was day after day in the theater cutting and fixing and pruning and changing and switching and worrying, sitting, hunched forward, making notes in the low box stage at right, where Lincoln would have gotten it.

I know now that *everybody* in the arts is forever a beginner. Experience counts for a great deal and very little. Every night onstage I feel I am starting from scratch, still not quite sure what I am doing and where I am going, thrown by the simplest thing that goes wrong. And there is that marvelous remark Jack Benny once made to me about performing in nightclubs. He said, "No matter how big you are, you have to get to the stage through the kitchen."

Tony Holland and I developed a scene which ultimately became a Second City classic. It was called "Model and Tailor" and originated one night in the improv section of the show when somebody called out, "Stitch in time saves nine." Tony remembered an ad in *Vogue* magazine showing a model standing on a pedestal while a man on his knees hemmed her dress. It worked brilliantly and we began expanding and opening it up in afternoon rehearsals. We tested it on audiences by slipping it in among the improvs. After the show, over coffee, we talked ideas together. Weeks of inspiration and honing created a tight and charming and seemingly spontaneous ten minutes.

The model, Rita, standing on a chair, starts out very snippy, impatient, saying, "Mr. Farber! It's 5:30!" In a while she confesses it is her thirty-third birthday. When Mr. Farber says, "Wonderful," she says, "I'm single. You know what that means around my house? It means I should better be dead, that's what it means. Nobody thought it was going to happen to me. I was picked Queen of San Pedro High—did I tell you that? Everybody figured I'd marry a doctor. The years began to pass . . . I figured I'd marry a lawyer or a dentist. I hit thirty. I said to myself . . . a CPA. Woke up this morning, I said to myself, 'Rita, you're thirty-three, you're single, face reality' . . . anybody, Mr. Farber. He walks and talks, he's it for me."

Mr. Farber tells Rita, "That's defeatism. You have a great future in the Lady Ida line. Age should have no terrors. In a couple of years you can model stylish stouts."

Rita tells him her former boyfriend might have made a good husband, but then she found out he already was one. She says models are treated like tramps, but do have souls— "They tickle us, we laugh, prick us, we bleed."

"That's Shakespeare," Mr. Farber says.

"It's *The Merchant of Venice.*"

"I didn't know you were such an intellectual lady."

"Verily."

Mr. Farber says, "I can guess where that's from."

"Same play."

On a first-name basis now, they talk about Meyer Farber's wish to be in the Peace Corps and his love of dancing—he has won five free lessons at the Fred Astaire studios—"Only in America could something like that happen."

He loses a contact lens and she finds it, saying, "Are you *lucky!* I had a friend once who spent two weeks on her knees . . . dropped it on a fuzzy rug." In the end he asks her to dinner and she accepts—"But you'll have to let me treat you to dessert, being it's an event"—so the audience is left thinking that just maybe . . .

Rita, the loser girl who cannot get married, was obviously a version of myself, and I played her again and again in Chicago, exploring her desperations in many incarnations in improvs and scenes. Though I did not imagine it then, she was to become my stand-up comedy persona, evolving into the urban, ethnic girl who is saying, "I'm not married and life is awful, so what's wrong with me?" That girl, in turn, has today become the loser girl who managed to get married and is saying, "Why is everything still wrong?"

Rita is the secret of my success. She works because people recognize insecurity and respond to it because everybody is like me, just a lot cooler than I am about their self-consciousness, their certainty that they will be found out at any moment.

I first realized that Second City was going to be a continuous battle when I discovered there was a new show every couple of months and everybody was competing to have their scenes included. Getting my scenes into the new show became a nightmare. In November I wrote in my diary, "I'm so sick of the constant pushing needed in this business; maybe I'm not right for it."

That same November Paul Sills left. He had never complimented me, never really dealt with me, just decided, "She's crazy, leave her alone." But it was Paul Sills who walked over and said, "You and Tony will be doing the first line, last line improvs from now on," and walked away. That was the premier spot in the show. The audience called out a first line and a last line and the style—Shakespearean, Old English—and it was up to the two actors to make a scene that fit between the lines.

The new director, who came out from New York, was Alan Meyerson. I knew for sure he had no sense of comedy when he put us to work on a Pierrot, Pierrette scene that was hopelessly stilted and formalized—and finally, after weeks of stupid work, the whole group rebelled. I had no respect for him and I doubt if anybody else did. We were like soldiers just arrived back from six weeks of combat, sleeping in swamps, and here was a new first sergeant telling us to clean our guns, telling us what was wrong.

Of course, he immediately hated me and pretty soon brought another girl, Irene, into the cast and soon it was, "Joan, let Irene do that with Tony" and "Joan, you don't do that anymore. Let Irene go into that with Bill." He even put her into the first line, last line improvs one night. And all this time she could not cut it. I decided, *If they want the new girl, they got her.* I withdrew from the show. Then there were a lot of phone calls from Bernie and the cast. I came back. Later it became clear to me that Alan had not been pushing Irene entirely for art's sake. Irene and he got married.

He was forever changing my place in the show and taking out my scenes. For example, when the lineup for the new Second City show was posted, "Model and Tailor" was not included. The paradox of my life is that I can be very pushy, but at the same time, I am truly timid. Making a fuss is against my nature. I did not go to Alan Meyerson and Bernie Sahlins with guns blazing the way I would now. It was tears running down my face and my eyes staring down at my fingers twisting each other as I said through sobs, "Alan, I have to talk to you. I just don't understand why 'Model and Tailor' isn't in the new show. I don't understand what you're doing. It's been working every night. It's not fair, Alan, it's not fair. Obviously, you must not need me. That's fine. I'll just go home. I'm giving two weeks' notice tonight." And I would be dying inside because the hurt was so tremendous.

I was not battling just because I was ambitious. In that rarefied, intensified atmosphere, all I lived for was Second City and what was happening on that stage every night. They were taking away my entire reason for being in Chicago, for being alive. When they took that stage away, there was no me left. And I had to fight for my rights with every weapon I possessed because I was alone with nobody to say, "Leave her alone, she's very talented" or "It's okay, she's Joan Molinsky from Larchmont." Second City neither knew nor cared that I was a person who had gone home at night to a beautiful snow-covered house with black shutters and a circular driveway. There was no photo mural of Tara over my bed.

Whenever these uproars happened, Alan and the producer, Bernie Sahlins, would tell me, "Calm down." And there would be long talks in which I poured out a list of real and imagined grievances 5,000 miles long—and then "Model and Tailor" would not only be in the new show, but placed just before the finale and be a huge hit, getting marvelous reviews.

Of course, when the scenes I had fought for were hits— when I was right—I wanted congratulations. I was hurt when the cast was not thrilled. I saw myself as noncompetitive and constantly a victim. In truth, of course, I was one of six major egos, each of them certain they were God's gift to American drama and sure their scenes were the best. Alan Arkin, one of the earliest members of Second City, has said, "We fought tooth and nail. The stage was a battlefield."

If I was obscenely pushy, that is what drive is—wanting the impossible, wanting it all, never knuckling under to an obstacle, pushing till you get what you want. I wanted to be a star, and J. Sondra Meredith at twenty-eight was not a team player. If I ever become somebody who stops fighting for my place in the spotlight, I will be finished. Let us not be sentimental about this. That is what reaching the top and staying there means in this business—*and* in the automobile business *and* the garment business *and* in politics.

If anybody is tempted to think, *Poor Joan Rivers, so insecure, so driven, so unhappy,* do not bother. Be glad for me. Thank God I am driven. Being driven is my energy source. It is my fun. I was having fun crying back there at Second City. I have always liked a good fight—your adrenaline is going and you are in there sparring and punching, especially if you have right on your side and you think, *We're going to win this.* I believe that where there is action, there is movement, and those ripples will eventually produce something positive. If I ever stop living in an Italian opera, if my life ever becomes steady and even, I will go crazy with boredom, become as fat as the Ritz. I am addicted to drama.

In December, to reassure myself and rebuild my self-esteem—and make some extra money—I performed twice at a sophisticated little Chicago nightclub called the Gate of Horn. The bright audiences liked me and doing my act was like a fix. It rejuvenated me, made me realize the whole world was not Second City, and let me be alone on the stage, soaking up *all* the love. In Second City's head I had committed a major sin. The inner group of Second City was very upset because they thought I was commercializing my art, cheapening everybody's image. A single! At a nightclub! But I needed that thirty bucks—it bought my perfume, because even in those days I liked Joy.

They put me down when I actually cared about the money and how much. They made me ashamed that I wanted to move forward, that I wanted to be a star. During my era Second City casts had no background of struggle in the theater. They had no terror. They had never been slapped down and told, "You aren't good." Still in their twenties, they were receiving a hundred fifty dollars a week, a lot of adulation, the title of artists—and they thought the acclaim was their due.

The core of the company had sprung full grown from the brow of the University of Chicago, where there was no theater program. Most of them had never intended to be actors. Their high calling was an intellectual, satiric theater, so pure and elevated it was separated from show business. To them, whatever came to Chicago from Broadway was passé and tired. Rodgers and Hammerstein were too commercial, a joke. Ethel Merman was raucous. Lucille Ball was beyond contempt—low class, loud, pushy, not for them at all. Their taste was an original German record of Lotte Lenya singing *The Threepenny Opera.*

They were always accusing me of going for laughs. "Too jokey, too jokey," they would say. Avery Schreiber also did not come out of the University of Chicago, and, when he was starting out and desperately trying to find his way, he was in a scene with Bill Alton and Tony Holland, who were golfers. Avery walked onstage playing a priest and said, without thinking, "I'm here to bless your balls."

The audience howled and screamed, and the cast never quite forgave Avery—or the audience itself, which should have gasped with shock. The moment punctured Second City's lovely self-image—a band of intellectuals entertaining highbrow audiences interested only in elevated, pristine comedy.

That whole Second City intellectual snobbery made me furious—their contempt for comics in general, their scorn for me in particular because I had actually played strip joints. When Dick Gregory, at his height as a black stand-up comic, came to see the show, they were all ho hum. I was the only one interested and spent a whole evening with him, going to a party at Hugh Hefner's mansion and then out to hear some black comics. He had just met Eleanor Roosevelt and kept talking about how she would not have had anything to do with him six years ago when he was a chauffeur.

The anger and bitterness in him were so great, you could see he would not last long as a comic. He could not keep himself from making a statement—and you cannot make statements through comedy. Your anger can be forty-nine percent and your comedy fifty-one percent, and you are okay. If the anger is fifty-one percent, the comedy is gone. Comedy is anger, but anger is not comedy.

No doubt, the Second City management basically considered me a troublemaker and, left to themselves, would have put me on a train to New York. But the Chicago audiences liked and understood me—and fortunately theirs was the definitive vote. Management had to acknowledge me, and in the midst of all this unpleasantness Bernie Sahlins, the producer, offered me a year's contract, which I refused. I just did not know whether I could stick it out that long.

I have always had this battle to be taken seriously by the show business establishment. The head of the William Morris Chicago office checked out the new Second City show, in which I was a leading actor—a professional performing first-class material. Afterward he came backstage and said to each person, "We'd like to represent you. Would you come up to my office?" He did not say anything to me. I did not fit into any of his female pigeonholes. Clearly, I was not an ingenue or a singer or a dancer. I guess he did not see a stand-up comedian on that stage. Or a comic actress. Maybe he did not realize I was acting, maybe he figured, "That's just Joan, being Joan."

I think the show business establishment to this day has been confusing me with my stage persona, seeing me as common clay and too much clay for them. That is my paradox: The common touch has won the public, but makes the establishment nervous. They believe I really am that woman on-stage, and how could that loud, coarse woman have acting talent and range, which requires artistry—which, in their opinion, I clearly do not have. Hollywood does not know what to make of me. No movie studio can figure out how to use me. Socially, I am an outsider. *Interview* magazine gave a *huge* party and at the door they handed out the latest issue to all the guests. The cover was a big drawing of my face and the lead story was on me. But they did not think to invite me.

In Chicago I would have given anything to have had a beau. I am not a solitary person. A boy who joined the cast, Dick Schaal—he later married Valerie Harper—liked me and we dated briefly. When Tony Holland and I went to see Melvyn Douglas in *The Best Man,* we had coffee afterward with the stage manager, a friend of Tony's. "Very attractive," I commented to my diary, "but I'm not for him. Bill Alton says winners scare me and I guess he's right." I still was not sure I was a winner and maybe they would find out I was a loser.

In December I gave a party in my apartment for the cast and their friends. After they left, I stayed up to clean my one room. At 6:30 A.M., just as I was going to bed, the phone rang and it was Nick Clemente. He was in Chicago, following his parents, who had moved to California.

Nicky stayed with me a week. Then, while I was doing a show, he left after washing all the dishes. I was very lonely—and relieved. The companionship, pretending the spark was still there, had been wonderful, but we both knew this was the end—and I felt terribly, terribly guilty. And sad.

That chapter was closing—the B & G, Harry Brent, the Adventurer Motel, those wars we had shared, the pain. Nicky had truly saved me from drowning. I would not have reached Second City without him, and now he would not be around for the good times that surely lay ahead. I knew he still loved me, but when I longed for romance, I was not longing for Nicky. I was different now from the girl whom he had put on the train to Chicago. That girl, who had grown up in a home where nobody communicated anything, let alone love, had almost no ego. At Second City, despite the battling—or perhaps partly because I was doing it on my own and winning—I had found an ego. I did not need Nicky's constant approval anymore. I was getting that from audiences and making my way alone in Chicago, paying my bills, living my life. I had become an adult.

I think Nicky, too, had realized some things. I think he had stayed an actor because *I* wanted him to be an actor. I think with me out of the way, his dream bled away to nothing. I think he understood, at last, that he had to go find his own life and not forever live mine. As a matter of fact, he went on to a great deal of success in Los Angeles. He became a major innovator in the advertising of books, introducing radio ads that dramatized scenes from the book. He became a vice-president in charge of advertising for all B. Dalton bookstores on the West Coast. He is now executive vice-president of the publishing house Price/Stern/Sloan.

During those months in Chicago I had continued to telephone my mother almost daily—a habit, a tie too powerful to sever. But gradually the calls became a pleasure, a reconnection. We talked only mother-and-daughter chitchat, never about my troubles, only my successes, and at her end there was none of the doubting, the unveiled hints, the guilt-o-grams. On the phone she could be my mother, a breath of love, of security, of the Larchmont house, of that part of myself which echoed her and which I needed to stay whole. The telephone line, I suppose, was a new umbilical cord, and my anger thinned down and my sympathy for my mother resurfaced—along with my sorrow for my father and my exasperation at their war over money which had crippled their lives.

I decided it was time to start giving my mother some good times and my father the first anxiety-free rest he had ever had. Just before Christmas, using money from my savings account—the first Molinsky savings in a long, long time —I brought my parents and Barbara to Chicago, paying for everything. I took them to dinner at the Drake Hotel, took them to see plays—*The Night of the Iguana,* Florence Henderson in *The Sound of Music*—took them to the ballet, to good stores for shopping—Marshall Field—and arranged for all their taxis and even slipped Barbara thirteen dollars for herself.

Of course, there was a thread of triumph in my pleasure. I enjoyed being in charge, proving, after all the battling about my career, that I was right and they were wrong. I loved playing the star in front of them, smiling with a becoming mix of pleasure and modesty when people in stores and on the street said, "You're the girl from Second City, right? We enjoyed the show."

"Thank you."

At Second City my family saw my reviews posted in the foyer, saw my picture in the program, saw a winner show, and heard the applause. Tony Holland came over to them. Bill Alton—Mr. Prep Respectability, a man holding an attaché case—said hello. When they left Chicago, I gave my mother some money and she looked at me and said, "You've got to get your nose thinned. It doesn't work onstage." She really was becoming show business.

Also in December Tony Holland left Second City and went to New York to make his fortune as an actor. I was devastated. I was losing my other half. "I wonder which is worse," I wrote in my diary, "to be lonely or to get very friendly with people, knowing they are leaving. *That* loneliness is the worst kind."

The day Tony left Chicago, I dyed my hair black in the tub because yet another William Morris agent, this time from New York, was coming to see the new show. If I looked different, if I was a new person, maybe he might sign me and make me a star. My hair came out black, all right, but it looked dull and awful and I decided to pour on baby oil to give it a shine. Well, it turned into a single greasy glob—like a huge, flat piece of plastic hair glued to my head. If Hurricane Zelda had blown my face off, that hair would have stuck. I looked like Prince Valiant. Again, the agent didn't sign me. He thought I had a malignant hair condition.

I began to work more with Avery Schreiber and Bill Alton. With Bill I developed a scene called "Dentist." One night in the improvs somebody called out "office party." I remem-

bered a dentist I had known in Larchmont who was pathetically sad, always pulling out pamphlets about Tahiti and Fiji,
the wonderful places he would never go. So Bill Alton played
a married dentist and I was his dental assistant, single as usual
and secretly in love with the boss.

It is New Year's Eve and after all the patients are gone,
they toast each other with spiked Lavoris and he shows her an
abstract painting he did—which she says looks like a tooth
"that needs a lot of work." He describes the exotic trips of his
dreams and she lets out the secret of her feelings for him.
Momentarily, they decide to run away together to one of
those far, romantic places—but their fantasy deflates as he
remembers that he is trapped in his marriage, and she sees
that she can no longer work there. So the scene was laugh,
laugh, laugh, sob.

On the real New Year's Eve management shortened the
program to include an extra, midnight show, and of course
they cut out "Dentist." That was a final irony, a last straw,
turning my life there irrevocably sour. That night I wrote in
my diary, "I feel so lonely when I see all the couples, the
dates, the married people. How lucky they are to be content
just being that. They probably envy me. As I left in my plastic
galoshes and carrying ten pounds of kitty litter, I heard somebody say, 'There she goes, I'll bet to her Mercedes.' Ha!"

It was time to leave Second City. Nothing more was going
to happen for me. It was time to return to New York. I had
been sending back reams of reviews to every name on my
rounds list and surely the Bon Soir would be waiting for me.
And I could always get work at the Second City company off
Broadway. My original contract with Second City was up in
February so I would wait till then, but said to my diary, "Between thinning hair and baggy eyes, I better step up my quest
for stardom. If only a star could be old, bald, and tired."

During my last show at Second City my Jax dress ripped
under the arm. I'm a great one for omens. I was right to be

leaving. And part of my bitterness is that only on this night, when it was too late, did any love finally come out. The business manager, Sheldon Patinkin, said, "I'll miss you, but even more, the show will miss you." Bernie Sahlins's wife, Fritzie, told me that people had been saying I was the best girl since Elaine May. During "Dentist," when Bill Alton and I started drinking the Lavoris, he stopped the scene, drank a toast, and presented me with a copy of one of his favorite books, J. D. Salinger's *Franny and Zooey.* I cried onstage. A person I deeply respected cared about me. And I did hate to leave Second City. It had been wonderful, it had been theater, and I cried for what could have been.

The next day, just before I left for the train, the cashier at the club came by to take the cat. I carried it down and put it in her car. I know this sounds stupid, but as the car drove away, that cat sat at the rear window and watched me all the way down the street.

13

IN NEW YORK I was Cinderella the morning after. I left Second City wearing glass slippers and my pretty ball gown and woke up the next day back in tatters. Nobody cared that I had been the queen of Second City. Most of the agents and managers on my rounds considered it an out-of-town credit and therefore meaningless. They acted as though I had been on a long vacation. It was the USO tour again—two steps forward, three steps back—only worse because I had tasted even greater success plus a little celebrity.

I moved right into my old grooves—right into the rent-free security of Larchmont. More than ever now, I loved that house. It was the place I had been young and aspiring, the place where I could be in touch with my dreams in their purest form, untouched by reality. And, now, after seeing me in Second City, seeing the reviews, seeing that I was making money, my parents changed their attitude enough to realize that I would never turn back—this was my life, good, bad, or blah—and if they did not stop the pressure, they would lose me entirely. So home became a haven, a pleasant place to rest, a throwback to my girlhood when my mother was always there for me.

Now my mother let me sit by the tub while she took a bath and listened to me when I talked about my work and my frustrations. Now she was all mother, protecting her young, instantly loyal when I was turned down at an audition. "They're fools, absolute fools," she would say. "You should call them again." I could talk to her, too, about whatever men came and went from my life and she loved being in on the

gossip and hearing last night's stupidities and suddenly I had
a sort of comrade, instantly loyal and caring for me as much as
I cared for myself. She replaced Nick Clemente. I think my
mother loved me and had fun with me, I think I became her
girlfriend. I was the only one who called her Bea and could
tease her. She never had a real girlfriend except me.

Right away I began the grind of rounds to managers'
offices and checked in with my long-suffering surrogate
mother, Mrs. Brown of Brown's Office Temporaries. She sent
me out to Eugene Gilbert Associates. Eugene Gilbert looked
like an inflated figure from a Macy's Day Parade—big, tall and
handsome with a lot of balloon in the center. He was dating
the Ry-Krisp heiress, who was very chic, very thin, and very,
very Jewish. If a flying saucer landed on her lawn, she would
tip it over to see if it was Lenox. Eugene Gilbert owned a
polling company called What Youth Wants to Know and he
had a network of students on every college campus and
housewives across the country who did his polling. It was a big
outfit with beautiful offices on Park Avenue near the Lever
House.

NBC gave him a huge contract to find out what American
youth wanted to see on television and Eugene Gilbert figured
that actors would love to work at night, tabulating the stacks
and stacks of reports from the field. I told him I could put a
team together like quicksilver. I rounded up my friends and
my sister Barbara and the job was like a social club, all of us
sitting in the big conference room laughing and talking.

But the reports were not coming in fast enough, the poll
was falling behind schedule, and the pressure for results kept
building. To speed up the process, Mr. Gilbert had us calling
his polling network on the phone and to please him, when a
housewife stringer in Kansas said she had only three surveys,
we tripled them to make nine. Then Mr. Gilbert himself pan-

icked and took Barbara aside, knowing she was the smartest, and told her to start bumping figures. We went into high gear —if we had 500 kids answering, we added a zero and made them 5,000.

I decided to be Jackie Kennedy and promote a little culture in the nation, arrange for American youth to hear more music instead of wasting so much time on basketball and sitcoms. My job was to tabulate the results of questionnaires into the long sheets of paper which would ultimately be bound and delivered to NBC, and never, before or since, has Leonard Bernstein had such an overwhelming response to Sunday afternoon concerts. All of America wanted more of them. He owes to me a major part of his career. Somewhere along the way, I want a short note from him saying:

> Dear Joan,
>
> Without your help, it would not have been possible.
>
> > Love,
> >
> > Lenny Baby

Throughout that period, in the back of my mind was the comforting knowledge that there was an escape hatch—a door already ajar which would lead to stardom as an actress. If nobody wanted me as a stand-up comic, surely Second City in New York would welcome the best girl since Elaine May, surely I could create another "Model and Tailor," another "Dentist," and have the same sweet celebrity I achieved in Chicago—and surely that would lead to a Broadway role, as it had for Barbara Harris and Alan Arkin and Tony Holland.

So, after about a month of looking at the sealed faces of uninterested agents, I went down to the club in Greenwich Village taken over by Second City and presented myself. They were mildly friendly and said, "Hi" and "Nice to see you," and then sort of shrugged their shoulders and went back to work. I was absolutely incredulous. *I* was the one who had been angry, the one with the grudge, not they, and here I was, willing to let bygones be bygones and they did not care. What would become of me now? My Second City identity, my only source of ego, my only hope, had just been stripped from me. Chicago was meaningless to agents and now at Second City itself.

One day, when my crow's-feet looked size eleven, I met Barbra Streisand on the street. By that time she was in *I Can Get It for You Wholesale* and she was very nice to me, very effusive, and said, "You must come over to my place tonight. Adolph Green and Betty Comden are coming and Lenny Bernstein will be there."

I felt two feet tall with Barbra looking down on me from the elevation of her new world, that charmed circle where I imagined the coauthors of *Bells Are Ringing* and *Wonderful Town,* and the symphony conductor, who had no idea I was his mentor, would be delighting each other with flourishes of their vast talents. They would be kind to me, of course, making a special effort for the shopworn hopeful who was a temporary file clerk at the Olivetti Corporation. I would have nothing at all to say to them except, "We have new Ko-Rec-Type at the office." I told Barbra thank you, but I was busy.

I was stalled in New York because I still had no slot. My act was too ordinary for a sophisticated nightclub, was not slick enough for the Copacabana, was not dirty enough for strip joints, and was not ethnic enough for the Catskills. I was not like the other girls developing comedy acts, because when Ruth Buzzi, JoAnne Worley, and Joanne Barretta came onstage, audiences knew instantly they were funny because they looked funny—JoAnne Worley screaming with her boas—and then, two thirds of the way through the act, the funny girl would perch on a stool and sing something very sad.

From the first second I came out onstage, audiences were confused. They did not know what to expect from a girl wearing a little black dress and a string of pearls, looking ready, not for comedy, but a date with an aging preppy. They waited expectantly for the obligatory torch song, but heard talk they did not recognize as stand-up comedy because it was not like Phyllis Diller or Jean Carroll, who were basically doing a woman's version of men's acts. Henny Youngman used a line: "My wife said for her anniversary she wanted to go somewhere she had never been before. I said, 'How about the kitchen?' " Phyllis Diller was saying about Fang, her husband —"Fang is so unmechanical. Have you ever seen anyone try to look at the engine through the ignition hole?"—which worked brilliantly for her because it came naturally out of a stage character she had created.

The way my mind worked, if I was funny, I would already be a success. So I must not be funny and needed to find some person or thing outside myself that would open a door for me —and, of course, I was willing to try anything. One day on my rounds I was in Jack Rollins's office and met Louise Lasser, who later played Mary Hartman in the nighttime soap opera, *Mary Hartman, Mary Hartman,* but she was then Woody Allen's girlfriend and an extremely pretty Village girl with dirndl skirts, ballet slippers, and a mane of hair down her back. While we were talking, she suddenly removed two thirds of that great hair from her head and straightened and fluffed it and put it back on. Immediately, I realized the cure for my career: wearing a blond fall, I could be beautiful like Barbara Harris and Zohra Lampert, like those glamorous, seductive women prowling Fifth Avenue looking like lions.

I also knew that I really needed a new act. But I did not know how to transfer my Second City improvisations skills to a stand-up single. I thought I needed a partner to stimulate me, to throw me lines to hit back. Misguidedly, I must have

thought a written act could be a sort of partner and give me a
sense of security, be something to instigate ad-libs.

My reflex once again was to look for somebody else to
give me success—a proven comedy writer who could reshape
me, make me fit into a show business slot. I found Bill Brown,
who was writing successful revue material for Julius Monk and
who went on to write the Broadway successes *The Girl in the
Freudian Slip* and *The Wiz.* For a percentage of my future stage
income, he created an entire act for me, a talk-sing monologue using bits of Gershwin's "The Man I Love" for transi-
tions between pieces of spoken comedy—and therefore chichi
enough to be approved of by my revue friends. It opened with
a piece on the brand-new area-code telephone dialing system,
allowing America to dial anywhere—and at that time driving
everybody crazy.

> I'm sorry I'm late but I was trying to call a friend of
> mine in Philadelphia with the new simplified dialing
> system—it's really wonderful—I dialed 211 and
> asked for this hotel in Philadelphia—211 told me to
> call information—that is 555-1212, but first I had to
> dial 411 to get the code number for Philadelphia—
> which is 215. I dialed 215-555-1212 and found out
> the hotel's number was 215-341-2345. I was calling
> from 212-682-6789 and my credit card number was
> 301-245-3578. 211 dialed 215-341-2345 calling
> from 212-682-6789 charged to 301-245-3578 and a
> voice came on and said, "Congratulations, that's the
> winning number for the Irish Sweepstakes!" . . . So
> now I'd like to sing my favorite number for you,
> "The Man I Love" by the late immortal, unforgetta-
> ble Cole Porter . . . I mean George Gershwin . . .
> "Someday he'll come along, the man I love . . ."

Predictably, no doors flew open. By early April of 1962
my career was still nonexistent. But that month I heard of a

tiny club called the Showplace in Greenwich Village, run by a woman named Jan Wallman who put on revues and acts and had her talent night on Monday. If she liked you, she would book you for a week. I picked myself up and went to the Showplace. It was a brownstone with a bar downstairs where Ruth Buzzi and Mama Cass were checking coats, and upstairs the living room-dining room area had been made into a single room with a little stage at one end. There was no way I could have suspected that I was starting the last lap, that I was on my way toward jelling as a comedian.

Jan Wallman was a big buxom woman, Jackie Gleasonish, a corseted woman who looked like a clipper ship under full sail and perceived herself as a slim wisp of a girl. She moved like a young dancer, extremely light on her feet, almost dainty, like a 200-pound hummingbird. Her face was pretty, very white skin, dark hair pulled back, and she wore dark and simple clothes but big jewelry and big, wonderful hats, sometimes made all of roses. The gay guys would go, "Oh, Jan, Jan, Jan, stunning, stunning, stunning." That first time, when I found her, I said, "Hi, I'm Joan Rivers. I'm a comedian. From Second City. I'd like to show you my act." She said okay.

So a few days later, at four in the afternoon, there I was in this little, shabby, empty club doing my Bill Brown act to this big woman who is deciding whether or not I am funny and if she does, she will let me perform free.

She watched me impassively and murmured, "All right, I'll let you know."

So then the socializing began, two or three nights a week dropping down to the Showplace to see Jan, being amusing, amusing, amusing till my head wanted to come off. And then I would stand in the back and watch Jan introduce the performers and would marvel at this hefty woman who floated through the club like Billie Burke in *The Wizard of Oz*, saying to customers, "Hello, how nice to have you here," in a light, breathy voice that made Marilyn Monroe sound like a truck driver.

Introducing the acts, she appeared in front of the curtain and, rising almost onto tippy toes, she delicately lifted her hands to quiet the room and said softly, "Good evening, I'm Jan Wallman. Now, with personal pride the Showplace presents Jerry Herman's new revue, 'Nightcap.' Won't you welcome them with me," and beside her face, she winsomely clapped her hands. Afterward, I would tell her, "The show is just great. Is there any room for me on the Monday talent night?"

"No," she would breathe, "but I'll let you know when."

After nine weeks she said to me, "You can come in a week from Monday and do six minutes, but no more. There's a long line of people waiting to go on that night." After that first shot I sent Jan flowers and a few weeks later got another ten minutes. By then Rod Warren was putting on a revue in the Showplace, and every night around six I would go down there and meet Rod and Treva Silverman and sometimes Michael McWhinney, the most admired of the young revue writers. After dinner I would hit the clubs to be friendly with the Jan Wallmans of the world—go to Trude Heller's, another club, just a wave and call out, "Hi, Trude, can I come in next Tuesday night?" Seemingly, my fate now was to be the queen of the freebies.

About once a week, desperate for a paying job, I would include Second City in my nightly circuit. Feeling stripped of all pride, I would say, "Can't you use me?"

"Yeah, we'll use you. We'll use you. But not now. Keep in touch."

"Well, here I am if you need me."

Then I would hang around a while to be seen, standing in the back watching Zohra Lampert being wonderful onstage, incandescent, a light shining from her. They still needed a girl to improvise, but they were not going to let this troublemaker in. They were going to get their revenge.

For a reason unimaginable to me then, the God of comics sent me David Fitelson for the second time. In the late spring I went to the wedding of my cousin, Allan Thenen, Aunt Alice's son, and there was David. He was grown-up and teaching now at the New School for Social Research in the Village. I was grown-up and the attraction was instantaneous and tremendous—a feeling now that all along we had been destined for each other. Even while I was married to Jimmy Sanger, I had been thinking of David out there, still available.

The affair started in again that same day as if the years between had never happened. Because we were older, it was even more intense. David had moved to his own apartment in Greenwich Village and was even more a bohemian intellectual and even more attractive, and this time we were serious about getting married and actually went house hunting in Nyack.

But because we were older, everything that was wrong with the previous relationship was even more wrong. David was writing his doctoral thesis and still constantly without money—which was even more infuriating and frustrating because that made marriage ridiculous and impossible. I wanted David to fit my dream, which was *Wuthering Heights*—the two of us separate and then he returns—Laurence Olivier come back with big bucks to claim me. When David Fitelson came back, he was even poorer than before.

By summer I was at the Showplace every second or third Monday, which was a tremendous relief. I had a nightclub that would let me onto its stage and give me an audience and, even though there was no money, it kept my ego alive.

Constantly searching, I had begun to experiment with my own one-liner routines, folding them in among the revue wit of Bill Brown's act. I was still singing my little bars of "The

Man I Love"—"Maybe I will meet him Monday, maybe Tuesday, maybe not . . ." but now I went into:

> With my luck I had to wait until Friday. I was with a
> USO troupe in Japan and I met Gansa Mishpooka, an
> ex-kamikaze pilot who felt that death had passed him
> by—all his life he had trained and trained to kill
> himself and then the war ended before he got his one
> big break. Finally, he put his arm around me, looked
> at me with those deep Oriental eyes of his, and whis-
> pered ardently, "Joan Livers, you're one ruscious
> rorripop . . . I ruv you . . . why are you raffing at
> me?" And I said, "Because you're tickring me."

Almost involuntarily, in the midst of my hodgepodge of
material, I was going back to my roots, returning to bits of my
Second City character Rita, the man-hungry, loser girl, and
even adapting pieces of the dentist sketch I had done with Bill
Alton. I sang, "He'll look at me and smile and I'll understand
and in a little while he'll hold my hand and though it seems
absurd, we both won't say a word . . ."

> How could we—he was the quietest dentist I had
> ever met and I was sitting there with my mouth filled
> with little cotton hot dogs. I loved him from the
> moment I saw him with the sun shining on his drill. I
> met him at a time when I was lonely and everything
> was empty and he came along and filled a big hole in
> my tooth. I knew that all I was to him was just an-
> other big mouth, so I had all my teeth capped, in-
> cluding those on my comb.

Mainly because of my "likability," my act was getting
enough laughs to confuse me and keep me lunging in all
directions, not seeing that Rita was the right course, the persona which could turn autobiography into comedy and touch
all women—the persona I did not even know I needed. When-

ever I did improvise away from Bill Brown's revue humor, falling into Rita's coarser stance and attitudes and voice, the revue purists like Michael McWhinney gave me hell. I was destroying myself, he said. I was working much too broadly, being much too commercial.

When something of my own did not work, Bill Brown would lecture me, "Goddamn it, when you're onstage, you're a warm, pretty person. Play to that! You're not a clown. You're not Milton Berle! Stick to the good material." I was terribly torn. I longed to believe them, to have an elegant, set act I could trust, but I knew with all my instincts that they were wrong. I kept on searching, searching, searching—kept on leaving the set material and improvising, trying out this and that, searching for I did not know what. A friend told me that onstage I reminded him of a car window filled with the faces of eager, peering dogs.

During all those months, since nothing much was happening in my career, a great deal of my time and attention and energy was concentrated on David Fitelson—partly because I had plenty of free time. The only person willing to book me was wonderful Jack Segal, a small, stocky Catskills agent with a card that said JACK SEGAL, PEP SHOWS, plus two little masks, Tragedy and Comedy. He never made me audition. All he asked was the usual question: "Have you got a car?" When I said yes, he guaranteed me forty dollars a weekend for anything from four shows to none at all. Jack had contracts with various places and threw me in when a gap had to be filled, but was really using me as a driver.

There were certain places you picked up acts—in front of the Stange Delicatessen and under the George Washington Bridge. You could always spot the performers. When you saw a woman with jet-black hair, eyelashes hitting Jersey, and holding a dry cleaner's bag of orange crinoline—you figured,

"That's her. I taxied men with barking suitcases, ventriloquists whose lips moved even when they were silent, and a trainer with three tap-dancing chickens who kept telling me his ambition was to have a line of chickens equal to the Rockettes. Coming home one night, a guy made out with a singer in the backseat. Every time I had to pay a toll on these trips, I would look around and the entire rest of the car was suddenly sound asleep and snoring.

The Catskills hotel audiences were—and still are—the worst in the world. The guests paid a package rate, so everything was free. The Jell-O was free, the shuffleboard was free, the show was free. Nobody in the audience had said, "Oh, great. Joan Rivers is here. Let's buy tickets." Joan Rivers was there, just like the shuffleboard. She was something the entertainment department had shoved down their throats, and they thought the peak of sophistication was saying, "I've seen them all and I've walked out on them all."

Before the show there were always announcements: "Please, the pool equipment is for everybody. All we ask is, the last one using it, put it away. As you all know, Mr. and Mrs. Neisbaum donated—and thank you again—a new set of oars for the rowboat. Harriet Schwartz lost her wristwatch around the pool area. Anybody finding it, please bring it to the front office. Sam and Gladys Katz are celebrating their thirty-fifth anniversary, so let's give them a hand. Now the brokhe and on with the show." Then the local cantor would lead the prayer for health and happiness and peace for Israel and the whole world.

I would stand in the back of the stage at Pinkerson's Bungalows, waiting to do my Showplace act and would look out at the 200 people with sunburned noses waiting to be entertained—a flag of Israel on one side and the flag of America on the other. I knew that they *wanted* to laugh and that I was going to fail them. So I had no confidence, and when you walk onstage without confidence, never meeting the audience's eyes, they smell the fear. Everything is affected—your delivery, your look, your stance—and when I am nervous, I stutter, so they always heard an act that was too long. They got a long bomb.

A good night for me that summer was half the audience laughing. The worst was the Benz Hotel where nobody spoke English and an interpreter onstage repeated everything I said in Yiddish. It was: "The beautiful Jane Green." Silence. Yiddish. Silence. "How quickly we forget." Silence. Yiddish. Silence. "She was married to Lamont Cranston, but he kept disappearing on her." Silence. Yiddish. Silence. Every line bombed twice.

But I was learning all the time—learning to adapt to audiences. I found a kind of a solution to the Catskills. Before the audience could hurt me, I would come out and say, "Tonight, this is not going to be a comedy act. It is going to be a lecture. I am going to talk about a lot of things. My first topic is that I am single. I have very high standards. If he doesn't have a pulse, forget it. Once I almost got married. See, this is my old bridal veil. I got as far as the airport . . ." That made it much easier because a lecture is not supposed to get laughs and sometimes I did better that way. Everything was unexpected and I could force myself to talk directly to them, make contact, because there was no pressure on me to have them laugh.

I was also learning a lot of negatives that have helped me tremendously. Never trust an audience. Never think they are truly your friends. Get their attention and their respect immediately. You are like a lion tamer on that stage, either master or victim, and there is no in between. Also I learned always to leave your car behind the recreation hall, preferably with David Fitelson in it keeping the engine running. I would get offstage fast and literally climb through a window, jump into the getaway car, and be gone before they realized how much they hated me—but praying that this owner would not telephone the next owner, praying that this owner was busy reviving little Moshe who had nearly drowned in the pool.

When I was paid later in New York by Jack Segal, he would shake his head and say, "Those reports! If I ever showed you the reports . . ." At the end of the summer, even I was too embarrassed to keep on. I told Jack Segal, "I don't think I should work for you anymore."

"Thank God," he said.

Since then, I have learned that certain kinds of success can ruin you. If I had been a hit in the Catskills that summer, I would probably not be where I am today. The struggle to make it in the mountains, the browbeating you suffer, defeats many comics. They wake up at age forty and find they are Catskills comics, locked into that groove of humor, sapped of the talent and drive they need to reach the next rung. Once a cruise comic did so well on a cruise ship that he went to his agent and said, "I'm ready for Caesars Palace." The agent answered, "As soon as it floats."

By the end of the summer my relationship with David Fitelson was growing complex beyond my ability to cope. I kept struggling to bring back that first bloom and rapture. Instead, fighting with David was like a disease in my life. I was exhausted and nervous, insecure, desperate for stability somewhere in my life, doubting myself as a woman, as a companion, questioning my ability to have a relationship with a man and my intelligence for picking this man—but unable to shake his tremendous grip on my feelings.

In September some of my financial instability was eased by an infusion of quick money. I received a call from the William Morris agent Bernie Sohn, who had arranged the Second City audition. He asked me if I wanted to make five hundred dollars. It was like offering me five million. He told me to be at Roulette Records at five o'clock. Vaughn Meader's

Nicholas Amplo, 1986

That poor girl, trusting her own amateurish, naive imagination—and a bunch of cheapie photographers—actually thought such fatso, fatuous pictures *(right)* might make some agent say, "She's adorable; we can get her work." The one above was posed for and picked by my first manager, Harry Brent, who then booked me into a strip joint.

The three loves I did not marry were Nick Clemente *(above),* "Mr. Good," who nursed me through the early agonies—Michael McWhinney *(top right),* a brilliant revue writer— and David Fitelson, my first affair, who later grew a beard and two pigeons.

(Above) My mother's friend "Aunt" Fanny Fields, a rich former English music hall star, kept telling her I had no talent.

Treva Silverman, my first funny and smart friend, helped me believe I could make people laugh.

These two brilliant actresses, in a scene from *The Goddess,* are playing a mother and daughter finding God—and hoping that by finding God, they will find an agent. My mother here is Ruth Buzzi, who later hit on *Laugh-In.* The show is *Talent '61,* a yearly showcase for young talent produced by Actors Equity.

I thought this was my way into show business—revue composer Johnny Meyer and I, two kooky kids, singing his cutesy-wootsie songs interspersed with my comedy routines of stolen one-liners. We bombed horrendously in the Catskills, boring a lot of bewildered Jews.

Here, at last, is a girl who is coming of age as a comedian and doing a piece of material that worked, called "Bride at the Airport." She is calling her fiancé in New York to tell him that her plane was diverted to Denver and that she will be late to the wedding—"How am I going to get married in an hour? Well...the baggage clerk is kind of cute."

Charles Spooner

(Above) At Second City in Chicago—a theater dedicated to unscripted comedy sketches improvised by the actors— I learned to trust what came spontaneously from my mouth. From left is the 1962 company: Tony Holland, Avery Schreiber, myself, Bill Alton, and Del Close.

I was a happy girl *(left)* on a 1960 USO tour of the Far East performing, for loving audiences, excerpts from hit musicals.

A 1964 act—Jim, Jake & Joan—billed "A Spirited Comedy Trio" *(right)* brought real success, but I was miserable and quit. Jake Holmes (top), Jim Connell, and I fought, and I was embarrassed by our material.

By 1965 I was totally
feeling my deeply personal
comedy *(above)*. Suddenly
I got on to *The Tonight
Show*, arriving, right, with
my manager, Roy Silver.

All photos this page © Joel Elkins, 1986

Thrilled to be made up by professionals, I had them double-anchor my hairpiece, which once dropped onto a rain-soaked highway and was almost run over. It became part of a routine about my car breaking down—"I now had a hundred-twenty-five-dollar wig that has Firestone across its forehead!"

On *The Tonight Show* as a last-second favor to Roy Silver—a throwaway—I was desperately nervous waiting in the green room, wrenching at my fingers as I went over and over my notes on what Johnny Carson would probably ask and what I would answer. On my lap is the sleazo pink boa I always wore, hoping it would glamorize the cheap pearls and the worn, shiny dress, bought for me at Jax by Second City in 1961 and, since then, my uniform for every performance.

© *Joel Elkins*, 198•

This is the moment when my life began, when seven years of rejection and humiliation paid off, when I got past all the people who were saying I was too old and would never make it. And suddenly, I had Johnny Carson there, feeding me straight lines and laughing. At the end of the show Carson said, "You're going to be a star." I did not realize he was talking to me.

album, *At Home with the First Family,* satirizing the Kennedys, was immensely successful, and Roulette wanted to do an imitation, *At Home with the Other First Family,* an evening with the Khrushchevs. When I got there, I found Buck Henry, who was then a writer on Garry Moore's TV show; George Segal, who had been appearing occasionally as a banjo-playing singer at the Showplace; Gwen Davis, a comedy writer; and Tony Holland, who had risen high above me and was very busy as a Broadway actor. For the next six hours we all sat and improvised and wrote the script. It was terrible. I played Mrs. Khrushchev, who was asked what she thought of Red China. I said it went well with a blue tablecloth.

Ready or not, we had to cut the record at 11:00 P.M. and we all insisted we would perform better in front of a live audience. They said, "Fine, fine, keep writing and we'll get you an audience." They took us to some sleazy recording studio and we sat at a long table staring bleakly at dregs of humanity. The record people had collected from the Broadway sidewalk anybody who would come in from the rain for a Danish and coffee. Bag ladies with kerchiefs and rolled stockings, pimps looking for their hookers, hookers hiding from their pimps, drunks, drugged-out musicians from nearby Birdland. Steam came out of clothes. And odors. As the record cutting began, Buck Henry murmured to me, "It's like making jokes to a police lineup."

We were all suckers. For twenty-five hundred dollars total and five delicatessen sandwiches they got themselves a hit album that sold in the millions.

That night I asked Tony Holland how to get back into Second City. He said, "Grovel. You're not groveling enough." I went down there the next night and started to cry. I said, "I'm desperate. I'm out of work. I need a place. Please." Maybe a lot of my bitterness about Chicago really comes from those months of both silent and vocal pleading and being put off and brushed off until I had to crawl in there

that night on my knees—in thorned knee pads—the best girl
since Elaine May eating crow that was not even cooked. And
still they only said, "Keep in touch."

That rejection—and others which followed—might have
once and for all confirmed my awful self-doubts and destroyed my ego, leaving me permanently fearful and tentative
onstage. But Jan Wallman and the Showplace saved me. I was
performing there regularly and in front of those audiences—
gays, New School intellectuals, other performers—I was beginning to improvise regularly, to dare to let my mind spin off
elaborations on set lines, let myself follow the laughter and
build little comic edifices, amplified each night with new ad-
libs, which were preserved on the tape recorder. They were
not wonderful routines, but my first step in the right direction.

> You know, I'm from Greenwich Village—that's the
> only place in America where a young man on a lim-
> ited income can live like a queen. Even our traffic
> lights are different—they say, STOP, GO, and SWISH.
> The Village is famous for beatniks—you know what
> beatniks are—the only people in the world who be-
> come incognito by combing their hair.

That was when the jelling really started—the winter of
1962 when I began freeing my mouth, letting things pop out
of it, letting it bring a bit of surprise and shock into the act.

But right away there was a new problem. After each show
my ad-libs were gone forever into the air, and spontaneous
lines have a special immediacy and emerge complete, perfectly polished, the choice of words precise.

Treva Silverman lent me a reel-to-reel Wollensak tape
recorder, a huge brute of a metal box weighing forty pounds,
with a skinny handle that cut into my hand. But it started my
lifelong technique of taping every show, replaying the act,
making notes, and using the new lines that worked. So for the

first time I was systematically—though hesitantly—inserting my own voice into the act.

Then two events occurred which forever changed my comedy life. First, Michael McWhinney took me to hear Lenny Bruce at the Vanguard in the Village. Lenny Bruce had absolutely exploded into the current world of sedate comedy. Boom! There he was, an obscenity erupting among the pleasant routines of the Establishment. While Alan King complained ruefully about doctors, Lenny Bruce rubbed his derisive thumb into every social status quo and became the focus of a national uproar, denounced by defenders of the public morality, called a genius by the stew of celebrities, college professors, hustlers, writers, jet-setters, theater people, agents, low lifers, that assembled to hear Lenny use every four-letter word and deride every propriety. Nobody could possibly be neutral about a man who said onstage:

> Guys are carnal, and if chicks really knew that, I think marriages would stay together. I mean, if you knew that about guys, would you really feel hurt if you came home and found your husband in bed with a chicken? Would you really cry, hurt? And that's the end of the whole marriage?
>
> WIFE: A chicken! (crying) A chicken in our bed.
>
> HUSBAND: Lemme alone. That's all.
>
> WIFE: *Don't touch me!* You want dinner? Get your chicken to get it, you asshole, you!
>
> In New York it's illegal—"seemingly sexual intercourse with a chicken." That's the literal wording. Now, how can you even fantasize that? Doing it with a chicken. They're too short. How could you kiss a chicken? I can't even imagine that.

Personally, I had only a mild interest in this shocking comic. I was very priggish. My mother had taught me that a lady does not swear, does not discuss sex and bodily functions. As a child, I thought Kotex was a radio station in Dallas. Onstage, I never swore or did sex jokes and in private I had no vices—did not curse, smoke, or drink alcohol.

The first night I saw Lenny Bruce, he came onstage in his Mao jacket, very low-key, a small, darkly handsome man with olive-tinged skin, delicate features, and a sensitive mouth— sexy like a Valentino leading man. He slouched about the stage with a hand mike, his voice at first conversational, reflective. But the pulse of his free association gradually increased —sudden, gleeful, evil, all-knowing grins igniting his face. His words—violent, obscene, wise, astonishing, appalling, liberating—rose and fell, paused and rushed, in musical cadenzas of blasphemy.

But I slowly understood that his message, in fact, was profoundly moral—he was showing us the cruelty and pain inflicted on the helpless by the religious and moral hypocrisy of the powerful. As much dramatist as comic, he delivered his sermons in opera buffa dialogues, mimicking the dialects of politicians, industrialists, jazz musicians, judges, derelicts, do-gooders, southerners, dikes, crooks, junkies—Cardinal Spellman saying to a delegation of lepers:

> Whatta you doing? You waiting for St. Francis? Look, I'm gonna level with you right now—that's a bullshit story. He never kissed lepers. He just danced with two merchant marines and we kicked him the hell outta the parish. Put yourself in our place. Would you kiss a leper? You try to kiss 'em and they fall apart.

One sequence that night impressed me indelibly, showed me a principle that is still a cornerstone of my act, showed me that words onstage can be used to shock and keep an audience awake, but at the same time those words can be spoken because they are basically meaningless. Lenny Bruce called out:

Are there any niggers here tonight? Oh, there's two niggers and—aha!—between those two niggers sits one kike—man, thank God for the kike. And there's three spics. One mick. One hick. One thick, funky, spunky boogey. There's another kike. That's two kikes, one guinea, one greaseball, one hunky, funky lace-curtain Irish mick. The point? That the word's suppression gives it the power, the violence, the viciousness. If President Kennedy got on television and said, "Tonight I'd like to introduce the niggers in my Cabinet," and every time he saw a nigger he yelled, "boogeyboogeyboogeyboogeynig-gerniggernigger," till nigger didn't mean anything anymore—you'd never make a four-year-old nigger cry when he came home from school.

That night some of the audience, in high moral dudgeon, walked out on Lenny Bruce and among the remainder I could hear every brand of laughter—startled, emancipated, guilty. Listening to truths that had been suppressed in my brain, to insights I had never crystallized, I was thinking, *Yes, yes. That's right. Of course. Well, sure. That's it.* And also he was hysterically funny with total control of his audience. The children were lined up to be fed. I was seeing Jesus.

Also, I was seeing myself through his eyes, confronting my own hypocrisy, the way I had lived the Molinsky lie of phony riches and, while hating it, used it myself as a facade and a refuge. Sitting in that nightclub, breathing the hot, heavy, smoky, electric air, I saw the essential tragedy of my family: their pretense of wealth was so central to their lives, they could not ever admit the lie, even to each other, could never let down and laugh behind closed doors and say, "Can you believe this? We haven't got a nickel and look how we're living, and everybody thinks . . ." Then it would have been our secret joke, our shared hoax binding us all together, and everything at home could have been wonderful.

The revelation that personal truth can be the foundation of comedy, that outrageousness can be cleansing and healthy, went off inside me like an enormous flash. It is still central to my stage performance. That night I realized the importance of getting down to basics: What are we *really* talking about? Why are we embarrassed about this? If that is all it is, so what? We need to know what we are *really* bothered about, need to get in touch with our true feelings and attitudes so we can deal with them.

Hypocrisy, pretending to be something you are not, will eventually turn into lies, one lie piled on another piled on another until your life is built on quicksand—until you become my mother and my sister, who always had to be the Molinskys of Larchmont and never found a way in life based on reality, never had the foundation to be happy. That is what my act is all about. If audiences can be honest and laugh about some parts of their lives—the problems of getting older, being fat, having the child leave home, being a woman, being ordinary—then they can be honest and laugh about all parts of life.

Lenny Bruce was the turning point for me. I never again did "Bride at the Airport." I was not a bride. I never again did the beatnik poetess and the Bill Brown act. I was not a cute little revue sweetheart. But though I understood what was wrong for me, I did not grasp what was right. The truth had been clear and compelling in Lenny Bruce's mouth, but I did not realize how difficult it would be, how terrifying, to find it and say it for myself.

Personal truth means to me talking about your pain, which means stripping everything away, showing all of yourself, not some corner of your life okay for audiences to see.

But the risk is awesome. When you open yourself up, talking about things that deeply pain you, perhaps the audience will not be your friend, perhaps when you bare your soul and say, "Here are my thighs," they may go, "Yeah? So? Waiter, another drink, please," instead of "My God, my God, you've been living with *this?*" That is a *tremendous* fear to overcome.

I had been hit hard by Lenny Bruce because I was already open to him, already moving instinctively in his direction by improvising and taping and developing my own voice. After I dropped the sketches and scenes from my act, I had about ten minutes of talk and I began going more into the soul of Rita, who was desperate for a man and wore low-cut dresses and put a dab of Day-Glo paint on her chest. But though my act was rooted closer to personal experience, somehow it was still coming from my head, not from any vein of deep feeling.

The second event crucial to my career came disguised as a catastrophe. I found out why David Fitelson had been sent to me. He was sent so I could break up with him. The fireworks, the terrible scenes, the battling, finally overwhelmed the good times and we separated, but after three weeks David came up to Larchmont and pushed his way into the house and took me onto the sacred ground of the living room and swore he could not sleep, could not eat, could not exist, without me. I agreed to try again. Then, after a month of trying again, I learned he had gotten one of his old girlfriends pregnant. During the three weeks that he could not live without me, he had bounced right into bed with somebody else! He had cheated on me! Don't give me that big my-heart-is-breaking scene in my mother's living room. That was not a suffering person.

I went to see him in his workroom in the basement of his family's Village house. He was still writing his doctoral thesis and the unnumbered pages were in piles on a huge wooden table. In my fury, I grabbed the edge of the table and tipped it over, spilling and scattering those pages like leaves in a wind.

We were finished, and I have never again in my life endured such pain. I had lost the one man I had wholly loved; I had lost my visitor's pass into the glamour of his father's house on Morton Street filled with the theater at the topmost level, lost my best friend, lost a living piece of a precious era of my childhood, lost the object of an intense physical attraction, lost my girlish illusion that when I met the man I loved, my life from that moment would automatically be a fabulous romance forever. I was left now with an endless, desolate emptiness.

Because it was my last link to David, because I could not believe that we were truly finished, I continued wearing the raccoon coat he had given me as a sort of engagement present —his father's old coat from the twenties, a wonderful flapper coat. In the next Showplace performance, I impulsively wore the coat onstage and stood there, empty, lost, fighting against tears, looking through the audience in the hope that he was there. Suddenly the terrible, raw truth came from my mouth: "I've just broken up with somebody and I think I'm going to die." Right away I knew I had better follow that up with something funny.

> I went out with a professor for five years. Do you want to know the truth? I hate professors. And their wives. Did you ever go to a professor's house? All the wives do is weave, weave—"That's a nice jacket." "My wife wove it." Haven't they heard of Brooks Brothers?

I felt a cleansing sensation, the hurt being washed away. My pain had found a channel and was spilling through, flooding me with a happy hysteria, goading me to speak fast and make everything funny because at any second I might begin to cry.

Five years I went out with this professor . . . But I just wasn't the kind of girl he was looking for . . . I wore shoes . . . I took baths . . . I should have known it wasn't going to work . . . First of all, while he was engaged to me his wife became pregnant . . . So I figured he wasn't sincere . . . Do you like this coat? . . . It was my engagement present . . . But I knew something was wrong when he told me to wear it in Jersey—during the hunting season.

I could feel warmth and friendship rising toward me from the laughing, happy faces before me, could feel us sharing my relief and liberation—and my sudden exhilaration. I knew in that moment I had found the key. My comedy could flow from that poor, vulnerable schlepp Joan Molinsky, the nerd I felt sorry for, who made me so ashamed I struggled to hide her like a retarded sister, shut away in an upstairs bedroom. At last I had become hurt enough, upset enough, angry enough to expose her onstage—and in my act from that night on, the pain kept spilling and spilling and spilling.

14

I WAS NOW ON a new plateau in my life. Performing my act was my therapy. When I verbalized my unhappiness, made it funny, and everybody laughed, I had a soothing space of relief —no problems, no anxieties, just a wonderful sensation of intense, almost physical contact with a roomful of friends. My blind, groping struggle had stumbled onto its goal: an almost family intimacy with the audience, just myself alone with my confidants. The discovery of that relationship, that way of treating audiences, was everything—and ultimately gave me a career.

In November I was finally accepted into the New York company of Second City. They brought me in with an insult— put me in the same dressing room with Irene Kane, who was the daughter-in-law of Mary Chase, who wrote *Harvey*—and *Bernardine*—and who later, as Chris Chase, collaborated with Rosalind Russell and Betty Ford on their autobiographies. They told us that in a week, one would be gone. It was seven awful days for both of us and I won out. And after those days —and months—of bitterness, it turned out to be an empty victory.

By then I was living for the Showplace and was divided, unable to devote my full intensity to Second City. And I had come into the company treated like an outsider and remained an outsider, a minor member gradually shriveling, never able to connect with anybody onstage, never able to find my Tony Holland. The New York show room was so large I could never get that lift from the audience—the almost shared creation— the excitement and exhilaration I needed to quicken my mind in the improvs. Pretty soon I was staying there for the money and that is what Second City became—my office temporary—and when you work solely for money, the spark and excitement go and the audience knows.

Twice a night, after each show at Second City, I grabbed Treva's big metal Wollensak and dashed five long blocks to the Showplace to appear as a "special guest artist." I thrived on it—loved that vision of myself rushing past couples—Joan Molinsky, fabulous gal, running alone against the winter elements, carrying her heavy recorder, going into the future, toward her art. Bull! I should have taken a cab. I was not starving.

At the Showplace, speaking directly and personally to the audience for the first time in my life, I was rapidly becoming Rita, the loser single girl bemoaning her life.

> The way my mother sees things, she has two daughters that aren't, as the expression goes, moving. She is so desperate to get me married, that if a murderer called, she'd say, "So, he has a temper." When a boy does come to the house, to impress him she puts out intellectual magazines like *Partisan Review* and the *Atlantic Monthly.* She even leaves a Bible open on the coffee table and writes "true" in the margin.

I could feel within me the core of happiness which stayed untouched by setbacks. Now I could go onstage and recite my calamities to my friends, the audience, and we could laugh about them together. There was the rainy winter Monday night when Second City was closed and I was coming in for a 10:30 spot at the Showplace. I limped onto Manhattan Island in my Buick, whose gears had been giving out one by one until only low was left, the engine roaring and spewing out a contrail of black glutinous oil smoke. Just across the bridge on the West Side Drive below the Cloisters, the low gear died and I bumped over the curb onto the shoulder and thought, *There goes my career in the Catskills.*

I *had* to get to the Showplace and, if I left behind my most precious possessions, the hairpiece and the Wollensak, they would be stolen by the men who strip parts off unguarded cars. In the rain and the dark, crazed because I might miss my performance, my head playing scenes of rapists stopping their cars and yanking me inside, I started walking. The hairpiece box was under one arm, the heavy machine in the other hand, the metal handle cutting into my freezing fingers, the wet wool coat weighing 500 pounds. I counted to fifty and then put the tape recorder down, rested, changed hands. During one of those switches, my numb fingers fumbled the box and the top fell open and the hairpiece, like a dead cat, flopped onto the pavement. Before I could pick it up, a car roared past, spraying me with more water and missing the sodden fall by inches. I tenderly returned it to the box and at the next exit ramp struggled off the parkway into the Bronx. Luckily, I happened onto some cops who were nice and took me to a subway station.

That night at the Showplace, damp, exhausted, besieged by anxieties, I went onstage close to tears, thinking, *Why me?* I felt that when anything started to go well—*bam,* something else blew up in my face. If my car was lost to me, I would be back to train schedules, back in Grand Central Station waiting for the 3:25 local that got me home at 5:30 A.M. I would be back to no independence, back to calling cabs, back to my youth, standing in front of the Larchmont movie theater waiting for cabs that did not come and I was afraid to go to a phone because Mr. Martino, the cabbie, might arrive.

Onstage I immediately talked about my car, telling my confidants out in front of me what had happened, saying to them:

Tonight I was coming down the West Side Drive and I'm all dressed up because I'm going to work and I have my wig right next to me in a box—you know, to keep it fresh—and suddenly the car stops . . . So I get out of the car and stand there saying little things like "HELP! HELP!" . . . And the wig is saying things like, "Help her! Help her!" . . . Nobody stops and I'm getting frantic and I begin waving with both hands and drop the wig and a guy drives over it . . . And I begin to cry because there is $125 that now has Firestone across its forehead . . . I pick it up and the guy screeches to a halt and says, "Sorry I killed your dog" . . . He gives me $10 and drives off . . . So there I am, it's 11:30 at night . . . It's pouring rain . . . I'm walking, a lone girl, against the traffic with a dead wig in my arms . . . Nobody stops . . . They're New Yorkers . . . They think I'm filming a TV show: "Keep driving, Shirley, she's just doing *Naked City.*"

When the audience laughed, I felt my bad feelings soften and gave myself up to the lift of their laughter—and thought, *This is good stuff and it's working and I'll kill myself if the Wollensak isn't getting it.* And there was more good news. The Buick stayed by the highway all night untouched. Everybody thought it had already been stripped.

In February of 1963, when Jan Wallman booked me for a full week in the Showplace for thirty dollars, I quit Second City. Of course, the minute I left, I was sorry. I had no money and had to work at D. G. Williams Co., dressing store window mannequins, but everything was tolerable because I was in love again. My group, my surrogate family, was still the revue crowd and our father figure was Michael McWhinney. He was the one who dispensed approval, who decided if you were worth admitting to the group. Sitting at his right hand was very important. He was the Charles Manson of the revue world and I adored him.

He was very WASP Connecticut—tall, blond, ruddy complexion, wore horn-rimmed glasses that he kept pushing up on his nose, tweedy, looked like a college professor—very leather patches—a charismatic man people turned and looked at. As a lyricist, Michael was a potential Cole Porter, writing songs that were beautiful, touching, mean, original, with great internal rhymes. He had a big, booming laugh, an irreverent, caustic, very dry wit, a brilliant, precise mind, and an insatiable appetite for gossip. Once Treva and I were trying to define who was in our group and she said, "The group consists of anybody that Michael knows the sex life of."

When I met him, he was in his mid-twenties, living alone. He had been an architecture student married to an elegant lady and had two children. His parents were rich with a huge chain of cemeteries and mortuaries in California. Their children had been brought up in the business and Michael could paint a corpse as well as anybody. When Kennedy was shot and the eternal flame was installed at his gravesite, everybody in California wanted one for their dearly departed and Michael's dividend check jumped $600 a month. At Christmas, he used to send gift certificates for free burials. That was his humor.

I basked in Michael's affection and aura. I was the person that Michael, the arbiter of humor and cleverness, had chosen to adore, which gave me an identity, something to *be*, even if it was Squeaky Fromme worshiping Charlie. I loved being with him, this man who was utterly romantic, utterly aware. There would be a rose left on my car seat, flowers delivered to me, a poem in the mail, a gift in elegant taste for no reason. He was my day and night improvisation partner who saw into the subtleties and absurdities of everything . . . both of us spotting the lady in the corner and knowing instantly the same funny thing about her—or the same sad thing. Our minds were like two little kids playing telephone, shmoozing and giggling into Dixie cups connected by a string of humor and affection. My first phone call in the morning was to Michael— and even when Squeaky had been with him all day, she would arrive home and immediately call her man.

Through my father's car repossessor friend, Stanley, I managed to replace my Buick with a beat-up green Valiant, so old the headlights had cataracts. Every morning, when I did not have an office temp job, I would drive down from Larchmont to pick up Michael at his apartment at the top of Manhattan Island, overlooking the Hudson River. In his tiny office, wonderful with a show biz clutter of filing cabinets, boxes of papers, posters of his revues, he would say, "Wait, wait," and search through bits of paper on the desk. "I want you to hear this. I almost called you at four in the morning. Wait. Oh, great. Here it is."

At the end of the day we would sometimes go back to his apartment again and while he worked with a composer named Jerry Powell, I would lie on the couch in the big living room, a pillow under my head, maybe reading a book, the Hudson River and Jersey spread out in front of me. The two of them would be setting to music the lyrics I had heard that morning, Jerry at the piano, Michael pacing or lying on the floor and writing. Rod Warren would call on the phone saying, "Listen to this." To me it was show biz at a top level. They were the next Richard Rodgers and Larry Hart at work—while Gertrude Lawrence lay on the sofa.

As in my whole relationship with Michael, I was living my dream vicariously, luxuriating in the glamour of being behind the scenes, being part of an exclusive fraternity, the privileged part of show business, the cherry on the cake. Also the act of creation fascinates me. You can only sit with a blank page and wait. You cannot press a button, cannot program it. Something either happens or it does not and if it does, where do you go from there? Everything comes out of smoke and mist and nothingness, a mystical happening, something to be worshiped if I was a Druid.

At a party one night that winter Michael and I announced our engagement. The news raced all through that little revue world. A few nights later we went to see Kaye Ballard perform and saw her backstage afterward. She said, "You two are engaged?"—and was hysterical with laughter. Like everybody else, she knew Michael was gay.

I had always known it, too, right from the start, and our engagement had started as a black joke. At that party somebody had told me to get rid of Michael—"He's gay and he's going to destroy you." I told Michael and he said, "Let's get them crazy; let's tell them we're getting married." But we so adored each other that it became a sort of reality—as though by desperately, desperately wishing, we could make it real. He was as frustrated as I was—one of the few gay men I have ever known who really hated being gay and hated himself. The only thing he took pride in was his mind and his work. It was a very sad love affair.

I became involved because of the determination that churns like an engine inside me, this credo of mine that willpower and intensity can do anything, can break through any obstacle. I felt so much masculinity in Michael, felt so physically attracted to him, that I refused to believe he could never function with a woman he loved. After all, he had lived as a straight husband for years and there were two little kids in Connecticut going "Daddy, daddy." I guess I really thought for a long time that the love of a good woman could convert Michael, really thought that I could save him.

He would put his arms around me and hold me and kiss me warmly. He would say, "I love you. There's no one like you," and be masculine and passionate, and I would tell him, "You're sending me the right vibrations."

He would say, "I'm not."

Michael and I would spend weeks together—shopping, cooking, laughing, playing house, writing, seeing and analyzing plays—like happy lovers. I never let myself wonder what he might be doing in secret. But finally, after an extremely intense winter, the two of us inseparable, there was a party at his apartment in the spring. After a while he said to me, "It's time you went home." I remember driving back to Larchmont, my body rigid with humiliation, my eyes hot and wet. There had been maybe thirty men in the room and I did not know which one it was, but signals had been exchanged and when I left that room, they all must have laughed, saying, "Doesn't she know? She's got to know. Everybody knows."

Gripping the steering wheel with white knuckles, I thought, *They were right to laugh. I am a joke!* I was in love with a man who was my dream—a man who looked right, who was right for me and my family, who had money, adored me, lived for humor, a man who had a happy place for me in his life— perfect except for one little flaw. He was a homosexual. I felt hot with shame. I, who prided myself on being honest with myself, who broke with David Fitelson because I knew he was the wrong man—I had let delusion take over, let wishful thinking convince me that this relationship could work—and now I had been told to get lost because my loved one was going to be a homosexual for a while. I felt slapped hard across the face.

I kept saying aloud, over and over, "What am I doing? What *am* I doing?" I felt entirely defeated, entirely inadequate —I who always believed there *must* be a way. But there was no way I could compete, no way I could lose ten pounds and get him. A homosexual is a homosexual is a homosexual. Torn by my mixture of anger and grief, I drove through the night, knowing this precious relationship was over, but still absolutely crazy about him. Besotted.

Michael and I continued to see each other, but the relationship faded back to what it should have been—an extremely warm friendship—and I wondered to myself why I constantly chose impossible men. Maybe I was picking men who would not stop my career, men I would not have to marry.

But I always loved Michael. I loved him till he died. Years later he was still phoning me, sometimes in the middle of the night, saying, "Only you would get this"—which is right away big flattery—and he would read me the wording of some *New Yorker* ad. The attitude was, "It doesn't matter whether anybody else gets it, because we know it's funny." He moved out to Hollywood and drank heavily. It was so sad because all of us had passed him by and he should have been the next Cole Porter or maybe Stephen Sondheim.

He was the rich boy syndrome. Free of any urgencies, he could sit back in his gorgeous home in the Hollywood Hills and wait for the perfect little couplet. One night, apparently very drunk, he fell from a grass terrace to the concrete driveway far below, landed on his head, and was instantly dead. They found grass under his fingernails, so apparently there had been a wild, clutching moment of terror.

Only a week before his death Michael called to read lyrics he had written for Angela Lansbury. He and Rod Warren were talking about a television special based on the four stages of a woman's life and they wanted her to play the aging woman. The song was a lament: she is writing her will. Giving away her money is easy, but the house is full of worthless, precious things that add up to a lifetime—the tacky little vase bought during a girlhood trip to Venice, the chipped teacup given by a lost beau. And she is thinking, *When I am dead, nobody will know the importance of these things and they will be thrown away. My life will end up in a waste basket.*

After Michael was gone, his brother came in and cleaned out the house. When his friends asked for little mementos, he didn't know what the hell they were talking about. Everything had gone out in the trash.

That summer of 1963, even though Michael and I had broken our "engagement," he and Rod Warren included me in their revue at the Falmouth Playhouse Restaurant on Cape Cod and I jumped at the chance to get out of New York and make even a little bit of money. It was staged in a small restaurant in the huge lobby of the summer theater, and every weekend Rod and Michael would come up from New York, where they were preparing the revue that would open in the fall at the Upstairs at the Downstairs. Julius Monk had split with the owner of the club, Irving Haber, who had then hired Rod and Michael to produce the shows.

Falmouth was a lovely, carefree summer. I lived with the other girl in the show in a room too small for a bureau and we would say, "We're in a little room with a drawer." On Sunday afternoons we would drive to Provincetown, where Dom DeLuise and Ruth Buzzi were also in a revue, and we brought wine and doughnuts and lay on the dunes and watched the sun come up.

I especially remember a sunny afternoon on a terrace, looking out over the vast green of a golf course with a little snippet of blue ocean in the distance. I remember myself in blue-and-white Bermuda shorts against tanned brown legs. Michael was writing a piece for me to perform in the Falmouth revue and he was pulling bits of paper out of his pockets and reading them to me—and we were laughing on the terrace, all sunburned. It was MGM movie time. The sketch was called "Crestfallen" and I was a drum majorette from the test group that did not get the Crest toothpaste. At the end of the sketch

I went off to be part of another test group, the girl who did not get the birth control pill.

In late August, to make a good salary, I joined a show touring European noncommissioned officers' clubs. So the golden girl kissed her friends good-bye and left them to complete the revue we had all been creating for the fall show at the Upstairs at the Downstairs. I had been totally involved, giving suggestions, very excited. Every weekend, with me at his elbow, Michael had been working on the lyrics. The mood, the unspoken promise, was that we were finally getting our shot at success, all of us rising as one out of New York's big gray mass of hopefuls.

Michael, Rod, Treva, and I, pals together, the four musketeers, were going to the Upstairs. Fate had decided that I would break through and be recognized in revues after all, and now at last it would be good-bye to grungy Greenwich Village and hello to that fabulous little Fifty-sixth Street boîte in the old Wanamaker mansion—a grand curving staircase, orange and pink lights on the stage, a little stained-glass canopy above the stage. This was going to be Jackie Kennedy coming to see me. This was going to be Second City to the fifth power and in *New York*. This was going to be *it!*

At the end of the tour I landed in New York and telephoned Michael and Rod and Treva. Everybody was thrilled I was back. They said, "The rehearsals are going great." Excuse me? My closest friends, who had been encouraging me for years, who had been saying, "You're talented, you're brilliant, you're wonderful," were now saying, "Oh, by the way, you're not in our revue." I asked each member of the group why. Each one said to ask the others.

But because these were the only friends I had, friends I needed to keep, I still went to rehearsals and listened and helped and judged. I was at the previews and present opening

night, celebrating the excited reviews and pretending I was
not being clawed by jealousy. Night after night I walked into
the Upstairs and saw, lined up on the stairs of this beautiful
nightclub, the stairs Mr. Wanamaker had used, men in dinner
jackets and beautifully, cleverly coiffed women in mink stoles.
There was a vibration in the air—wealthy people pulling up in
limousines, laughing, talking to Treva and giving her cards—
and I was standing to one side, getting ready to go down to
the Village. Soon Treva went off into television writing, hired
by Carol Burnett. Michael and Rod were busy on the next
revue and Roger Whittaker had just written them up in *The
New Yorker*, and the *Times* was interviewing them over lunch at
the Plaza. They were new, flash names in New York and could
wear coats with scarves tossed over their shoulders.

I understand today why they did not include me. Once
again, I was not right for somebody's slot. They wanted girls
who would disappear into their bland, faceless ensemble. And
they wanted singers. I was okay in a Falmouth restaurant,
semitalking, but the truth was, if I had had to sing on key to
save six million Jews from Hitler, they would all have been in
the ovens a year earlier. My singing voice was Lauren Bacall
with a cold. And if there had been a song in my throat and I
was included, maybe for two weeks I would have gotten my
laughs by lifting a finger and cocking an eyebrow. But then
Joan Rivers would have found she got a bigger laugh when the
eyebrow went up and she flashed at the same time.

But the irony that fall of 1963 was beyond anybody's
imagining, beyond even my overripe fantasy. Michael and
Rod and their glorious success were, in fact, the final flare of
something passing. It was I, sick with envy, who was part of a
future which was going to drown out the precious revue world
with raucous reality.

On the Upstairs stage were six beautifully elegant kids—

the boys in short hair, full dinner jackets, patent leather pumps, the scrubbed girls in black evening dresses and long white gloves—all faceless, homogenized WASP, singing without a microphone inbred songs about such things as Con Ed and the end of the Brevoort Hotel. When President Kennedy was assassinated, what the revue crowd discussed was the end of Vaughn Meader's career imitating the First Family. I left that irrelevant, antiseptic scene each night and traveled downtown to Greenwich Village and Bleecker Street and entered a world almost of delirium.

In Greenwich Village Bleecker Street was a beatnik ginza. It churned with raffish energy, a spectacle that assaulted and amazed the senses—sidewalks mobbed and overflowing into the street, long-haired scruffies jostling Bronx bagel babies jostling collegiate slummers. It was a hippie heaven where beats and flower children could strut their rebellion and where exploiters could rip off the gawkers. Little shops no wider than an alley or tucked downstairs in a converted cellar sold hideous beat artifacts like kitchen-made jewelry and tie-dyed clothes. There were coffee shops with fake, arty bohemian decor and huge gurgling espresso machines hissing and gleaming like small locomotives. There were the coffee shop nightclubs which offered ice cream and sandwiches and entertainment—places like The Bitter End with its owner, Freddie Weintraub, out front, hawking the civilians in to see the stage show and the freaks. Down the side streets, where the original Italian neighborhood lived on, you could see the separate little social circles of women and men sitting on stoops and chrome kitchen chairs, taking the Indian summer air. It was all a fabulous zoo.

In that raw, rough Village, people knew the Vietnam War had started and that boys were being shipped away to die. In the coffee shops—the successors to Phase 2—straight kids in dirty jeans and open shirts were moving amplifiers and loudspeakers onto those little stages and blaring out protest and

anger and rebellion—singing about what the fuck are we getting killed for.

Almost every night of the week a different coffee shop
held a hootenanny, a new version of the talent night where
you could perform for free. They were a frightening world I
did not understand—a heterosexual male society out of control and dangerous. That thundering amplified noise—and
LSD, and pot—seemed in control. People's looks were scary.
When I walked into the communal dressing rooms, if those
eight raunchy guys had not been holding guitars, I would
have thought they were going to kill me.

I did not, of course, know that this was the leading edge
of my own future, that it would overwhelm not only the revues
but the traditional comedy of the 1950s, the Bob Hopes and
Danny Thomases and Milton Berles who had staffs of writers
turning out what I had thought was comedy. Nichols and May,
mingling acting and comedy, had been the dignified pioneers,
and then Lenny Bruce had blown away all reserve. Now we
young comics, along with the country, were being liberated to
go our own way, to develop our own very personal comedy,
which we learned to write for ourselves—current humor
describing human behavior by describing our own behavior,
material nobody else could perform. It would leave far behind
the one-liners I had once so avidly written in my notebook:
"She was so anemic, when mosquitoes landed on her, all they
got was practice."

Comics were used at the hootenannies to fill the break
while the next band set up its equipment. On Monday nights I
did the hootenanny at the Café Wha? On Tuesday nights I was
at The Bitter End, Thursdays at the Café Au Go-Go, Saturdays at the Café Bizarre. On Wednesdays and Fridays I
crossed the meridian of Seventh Avenue and performed again
for fifty-five gays at Jan Wallman's new club, a clone of the
Showplace, called the Duplex. Everywhere I was working for
free and was grateful to be allowed to do it.

The Bitter End was the Palace Theater of that circuit. Its decor can best be described as "early subway." No liquor was served, just cider and ice cream sodas. And if you did not mind touching the utensils, you could order food off a dirty menu that had a life of its own: It walked toward you. And the toilet! Better to burst a kidney. There was never a mirror in the big battered communal dressing room until I asked for one. Peter, Paul, and Mary had worked there for a year and never needed a mirror. At The Bitter End you were what you were and you sang from your feet through your body.

The epitome of this new look and world was the owner, Freddie Weintraub. He had graduated from the Wharton School of Business, worked his way up to managing a chain of eighty-one children's furniture and toy stores, and had a sub-urban, country club life with wife and kids. He chucked all of that for truth and beauty, which meant going to Cuba and being a nightclub pianist. Back in New York, he bought The Bitter End, installed a big sound system, accompanied the music with light shows, and invented the hootenanny. The Bitter End became a hangout for folksingers, who attracted beatniks—who attracted gawkers.

Freddie was as wild-looking as anybody—a huge man, well over six feet, imposing, burly, never in a tie. His rebel-lious statement was to grow a beard, so he was all hair in a big fur Russian hat and a big coat with a fur collar. A sixties hippie who went home at night to a fabulous Village apartment, an ex-Playboy Bunny wife, and a maid, Freddie was a natural star. He dominated a room with his big voice, bigger manner—"Okay, let's cut the shit. What's the bottom line? What do you want? Okay, you got it. That's it." Freddie did his business with his feet on his desk and was very successful. With a partner, Roy Silver, Freddie was also into management. He took on Bill Cosby, who was appearing at The Bitter End, to try out new material. From the hootenannies, Freddie and Roy got the Serendipity Singers, who Freddie kept working for six years on the strength of one hit record, *Don't Let the Rain Come Down*. Freddie managed my friend from the Showplace coatroom, Cass Elliott, now of The Mamas and the Papas. Bobby Zimmerman, a thin, withdrawn, skulking kid with a big scarf, had been filling in for ten dollars a night. Roy Silver took him over and Bobby Zimmerman became Bob Dylan.

Freddie Weintraub, like everybody else, had his slipups. Two guys named Simon & Garfunkel came up to The Bitter End office with a tape of songs they hoped the Serendipity Singers would record. They also wanted to sing at a hootenanny night. Freddie said, "With a name like Garfunkel, get out of here." A couple of years later, a secretary in the office listened to the tape. It was their entire *Sounds of Silence* album, which had just been released and went on to sell millions, year after year.

I would go to The Bitter End during the day and get a piece of paper with a number on it telling me when I went onstage—like at a bakery. That night, in my little black dress, I sat on a bench against the wall opposite the stage in a line of maybe fifteen scruffy musicians, comics, and girl folksingers wearing necklaces made of fingernails. The hootenannies started at 8:00 and continued till midnight and later, and you did not dare leave, because they might change the order. So you sat through hours of anticipation and fear and jealousy, thinking, *This guy is doing great jokes . . . that guy is taking too long . . . everybody will go home before I get on . . . will Freddie Weintraub like me and book me? . . . will Jack Rollins leave before I go on? . . . will I remember what I'm going to talk about? . . . do I look fat?*

But there was also tremendous excitement. You felt ferment all around you, felt talent poised to break out into the big time. Everything was new, the sound, the look, and everybody came to see it—the *Tonight Show* people, agents, managers, bookers for the Sullivan Show. At any moment one of us could be plucked out of there and become famous, and you discovered that those weird hippies with long hair and beards were already selling records in the millions.

On that bench with me at one time or another were comics Dick Cavett, George Carlin, David Frye, and John Byner. Richard Pryor, skinny, brilliantly shocking, was right there on the bench, too, with jacket sleeves lengthened so many times, he looked like an admiral. Woody Allen, who had been a writer for *Your Show of Shows* and loathed performing, went onstage ashen with fear. Before the show, one of his managers, Jack Rollins or Charles Joffe, had to stay in the dressing room with him to keep him from escaping through the window.

When I finally did get on the stage, my heart would fall. I could not imagine that those people in front of me would be my friends tonight. Looking out, I saw strangers, no tables of six gay guys carrying dance bags, just roughnecks—as my mother would have called them—with artsy-craftsy dates, girls who had woven everything they wore. They were frightening to me because they had chosen a life I did not want, a life of free love and truth and no possessions. I was alone in a foreign country.

But the raw newness of this world was cutting me loose too. The process had been started by Treva Silverman and my revue friends who liberated me from Larchmont, from everything I had been taught about everything, from all the oughts and shoulds that had been holding me down—ropes, ropes, ropes, ropes. And from then on, year by year, a rope was cut here, a rope was chopped there—and now it was happening in a rush, until eventually I was able to go up—like a big fat balloon.

Talking about myself to these new, straight audiences, I was even more free, more honest, more able to say onstage the things that girls think about. I would start out cute, telling them, "I dread going home through these rough areas. I stop at a red light and a wino wipes my windshield. I'm scared to death. I'm on a bike." I talked about being fat as a child, said, "Because I was so fat, nobody could get close enough to me to find out I was fun. So I began to retreat into myselves."

Then, in among the cute, I now threw in lines about birth control: "A friend of mine was taking the pill and was in great trouble because they said, 'Take one a day,' and didn't tell her where to put it. Every night she put it in her ear, and the next thing she knew, she was eight months gone." And then there would be more cuteness and suddenly a little talk about going to the gynecologist: "I don't trust a gynecologist who, while he's examining you, goes kootchy koo." Pretty tame today, but in those days they were taboo subjects and even at The Bitter End there would be some gasps—but also laughter. I ended the act saying, "If you liked me and know any agents, please remember my name is Joan Rivers and I put out."

I was not a major success at The Bitter End—still a bit too tentative and giggly—but Freddie kept letting me come back. He used to ask people what they thought of a new performer. "Liked" was the kiss of death. "Loved" or "hated" interested him. At least the performer had aroused emotion. It was the first time being loathed by some people was my big asset.

Freddie was managing a husband-and-wife singing team, Jake and Kay Holmes, until Kay went off with Roy Silver. Freddie, who was basically a nice guy, broke up his partnership with Roy and told Jake, "I can't get Kay back for you, but I can get you a new act." Freddie hired me and Jim Connell, a clean-cut comedy writer and comedian I had known at the B & G. Freddie named the act Jim, Jake, & Joan, and I said, "Who's going to play Joan?" When nobody laughed, I should have realized we were in trouble.

Jim was tall, gangly, Irish-looking, wore glasses, and had brown hair with a sort of wimple. His humor was okay, but not my kind. Jake Holmes, thin, handsome, wiry, intense, totally sensitive and hurting, was the poet. That was how he saw himself and that was how others perceived him—except for me. Kay had left him. Jake was suffering and continued to suffer—an open wound with a necktie. You always wondered, "When is Jake going to do away with himself?" Obviously never, because he has become a hugely successful composer and singer of jingles for commercials.

We wrote our act and rehearsed it for a month and Freddie helped us and paid us forty dollars a week. While we rehearsed at The Bitter End, The Mamas and the Papas were headlining and I loved Cass Elliott's voice. She was not just big in person, but big in spirit with a huge laugh and very friendly to me. She was very sexual, too, which did not fit her at all, and was already living a free life and into the drug culture that was all around us. She was really one of the great flower children of the sixties.

Jim, Jake & Joan started performing as an opening act for the Simon Sisters, who sang folk music in dirndl skirts and off-the-shoulder blouses, and they did not knock me out. "Winken, Blinken, and Nod" was their big number. Lucy Simon was pretty, but I liked the big, lumpy, gawky sister, Carly, who wore flats so she would not look so tall and had huge teeth and those big hands with short nails that are so unfeminine. She had great generosity of spirit and being the less good-looking sister made her more open and vulnerable and accessible to becoming a friend. We had a lot in common, both of us coming from upper-middle-class backgrounds, both from good schools and suddenly here in the Village, both ambitious and oddities—I walking around in my silk stockings and pumps, clutching my proper handbag and sweet little gloves.

Carly and I and Cass Elliott, I think, spotted each other

for what we were—women trying to get by on inner beauty—
heavy thighs and inner beauty. And then, of course, Carly had
to spoil it all by losing weight and becoming a sexpot.

Jim, Jake & Joan were promoted to a middle act and we
ended up headlining at The Bitter End during the summer.
We did a guest shot on a local half-hour variety show called
The Beautiful Phyllis Diller Show and auditioned unsuccessfully
for *The Tonight Show,* now hosted by Johnny Carson. Everything was terrific—money was coming in, we were Freddie's
guys, I was the queen bee of Bleecker Street, headlining at the
Palace. I could pop into any club, bar, grocery store, shop,
and they would say, "Hi, how are you? What's happening?" I
loved the absurdity, the blasphemy—in a way, the honesty—
of that Bleecker Street world. Somebody would shout to us
that a tour bus was coming by and we would run outside onto
the sidewalk and watch Jim Connell give the tourists a show by
kissing Wally, the black doorman, full on the lips. That way
the tourists got a twofer: homosexuality and miscegenation.

Jim Connell's father—very straight and Irish—refused to
come to the Village. The last time he had been there was when
the doughboys came marching home in 1918 through the
Washington Square arch. Jim kept telling him, "It's safe. It's
okay." Finally, the father relented. Just as this dignified man
in a gray suit approached The Bitter End, a guy jumped out of
a doorway and yelled, "Hey, Pops, wanna have your picture
taken with a fag?"

After Jim, Jake & Joan had been headliners for a while, we
began to realize that we did not like each other very much.
Freddie had shoehorned together three solo performers
whose daily writing sessions were now abusive arguments. We
fought about what was funny and every suggestion was wrong
and not funny. We even argued about the number of lines we

each had and Jake, who was a very good songwriter, decided he was funny, too, so we had to have equal punch lines.

The outcome was sophomoric humor I felt was beneath me—a cheap West Side revue. In one sketch we were three babies in a hospital nursery, wearing bonnets and speaking with a lisp:

JIM: Welcome to the ward. How long have you been a baby?

JAKE: Two days.

JIM: Wow. You sure don't look your age. How do you do it?

JAKE: I'm a caesarean.

JOAN: A caesarean. I hear they're a bunch of cut-ups in the caesarean section.

That gives you a general idea of the quality. I hated putting that stupid bonnet on my idiot head and pretending that I enjoyed it, pretending I thought this was funny. I wanted to say to the audiences, "Oh, please don't judge me on this."

The only relief to my unhappiness came between shows, once again running with my Wollensak back to the Duplex, back to doing a single, back to what had been getting me nowhere in my career. But deeper than my embarrassment in Jim, Jake & Joan, I think there was within me a primal understanding that I could only be happy alone onstage, talking one-on-one to the audience. What I know for a fact is that my entire body began to rebel. Pimples spread out over my back, not genteel little zits, but big reddies that blossomed into gross yellowies. At The Bitter End, in my dress with a plunging V in the back, I looked as though my body was inside out. I tried creams, astringents, lotions, long hot baths—and still the pimples spread up my neck and down my arms till I had to buy a long-sleeved turtleneck sheath.

When I showed the outbreak of pimples on my back to

my father, the doctor, he said, "It's nothing. Put Calamine lotion on it."

The act I hated kept getting bigger and bigger—a paradox that was tearing me apart. This cheesy revue was restoring my dreams, was establishing me in show business, was delivering everything those thousands of hours of rounds had never won. I now had Freddie, my swinging manager, and even Irvin Arthur was behind me, booking us for a tour. I was, at last, on my way—and miserable.

In late September Jim, Jake & Joan opened for Trini Lopez in Chicago at Mr. Kelly's and received wonderful reviews. In Indianapolis we opened for the singer Fran Jeffries. By then, the three of us were barely talking. We walked to the club in single file and returned to the hotel in the same formation. Onstage I hated myself, hypocritically smiling at them, knowing we had not eaten a meal together in three weeks.

After Indianapolis I went to see Freddie Weintraub. I thought he must like me. He had picked me for the act, come to rehearsals and laughed, sent us on the road. I also thought I was Miss Hotshot. I told him things were not working out for me and I wanted to leave the group. Freddie said, "Fine. We'll get another girl." Just like that.

I said, "I've got my own act. Would you continue to manage me?"

He shook that big head of his. "No way," he said. "I'll manage you as a writer, but not as a performer. I don't see you ever making it as a single."

15

THOSE WORDS KEPT ringing in my head—"I don't see you
making it as a single"—the pronouncement of Freddie Weintraub, a man famous for spotting talent. It was only a little
consolation that they were unable to replace me in Jim, Jake &
Joan. Freddie tried several new girls, but soon dissolved the
act. Maybe they were not very good—or maybe their names
did not begin with J.

I returned back to the one place where I fitted in, where I
was not an overaged, slightly-used-up, unmarried loser. I
went back again to the Duplex and Jan Wallman, who kept
letting me be onstage two or three nights a week as a special
guest artist. My skin cleared up and I became one of a lucky
group who were her children. She defended us, told drunks to
be quiet while we performed, booked us even when audiences
hated us, and on Thanksgiving invited us all to Thanksgiving
dinner at her apartment.

I loved Jan. I loved her because she was like me, trying to
live her dreams, working during the day as a bartender so she
could be a little impresario in front of her audience, making
her breathy little speech, "Good evening. I'm Jan Wallman
. . ." She once told me she believed that if she was a good girl
she would go to the Blue Angel when she died.

The shows at the Duplex started at 10:00 and, on a big
night, went to 3:00 A.M. The address was 55 Grove Street in
the Village, a brownstone you entered from ground level into
a bar and then climbed steep stairs to the Duplex on the
parlor floor where there was room for about eighteen tables
and a service bar against the left wall. The Duplex had no

stage, just an area at the far end with a drapery covering the wall behind it. The one unisex bathroom was at the rear of the performing area and during your performance somebody would suddenly walk across the stage in front of you and then, if it was a very quiet moment, you could hear a slight *wishhttt.* Next, always on the punch line, the toilet would flush. It was a little like performing in somebody's apartment living room, with lights.

The revue world had been an MGM movie, but comedy in the Village evoked no fantasy. It was grubby. Gritty. There were roaches. The dressing room was two flights down the back stairs: a table and couple of light bulbs in a basement room where they had the tin lockers for the help and stored the liquor. There were rats down there and I rarely used it, changing and doing my makeup in the bathroom and then making my entrance from the cellar stairs. One night I was standing there, waiting to be introduced, and a lesbian came up behind me, grabbed me, and kissed me right on the lips. I was in such shock, I just stood there. She said, "I've been watching you for a long time. You're swell." Then I walked onstage. That did not happen to Judy Garland in the movie.

In addition to retreating into the Duplex, I auditioned again for the Johnny Carson show, where there was a new talent coordinator, Shelley Schultz, who had seen me in Jim, Jake & Joan. I received the standard brush-off: "Thank you, but your material is just not right for us." I persisted, told him I could have new material in two weeks. Shelley said, "We just don't think you'd work on TV"—more deathless words to mingle in my head with Freddie Weintraub's verdict.

In November 1964 Jan booked me into the Duplex show for a week—my first extended run and a tiny showcase to which I could invite agents and managers. I decided the time had come for an ultimate effort, really a frightening test that might prove what I suspected—that all doors were now closed, that in the minds of the men who could open doors, I was a pathetic never-will-be. I bought fifty postcards and blanketed my past, sending a card to every one of the names who had once carried my hopes: Irvin Arthur. Freddie Weintraub. Jack Segal. Marty Erlichman. Charlie Joffe. Bob Shanks. Jack Rollins. Paul Keyes. Roy Silver. Tony Rivers. Every agent or secretary or manager, large and small, that I had ever phoned or waved to or used their ladies' room. Julius Monk. Irving Haber. Lenny Jacobson. This is your life, Joan Rivers.

The card read:

> Hi! I open at the Duplex, 55 Grove Street, for one week beginning November 15. Come and see me. I'm looking for agents, managers, whatever. I'd really like you to come down. My treat.

Nobody came. Each night I waited and not one person cared enough to appear. I understood that after seven years in the business, nobody was going to come anymore, that everybody had looked at my invitation and said, "Oh, she's still around and who cares," and thrown it into the wastebasket. I had run out of people to court and this was going to be it now, carrying the Wollensak and going every night to the Duplex until Jan found somebody newer or younger or brighter—or the club closed and Jan had no club. I thought, *My life is going to be nothing.*

On Thursday night I went onstage. The room was almost empty—just five gays, but sitting in the back with his wife Kay, Jake's lost love, was Freddie Weintraub's former partner, Roy Silver, the man who had the whole ball of wax, who had the muscle to get me my break, who was now the hot manager in town with the hot comic, Bill Cosby. This was not Harry Brent, not Lenny Jacobson, not anybody I laughed about. Here was the real thing, a manager I looked at and thought, *Wouldn't it be great if . . .*

JoAnne Worley and her boa were the opening act. Then I came on. Showing Roy I was fabulous, I quadrupled my energy, swished that skirt, flashed those crinolines, juiced that personality. I made JoAnne Worley seem like Marcel Marceau. But nobody can win in front of an audience of seven, even if five are gay. I felt I was babbling in a vacuum with no sense of an audience, no sense of a relationship—especially when one seventh of the audience walked across the stage on his way to relieve himself. At the end the reaction was so thin I could hear the individual hand claps. All those postcards, maybe my last chance, had brought only one person, and he had seen a horrendous night. I sat down at Roy's table almost suicidal.

Roy smiled. Roy said I was wonderful. Roy said he wanted to manage me. Roy said I would have to work on the act with him every day and do exactly what he said. I broke down. I could not speak for a long time because my throat was full of tears. At last, here was somebody who had seen something, a voice in the wilderness—and I was so *grateful.* How nice of him! How kind!

I kept looking down and away because I was embarrassed that this meant *so* much to me. Maybe if he saw that I was this desperate and defeated, he might change his opinion. And then I was able to speak and tell him, "Anything," and I hoped he did not notice there were tears streaming down my cheeks.

Roy was a hustler—medium height, slim, dark hair, smooth-faced with a biggish nose, horn-rimmed glasses—a New York Jewish boy. He talked hip, fast New Yorkese, the latest phrase always on his tongue, very Mike Toddish, very avant-garde. Had once been married to a black girl, which for a Jew in the sixties was wild. The way he made his start in management was brilliant. His one client, a folksinger named Jimmy Gavin, was almost totally anonymous and agent friends at GAC told Roy to get a star, so he could come into offices as a heavyweight. Some newspaper discovered Veronica Lake working as a waitress at the Martha Washington Hotel, which was not where Jackie Kennedy ever chose to stay. Roy cornered Veronica in a dry cleaner's, convinced her to make a comeback, signed her, sent her to Elizabeth Arden on borrowed money, had a meeting at GAC, and got her the lead in a road company of *Mary, Mary*.

After the tour, everything fell apart. Veronica was an alcoholic and her idea of recreation was being the big celebrity in ports like Galveston, Texas, where she could meet merchant marine sea captains just off a long voyage. They would have thousands of dollars in their pockets and she helped them spend it. I guess that was better than waiting tables at the Martha Washington. But by then, Roy Silver was established as a manager. The night he came to the Duplex, Bill Cosby had just signed to play in the TV series *I Spy*.

In the beginning Roy and Freddie Weintraub had managed Bill Cosby together. According to Roy, when he and Freddie split over Kay, Freddie kept the Serendipity Singers, who had a hit record, and Roy took over the relatively unknown Cosby. That is typical of show business. Everybody is an expert and nobody can predict anything.

But Roy and Freddie did one thing right—their instincts were that Cosby should work white, use no material about being a black. Later, just before the first script for *I Spy* was to be shot in Tokyo, Roy, with his heart in his mouth, told the producer that Cosby would get sick and miss the plane unless all black stereotype dialogue was removed. The producer had to give in. On the long flight to Japan, Roy sat next to the producer, who said only one thing to him: "Pass the salt."

I'm sure Roy came to the Duplex that night out of pity. He had already watched me perform at The Bitter End and had probably been saying like everybody else for six years, "Poor Joan, she'll never make it," which made it almost impossible to say now, "Wait a second, something's working here." People who think they have the pulse of America do not want to admit, "Gee, I was wrong and she was right." They do not want to be bothered.

But this time Roy listened just for himself, not judging me against other women comics and past images of me, not considering what a club owner would think of my material. Roy saw me plain. His instincts told him the country was ready for something new—ready for a woman comedian talking about life from a woman's point of view.

The next morning he tried to find me an agent. By late afternoon he was calling his friend Marty Littke at William Morris and asking, "Tell me about Joan Rivers. Why can't I get her an agent?"

Marty Littke said, "Because everyone has seen her. She's been on the Paar show twice and there's absolutely no interest in her anywhere." Roy, bless him, was not discouraged. He asked Marty, as a favor, to sign me. Marty agreed to come down to the Duplex sometime and have a look.

Then Roy, who wanted to be Jack Rollins, began to work with me. Roy was smart enough to imitate Jack, one of a past era of creative managers who lived, ate, breathed with young clients, knew their acts inside out, studied them every night. From then on Roy was always at the Duplex, sitting with a pad making notes, while onstage I talked about the death of my wig on the West Side Highway and how I went to a wig farm to find another one among all the gorgeous wigs running around.

> I was set to get a stunning one—long blond silky hair—when suddenly I felt something licking my hand. I looked down and it's the runt of the litter. How can you say no to a little cross-eyed wig that's looking up at you with love in its eyes. I figured with love anything can be made pretty, so I took it home

and bought a book called *Training You to Train Your Wig* and I say to it things like "Set! . . . Curl!"

Every day, sometimes at 6:00 after office temp work, Roy and I met at his office and listened to the previous night's tape on Treva's Wollensak, taking off ad-libs, discussing them, putting them down on paper. He would say, "Go more for this," and we would ad-lib on those themes and write down more. He kept saying, "Broaden it out. Broaden it out." Instead of one experience with a boyfriend, he wanted three—with other boys. We expanded a routine about my hairdresser, Mr. Phyllis:

> My mother would sit in his chair in his shop crying, "Oh, Mr. Phyllis, neither one of my daughters is married. A good man is so hard to find." And Mr. Phyllis would cry into her teased hair and say, "Don't I know. Don't I know." Poor Mr. Phyllis. He was robbed. Thieves broke through his stained-glass door and stole all his valuables—including his roommate. They thought he was a piece of pop art.

Roy was the element I had lacked, the outside ear, the editor, able to give my nonsense a real shape, the hard polish of a pro. For the first time in my life, I was physically, systematically constructing a stand-up comedy act, instead of machine-gunning jokes—if you do not like that one, how about this one? And, again, Roy's instincts were right. He kept saying to me, "Take it away from the *Partisan Review.*" He wanted me to be strong, even if it meant being outrageous. He knew it was time for a woman comic to joke about things not mentioned in polite society.

I was becoming a nice Jewish girl in stockings and pumps saying onstage what people thought but never said aloud in polite society, a girl talking about gynecologists, about having an affair with a married professor whose wife got pregnant, talking about the pill being a laborsaving device, about my gay hairdresser whose mother wanted a girl—and got one.

Today, all this seems very tame, but in that era such talk was shocking onstage. Several times I did free shows out at a place called Pip's in Sheepshead Bay. The owner, George Schultz, a sort of Long Island Jan Wallman, loved comics. After my third appearance there I went up to him and asked, "Is there any chance of getting a booking here?" He answered, "Let me give it to you straight. I like you, but you scare my partner."

Even four years later, when I was pregnant and appeared on *The Ed Sullivan Show,* CBS would not allow me to say the word *pregnant.* It would be indecent. After much consideration, they came up with a solution for the embarrassment of my huge stomach. They had me say, "Soon I will hear the pitter patter of tiny fee.."

But this material was not too strong for the Duplex, where Jan never had a rope because the customers would just fly over it. Performers on their night off, the intelligentsia from NYU and the New School, all came and kept saying, "She goes too far . . ." and kept coming back, and night after night I was feeling those shock waves of laughter, luxuriating in the appreciation, getting that soaring sensation of lift-off. At ease now, I was really beginning to improvise—but still needed that Second City partner, needed a friend beside me to trigger the ad-libs and comfort and support me. Since I did not want a companion onstage and the partnership of a written, set act had not worked, I decided that the audience could be my partner.

I started up conversations with people, politely asking them, "Are you married? Single? I'm the last single girl in Larchmont. My mother's desperate. She has a sign up, LAST GIRL BEFORE TURNPIKE." I was tentative and still anchored on top of a stool in front of a microphone I did not dare touch, but those tiny relationships worked as improvisational kickoffs, and I was not afraid of what people might say, because in Chicago I had never known what would come out of Tony Holland's mouth. I also learned that if I made even one friend in the audience, then I did not care if the entire rest of the audience turned against me.

I had two barometers telling me I was on a very right track. One was the nightclub critic of *Cue* magazine, Eugene Boe, a big, burly, booming-voiced Phi Beta Kappa from Harvard who began turning up at front tables. He gave me my first major review:

> Joan "Second City" Rivers, in the late hours at the Duplex, is a very funny femme in search of an act. Her unmeasured monologue contains some of the sharpest, smartest talk to proceed out of the mouth of a babe since Elaine May. Female comics are usually horrors who desex themselves for a laugh. But Miss R. remains visibly—and unalterably—a girl throughout her scream-of-consciousness script.

I was *very* excited. Gene Boe was a major respected nightclub critic in New York. *Cue,* one of the city's most powerful entertainment magazines, giving listings and reviews of every event in New York, had compared me to Elaine May! A friend had the clipping enlarged and I brought it home and put it on my wall. I thought it was a booking review, that Irvin Arthur would soon be on the phone. What it did was bring twenty-five extra people down to see me, including Jack Lemmon, who was so tired he fell sound asleep during my act.

The second sign of my success was Michael McWhinney. Though our romance was over, I still worshiped him. Michael would sit up front and cover his ears and put his head right down on the table, groaning with disgust, while I bemoaned on stage having to buy nine bridesmaid dresses, all green, all acetate—"Where can you wear a green acetate bridesmaid dress? How many Puerto Rican proms can you go to?" Afterward he would say to me, "My God, what are you doing? What *are* you doing!"

He went around telling everybody that I was going commercial, destroying myself. Destroying myself from what? I was not in their stinking revue. He was furious because the birdie was flying away from his prison. My answer, if I had known it then, would have been something William Randolph Hearst said: "If you write for the masses, you eat with the classes. If you write for the classes, you eat with the masses."

So, professionally, I was happy with Roy. Somebody besides Jan was saying, "You were good tonight. That worked tonight." I had a winner coach I could talk to. Bill Cosby's manager was talking to me about my act in front of the Duplex and right over there Jack Rollins was doing it, too, with *his* new little fighter, Dick Cavett.

At that time the Duplex was a special cocoon where a small group of emerging talents were making their mistakes in private, so to speak. We respected each other, had coffee between sets, ran in to see each other's acts, asked each other, "Is this funny?" There was Dick Cavett, there was Linda Lavin, who was singing then, very sexy in a lace body stocking. There was JoAnne Worley, who hit big on *Laugh-In.* Woody Allen was there once in a while and Rodney Dangerfield. All of us were unknowns. One cold December night I was on the sidewalk when a sailor and his girl stopped and looked at the show bill outside the Duplex. He said very sarcastically, "Linda Lavin . . . wow! Joan Rivers . . . wow! Dick Cavett . . . wow!" And walked on.

The comics' acts were all self-deprecating. Dick's persona was the barefoot boy with cheek of tan just arrived in New York City from Nebraska, and he had great lines. He lived in a boardinghouse where the landlady was so mean, she sold the boarders their mail. He went to the Stage Delicatessen and ordered a chopped-up liver sandwich.

Unfortunately, Dick was probably too cool, too intelligent, too airy, too classy, to be a stand-up comic. He was perfect for television, but would never have made it big in nightclubs. But he was very witty. There was a guy in the talent nights at the Duplex who started out in a regular suit, and, as he sang *Pagliacci,* gradually put on clown clothes and full clown makeup. One night there were only six people in the audience and Dick said to him, "Listen, there's half a house tonight, so just do half your face."

Dick and I became good friends and actually tried to form an act together, be another Mike and Elaine. That was the era of the radio program *Monitor* and we improvised tapes and tapes for NBC, but they never used us. His big chance as a comic came when somebody performing at the Plaza Hotel— Abbe Lane's chihuahua, maybe—got sick and Jack Rollins sent Dick up to fill in for two shows. He left the Duplex, very snappy in a tuxedo, except that he had on brown cordovan shoes. He kept saying, "It won't matter. The lights don't hit that low." After the first show he came back. Nobody ever asked what happened.

When Woody Allen was not at The Bitter End, he was at the Duplex, talking very slowly, lots of nervous ticks, smacking his lips while he gathered his thoughts. He never improvised, always came in with set material and wonderful things came out of his mouth. He said he did not believe in an afterlife—although he did plan to bring a change of underwear. When he played softball, he would steal second—but would feel guilty and go back.

I was jealous as hell of Woody. Terribly jealous that New York intellectuals were beginning to make a big fuss over him and then would leave the Duplex before I came on. And I would wonder, *What am I doing wrong now? What's the next fleece I have to find?*

But compared to Rodney Dangerfield, I was Little Mary Sunshine. His jealousy festered right on the surface as he constantly knocked Dick Cavett, sneering at all "intellectual comics." It was impossible to avoid a run-in with Rodney. I was using a joke based on Irvin Arthur's telephone habits: "I called my boyfriend at work and he put me on hold for two years." Rodney said I could not do that joke. Telephones were his premise. He was very angry. I said, "Okay, we'll divide up the premises. I'll take marriage, dating, family, children, and pregnancy. You can have telephones, movies, and current events." He saw no humor in that. He was too angry to have humor about himself.

Rodney once said, "Half the fun of winning is seeing your friends lose," and he would talk during other comics' acts. We all have anger, but Rodney's filled that poor little room. I do not like him, but tell me he is playing somewhere and I will get dressed and run to see him. I have *tremendous* respect for Rodney as a comic—he has the most brilliant, the most inventive, the meanest humor—and he makes a fool of himself. There is a lot of me in Rodney and vice versa.

He talked to me about needing a hook, saying you must have one so they will remember that and identify you. Jack Benny was cheap. Joe Penner had "Wanna buy a duck?" Rodney found his hook working at Pip's on Long Island. One night a sleazo mafioso came in after a big fight with a whore. He said to Rodney, "Jesus Christ, even with hookers I don't get no respect." So that became his signature line. "I don't get no respect." When his sister, a schoolmarm, heard Rodney, she corrected him. She said, "Excuse me, Rodney, but it's 'I don't get *any* respect.' "

I thought a hook was low-class, so it took me years to find mine and it just came naturally. Much later, when my act had really become gossiping over the back fence with audiences, I slipped into "Can we talk?" I said it so much, so automatically, it became my identifying line. People began to know

who I was—"Oh, yeah, she's the one who says 'Can we talk?' "
I hate saying it—I do not like anything that's consciously
done. It is too manipulative. But that hook lifted me off a
plateau in my career, and what really took me through the
roof was talking about personalities. Dear Elizabeth Taylor, I
owe a lot to you. Love, Joanie.

Without an agent to book me, there were no jobs beyond
the Duplex. Finally our great white William Morris hope appeared—Marty Littke, who was going to sign me because he
was Roy's friend. All through Linda Lavin's act, Marty talked
to Roy and afterward in the basement dressing room, Linda
turned on me, raging like a gutter bitch, "You keep your
friends quiet!" The next evening Linda Lavin, very sheepish,
came to me with roses and said, "I'm sorry I yelled. I was at
William Morris today." She, not I, had been signed by Littke.

That same week Roy called up Shelley Schultz at the
Carson show and said, "You've got to see her again." Shelley
did it for Roy—and this time came down to my natural habitat,
the Village. He sat through the show expressionless and told
Roy, "I told you before, she's not right for the show. She's not
right for television." He also told Roy, "This is the end. No
more." I was the hit of the Duplex, the queen bee, and audiences were giving me tremendous responses, but nobody in
the business thought I was funny.

So in late November of 1964 I was still plodding around
the Village with that Wollensak, still wearing that Peck & Peck
coat, still driving that battered car, still wearing the Jax dress
from Second City. They were even sorry for me in the office
temporary world, wondering why I was still there.

One morning I lay on my bed in Larchmont asking myself
what was going to happen. Here I was, six years after *Seawood*,
no real career, no man in my life, and not even enough money
to buy Christmas presents. The phone rang beside my bed. It

was Jorn Winther, the director of the Phyllis Diller show, who remembered me from the Jim, Jake & Joan guest shot. He wanted to hire me as a writer on the show for three hundred dollars a week. In five minutes I was in that Valiant and on my way to ABC. Now the joke was going to be on everybody, including me. Instead of starring in the great American play, I was going to *write* the great American play. And who would have thought it could all begin with a stupid little mouse named Topo.

The previous winter, during my "love affair" with Michael McWhinney, I was sitting on the floor of his apartment, waiting for a pot of artichokes to cook, when Michael laughed uproariously and said, "Can you believe this? They want me to write 'Topo the Mouse' for Ed Sullivan for $500." They were asking Cole Porter to sell out. Well, I was born corrupt. I said, "I'll do it. I'll do it." I lay on the floor and wrote a sketch about this comic Italian puppet mouse, with a little Italian accent, who had become a semifad in America. I had him asking Ed Sullivan to explain football: "I don't get it, Eddie." I put Topo in a little football jersey that said 1/4. When the artichokes were done, so was I. We turned it in under Michael's name and he promised to split the money. They liked it and commissioned two more, and I did one and then Michael decided that, since he was Cole Porter, he shouldn't be bothered with such nonsense.

But something important had happened. I believed for the first time that I could actually be a writer. I did not see myself as one of those lofty authors who sit at a typewriter and do not move their lips—but I could be funny on paper and had proved it on the mouse level. That was confirmed when, after my Topo credential, Treva Silverman consented to do a sketch with me for the new revue at the Upstairs at the Downstairs. We wrote several, sitting and laughing and giggling and ad-libbing—in fact, using my Second City techniques. So at last I was learning how to tap the big balloon of nonsense inside me—a misshapen balloon in a misshapen body—learning how to put a tube down into it, so the foolishness came flying out onto a piece of paper.

At ABC, searching for the offices of the Phyllis Diller show, I walked through miles of corridors, past the offices of the Les Crane show, a late-night talk show, and finally, way in the rear, found a large room divided by low partitions, like an insurance firm. I introduced myself to the secretary-production assistant, Carol Cohen, who said, "Welcome aboard, Joan. You have just joined the *Titanic after* it hit the iceberg."

The staff was only four. Besides Jorn Winther, there was Carol and Claibe Richardson, who did the music—a go-getter who went on to write the music for the Broadway musical *The Grass Harp.* The show was mini *Ed Sullivan,* taped during the week, aired at 10:30 on Saturday nights with Phyllis Diller hosting and doing a monologue. She flew in from the coast just in time to go onstage, arriving in a big mink coat and followed by this skinny guy with thinning hair, a caddy who carried her book of jokes, which was as big as ten phone books. She would say, "I need a joke on doors," and he would turn to D. I was very impressed.

But what permanently influenced me was Phyllis Diller's warmth and charm. She made it her business to know everybody's name and go over and say a word to them with no condescension in her voice. She treated me as an equal, as a peer, as a professional in show business—not a nonperson.

The next week Phyllis Diller decided the show was not worth the trip and dropped out. So we changed the name to *Show Street* and brought in guest hosts. I loved the job. We laughed at everything—laughed at the budget, which was about $1.20, laughed at the backdrops on the set, which were

enlarged posters, laughed about bringing light bulbs from
home for our office lamps. We laughed at the ragtag audiences we roped in from the streets for taping the shows—and
laughed at having to spray the seats with disinfectant afterward. We could even laugh at our problems collecting our
salaries. ABC was almost bankrupt and I had to go around to
headquarters and beg for my check like a little grocer dealing
with Harry Meangrass. It was we four against the world. We
never spoke to the Les Crane people. It was a camp atmosphere. The buff team at Camp *Show Street* fighting the gray
team, which was ABC.

But everybody liked us. One of the guys in the ABC
newsroom knew I could not afford a parking place, so he gave
me a big sticker that said ABC NEWS, which let me park anywhere. One day a cop watched me park my ruined green
Valiant in an illegal zone. When I flipped down the sun visor
so the sticker showed, he began to laugh. He said, "The car is
the news—that it runs."

To find acts, we advertised in *Variety* and *Show Business* and
into our office trooped the shabby sad sacks of show business.
I remember a woman puppeteer who kept saying, "I just don't
know what's wrong with the little fellas today. They just don't
want to talk to me." These people auditioned right there
among our tiny cubicles, the sweat breaking out from the
tension as they performed while we watched from our desks. I
saw them as kooks. They forced me to wonder whether I was
actually one of them—a kook, too—threadbare around the
edges, hanging on in the business against all reason.

I loved being a professional writer by day, loved being
able to get Milt Kamen to host a show, loved seeing him again.
My fourth week we had Zsa Zsa Gabor. She treated us like dirt.
She was at the Waldorf Towers and I came over to discuss the
script with her. Halfway through, she said, "Darling, my hem
. . . I just stepped on it. Could you help me a minute, Joan,
dear?" She just happened to have a needle and thread right

there. Then she said, "Oh, excuse me a minute," and disappeared for two hours. I telephoned Claibe and said, "She wants me to hem her dress." He said, "We need her for the show. Consider yourself the Betsy Ross of ABC."

Next she demanded that our itty bitty, dirt-poor show hire a Rolls-Royce to take her to the studio. Claibe and Carol and I got on the phone. Finally Carol's mother finagled one from a friend. An hour before the taping, Carol's phone rang. It was Zsa Zsa. She said, "The Rolls is here." Carol said, "That's wonderful." Zsa Zsa said, "But how will my maid get to the studio?"

At the studio Jorn described the trick shot he wanted to use as an opener—Zsa Zsa apparently emerging from a champagne glass. We showed her the two cameras, showed her how we would superimpose one picture on top of the other. She did not understand. She kept saying, "But, darling, I'll never fit in the glass." Zsa Zsa, however, was very shrewd. She knew herself, knew what she could do and not do, knew what lighting made her look glamorous, knew what was expected of her, and delivered it—which is the sign of a pro. And she was very careful. She checked every light, every angle. We were going to send her out in the audience to answer questions and she wanted both the questions and the answers in advance: "What do you consider a good housekeeper?" "The wife who keeps the house after the divorce." There was no way she could slip up. She made only one major mistake—allowing herself to be booked on *Show Street.*

Zsa Zsa was naturally funny; everything came out funny and I just followed her around, saying, "That's funny. Use that." At the end, she asked me to come to Los Angeles and write for her. I guess she had more dresses that needed hemming.

All during December *Show Street* was my life preserver, though I sensed it might sink at any moment. People would say, "What are you doing?" I answered, "I'm writing *Show Street,*" and they said, "Oh, is that still on?" But I kept telling myself, "No matter what happens, I've got the writing now. I'll be able to live like a person." All my money, however, was going out for new tires and for capping my terrible yellow teeth which were a mosaic of fillings and still rotting. Whoever married me was going to be marrying a dentist too.

The week before Christmas, at the ABC Christmas party, a vice president of ABC told us, ha, ha, ha, the show is cancelled, you're all fired. I was sorry but unsurprised and felt fortunate compared to Jorn Winther. I was haunted by the memory of a night he invited his little staff to his house for dinner. He had six kids, and on a blackboard in the playroom was written a list of all the payments he had to make for his family—Sears, life insurance, Con Ed, the mortgage, etc. I realized that Jorn, the producer-director-father-figure, was counting pennies and I thought, *My God, he's as desperate as we are,* and now, with the show off the air, he did not have Larchmont to go home to.

Throughout *Show Street* I was performing regularly at the Duplex. Roy Silver and I both felt the act was truly coming together and getting slick, felt that it was ready now to be an opener at the Bon Soir or the Hungry i in San Francisco—felt the time had come to invite the man who booked that circuit, Irvin Arthur.

He came in the week before Christmas—the first agent I had gone to, the man who had been watching me all those years, my boss in the office who let me go off to auditions, an honest man I respected for his taste, a man I liked and thought liked me, even though I had driven him crazy with phone calls. Mr. Arthur! It was very emotional for me. He had not seen me do a solo since before Chicago and I thought, *Wouldn't it be wonderful if we came full circle and he said, "You're ready and I'm ready."*

Roy Silver was busy that night and Irvin sat alone at a table in the rear and left immediately after my act. I caught him just at the door and called his name and he turned back toward me. Standing there alone, I asked him straight out, "What do you think, Mr. Arthur? What do you think?"

He looked embarrassed. He said, "What can I tell you? You're too old. Everybody's seen you. If you were going to make it, you would have done it by now."

My face must have died in front of him, the pain pooling in my eyes. He started to leave and then swung back again and tried to soften the blow, saying, "Hey, I could be wrong. I told the same thing to Peter, Paul, and Mary."

16

ON NEW YEAR'S EVE the defenses that sustained me—my ability to discount my highs and reduce my lows—finally found their breaking point. At the Duplex it was a typical New Year's audience—ruffled blouses and corsages, teased hair and doe eyes and stupid paper hats printed with HAPPY NEW YEAR 1965 —all "New Jerseys" who had said, "Let's go to the Village," and suddenly found it was 10:30 and they had to get into a club somewhere. They were drunks and neckers—and it is hard to make somebody laugh who is French-kissing. I lost my authority onstage. My words came out in the wrong order. I stuttered. I became tentative and the animal smell of failure went out and everything became worse and worse and worse. The Jerseys began talking through me as though I was a cocktail pianist and I felt right back at the Show Bar.

I thought, *What the hell am I doing here? A thirty-one-year-old Barnard girl, an honors graduate, trying to be liked by people I would otherwise never let into my life. I would not date that boy. I would not talk to that girl. Why am I in agony because they are rejecting me? Why am I torturing myself? It's madness. I've got to get out of here.* But I knew I cared deeply whether they liked me, whether they laughed. These people who were having none of me came from the real world. Only if the real world liked me could I go on performing, could I make a living doing the one thing I loved.

After the show the piano player, the waiter, the other performers, hurried away to their dates and homes. Dreariness took over. Any nightclub without people is from Hieronymus Bosch. The only glitter had been from the stage spotlights and now the harsh working lights were on. Jan sat at a table counting the night's receipts—the first time I had seen money in front of Jan for many weeks. She said, "We certainly had a good night," and offered me some champagne from an unfinished bottle.

Nobody was there to worry about me—worry that it was three o'clock in the morning and would I be all right walking the long blocks to my car and would the engine start in this cold? *You're on your own, sweetheart,* I thought. I shrugged into my black coat with the green dots I had bought at Peck & Peck when I was hotel hopping with Nicky. It smelled like a nightclub—stank of beer and cigarettes and staleness. The Duplex was a tiny place and if only one girl—or boy—wore Here's My Heart perfume, everybody left wearing it.

Out on the desolate street there was no limousine at the curb, no top-hatted gentleman inside it going tap, tap on the window and calling to me, "Mon car, lovely mademoiselle. Mon car," just a bitter wind blowing off the Hudson River— that cold which makes the teeth ache and the eyes water. The Wollensak was pulling my arm out of its socket. Only a halfback would call it a portable recorder. Why was I lugging the stupid thing? For what? For nothing!

I used a parking lot that closed at 9:00 P.M., sneaking in at 9:30 to park free. My Valiant sat alone in the huge area. I pressed the starter. The engine turned over—reluctantly, lifelessly. It turned and turned—began to, slow—as though the battery was dying. Then the engine coughed and caught, gasping and choking as if the engine was full of phlegm. The heater—and therefore the defroster—was broken, so I was no warmer inside the car, just out of the wind. At least it was too cold for frost to form on the windshield.

I headed up the East Side Drive and at Ninetieth Street, traffic came to a standstill and I could see three stationary corridors of red taillights snaking far ahead and out of sight. I sat wondering whether to turn off the engine to save gas or leave it on for the faint warmth that might seep back through the many holes.

I looked out at the other cars packed in around me, trapping me. Every one of them held couples. The whole world was couples that New Year's night—coming from someplace nice, coming from normalcy, from security, from caring —not from a roomful of people who did not like them. I began wondering if I would ever get married and whether I was too old to win the Jewish prince. Well, maybe if I could find a Jewish widower prince. . . . But nobody would want a dumpy, haggard, fake-blonde performer living on crumbs of hope. The marriage door, like the others, was closed. There was no way out. Not marriage, not acting, not comedy, and apparently not writing. I felt as stuck in my life as my car was stuck in the traffic.

Suddenly, I was terrified—the fear that squeezes the heart, turns the stomach raw. It was too late to turn back in my life. The bridge was hacked off behind me. I had nowhere else to go but show business—and I was going toward nothing but more letdowns, toward nothing but the words of Freddie Weintraub, "I don't see you making it as a single," and Irvin Arthur's "If you were going to make it, you would have done it by now."

I had always thought, *It's going to happen. It's going to happen.* Now I let myself realize, *Maybe it really is not going to happen.* After seven years of rejection, seven years of slipping back to nothing, hope had leached away. Any day now Roy Silver, like everybody else, was going to get discouraged and dump me, because money only came when Jan Wallman opened her pocketbook and took out some fives and ones. Bill Cosby was in California now and Roy would soon want to be with him and then there would be absolutely *nobody* left.

I had this flash picture in my head—what I would be like in ten years. I would be in the same car, the same coat, with the same Wollensak. And alone. And taking on that look women get—the mouth tight and the upper lip mushy with vertical lines, two deep creases from the nose to the sides of the mouth, indentations in the throat with the cords beginning to show, puffiness around eyes that don't laugh. It was the look of defeat I had seen at the *Show Street* auditions and the tryouts for *Talent '60* and *'61,* when actors in their fifties and sixties waited among the kids. I had seen it in salesladies I had known at Lord & Taylor, women who had given up show business, but never taken a good job because they always thought they would go back into the business.

That New Year's sealed into me forever the insecurity that keeps me constantly on edge. I know to my marrow that you cannot rely on anything, even while it is happening. You cannot say, "Okay, I've reached this level." You have reached no level. You get up the next morning and you are at the bottom all over again. You have your talent on this day, but you never know whether tomorrow you will be able to look at something and make a joke of it—whether you will still have that gift that came from nowhere and may disappear into nowhere.

I sat on the East Side Drive for at least an hour. People got out of their cars and a man came by and said there had been a terrible accident, four people killed. I could imagine the police cars whirling out their red flashes against the white ambulances, the tangled cars, the forms under sheets.

Suddenly I felt very ashamed, felt embarrassed by my self-pity, by my shallowness. Up ahead they were counting corpses while I was alive, healthy, smart, able to make my own decisions, able, in fact, to do anything I wanted to do. I had chosen this life, had even chosen, in a way, to freeze in this ridiculous car. Nobody had ever made me any promises— except maybe myself. I was master of my fate and if I did not like it, change it. Just stop wallowing!

I reached home at first dawn and tiptoed past the beautiful furniture of that marvelous house which was not my home and yet was home. Maybe it was not cute to be living there still at thirty-one, but it was delicious to be there—"the place," as Robert Frost said, "where they have to take you in." And I could get into my bed and it was warm and I could pull the covers over my head and forget everything.

Once again I had confirmed for myself that this was the only life that offered moments of happiness, offered the camaraderie with other performers, offered the reward of relief and exultation onstage. I went back to my rut, plugging away, doing some temp jobs, working with Roy, performing at the Duplex. Maybe I had chosen this existence, but there was no cookie anywhere in it.

Roy, astoundingly, remained determined and true to his character, the New York hustler. One day in January he telephoned Shelley Schultz at *The Tonight Show* and said, "Never mind Joan Rivers. I've got another girl. Her name is Joan Molinsky. You'll love her." Shelley said okay, bring her up. When I walked in, he turned sixteen shades of crimson and started yelling at Roy and, very, very angry, slammed out of his office, leaving us standing there. I returned into the reception room and stood in front of the secretary's desk and did my entire act for the girl, who was eating her lunch. I figured maybe if she laughed, she would say to Shelley, "That girl is funny. Oh, God, you're wrong. She's *funny.*" The woman just sat there, gumming down her tuna sandwich, sipping her coffee from a paper container. "The hood of my car has been up so much . . ." Sip. ". . . the engine's sunburned." Munch.

In early February my savior, Jorn Winther, now a director on Allen Funt's *Candid Camera,* called and offered me another job as writer. The next day I was interviewed by Allen Funt in his office, very show biz, all around me projectors and screens and speakers, and Allen hired me on the spot and was quite affable. I was extremely pleased. This would be a terrific writing credit—could go right next to "Topo the Mouse." On the way out, I introduced myself to the secretary—"Hi, I'm Joan Rivers." She said, "I never bother to learn names. Nobody's ever here long enough."

Right away I discovered why. At *Candid Camera* I was no longer Joan Molinsky, spy courier, carrying the battle plans across the border in her shoe. I was Joan Rivers working at Gestapo headquarters. I shared an office with the other writer, Bernie Orenstein—who went on to produce *That Girl, Sanford and Son,* and *What's Happening!* As soon as I walked in, Bernie said, "Be careful, the whole place is bugged."

There was an intercom, a brown thing with a meshy front, and Allen Funt had a big console on his desk with buttons he could punch and tune in to any office. When Bernie and I laughed, suddenly out of the speaker would come Allen's voice: "I guess you have so many ideas, you can afford to have a good time." One writer, while he sat dreaming up ideas, kept hitting the keys with two fingers so Allen would think he was busy. I even stopped talking in the ladies' room and told people, "Don't talk on Fifty-fifth Street till you hit Fifth Avenue."

Bernie and I started bouncing ideas off each other, but Allen liked to divide and conquer by making everybody frantically competitive. He shouted through the loudspeaker, "Bernie, get in here," and I sat at my desk, wondering whether Bernie was telling the ideas we had thought up together, whether he was saying, "How about a talking goldfish?" Later Allen screamed at me on the intercom, "Come in here, Jane." I was never more to him than the girl whose name began with J—Jenny, Jane, June. I stood in front of that huge desk of Allen's—the shorter the man, the bigger the desk—and he stared at me across his plate of carrot sticks, a chubby, mean Bugs Bunny, looking at me with little eyes. I was crazed, knowing I *had* to come up with an idea. When I suggested something—"How about a man's wristwatch that turns his skin black?"—he said, "Somebody was in here ten minutes ago with that idea. What the fuck's the matter with you?" I stopped trying out ideas on anybody and *never* left my yellow pad on my desk, always took it with me to the ladies' room. I felt utterly alone.

I am sure I was wrong about people stealing ideas, but that was the atmosphere there, everybody suspicious, frightened, under devastating pressure, their jobs in jeopardy every minute. After twelve years on the air Allen was desperate for new *Candid Camera* stunts, so he kept squeezing people, and when they were dry, hired somebody else. Everybody was disposable. I was the Kleenex of writers. He fired people on a whim during tinhorn furies and occasionally fired, rehired, and then fired somebody all in the same day. Once he came out of his office and found a guy standing in the hall doing nothing, so Allen walked right up to him and fired him. The guy said, "I don't work for you." He was a kid delivering coffee.

Allen systematically assembled people who were dependent on the job and on him—people like Jorn Winther with his six kids and a blackboard full of payments, people like me, desperate for the money. Allen could only be relaxed with people who were uncomfortable. If somebody was not living in constant fear, Allen could not be comfortable and he ground in the terror with all sorts of petty cruelties. At Christmastime he divided the mandatory employee gift list into two columns: the B group and the A group, which received better presents. The list sat on his secretary's desk where anybody passing could glimpse it and see the names crossed off one column and moved into the other, always A's being demoted to B's.

Around the office Allen Funt was called "The Big A" and

"Zeus." People gobbled up stories about him—like the day President Kennedy was shot and the telephone operator refused to answer with the ritual "Smile, you're on *Candid Camera.*" Allen bawled her out and refused to close the office so people could go home. The producer of *Candid Camera,* my old friend from the Paar show, Bob Shanks, called in all the film crews from the field. Allen screamed at him, "That's a half-day's work. That's money out of my pocket." With a stream of profanity, he insisted they still needed footage for the Sunday show.

Bob told him there would be no show on Sunday.

Allen screamed, "Of course there'll be a show."

Bob said, "Allen, I don't know how to explain to you the gravity of what's happened. The President of the United States has been shot."

"Well, I can't control that," Allen said.

It was the beginning of the end between them and a few weeks later Allen fired Bob, saying, "I'm sick of Khrushchev running things. We're going back to Stalin." Bob wondered who had been Khrushchev. Allen always thought of himself in world terms. Lyndon Johnson did not have to fire Bobby Kennedy, who had the grace to quit.

Every day at 6:00 P.M., the hour everybody else was going home from work, Allen held a staff meeting on a lower floor in his combination den-gymnasium. It was like descending to the third level of hell. Nobody frisked down those stairs. Somebody was going to be screamed at, going to be "it."

We assembled in a circle, seated on a sofa and chairs, and waited in silence. Allen was having a romance with the secretary he later married, the lovely Marilyn, and to help lose weight he had had a sauna installed. Materializing from it for the meeting, a bald, sweaty, pink little man naked under a terry-cloth robe, his plump little feet in thongs, he took his place in his special chair, and sometimes, whether by design or accident, his robe would slip, leaving his genitals in plain view.

There was another long, silent wait while Allen puffed on a cigar and gazed at the ceiling. Then, looking at nobody in particular, he said something on the order of, "I can't tell you the fucking garbage you people are turning out. It's an all-time low for *Candid Camera*. I'm going to have to fire some people. Okay, what did we all do today?" I had just found my way to the ladies' room and already my job was on the line.

The film guys from the field reported in, saying, "I think we got something really good, Allen." He said, "I hope the hell you did, because what you got yesterday was shit." Then he wanted to know what we had for tomorrow. Sometimes he liked an idea and even praised somebody. But on my third day I was "it" and when I came up with some stupid idea, he turned to the staff in general and railed, "What the fuck am I paying this cunt for!" Fixing me with his sadistic eyes, he said, "You asshole, we did that two years ago. You better come up with something, Jennifer, or you're getting out of here." That is where I learned all the language I use onstage today.

Right away in those meetings I learned *never* to volunteer a thing. Whenever Allen stopped to eat his carrots, there was absolute silence—except for *chomp, chomp, chomp*—while everybody sat terrified, clammed up, waiting for Hitler to swallow. What I could never understand—this was a man in love. When a person is in love, that is when they are the nicest, that is when the King pardons the prisoners. They open the Bastille gates and say, "Come on out. Francis the First is in love." Allen the Last had found the woman of his dreams, had created a hit show—so he must have been at the height of his warmth. I am glad I was not around when the show was failing and the marriage went on the rocks.

I felt very unfunny at *Candid Camera* and originated little for the show. I remember a stunt with a sugar bowl. A guy sitting in a luncheonette poured the sugar and dirt came out.

He called the waitress and said, "This is dirt. It's filthy." She said, "What are you talking about? It's fine," and she pressed a secret button and only sugar came out. When he tried it again, dirt came out.

But everybody's ideas were just springboards for Allen Funt's extraordinary imagination. In his work, he was a genius, right down to the smallest details. He would say, "No, no, don't make it a coffee *cup*, make it a coffee *mug*"—and the stunt did work much better. I would think, *Wow, that's why he's behind that desk.* He had a total understanding of what he was doing, knew when something was right. I never once doubted his ability and had complete respect for him professionally. He made America really laugh for years and years.

Candid Camera was especially sad and sour for me because it was my father's favorite television show. He always tried to be home on Sunday nights for *Candid Camera,* and, sitting in his big easy chair, he would roar with laughter. It was the only time he and I ever laughed together. With every other person, he was a chuckling, joking man, but the only thing we were able to share was *Candid Camera*—and now that had turned to ashes for me.

But I still had my therapy, still had the stage at the Duplex, a center for my universe. In a curious way, failure was setting me free. Since show business considered me too old, too shopworn, too shocking, there was nobody left to please except myself—and that, of course, is the real secret of pleasing the audience. When you enjoy what you are doing, they will enjoy it with you.

I entertained myself by being even more conversational, more spontaneous, more outrageous. Without knowing it, I was putting my finger on a new course of public concern and consciousness. The rebellion of Bleecker Street—The Bitter End—was spreading out into Grove Street and far, far beyond. The pill had brought on sexual liberation and new honesty for women. The assassination of Jack Kennedy and the Vietnam War were making the whole country outspoken, cynical, rougher. There was national pain, national anger, national protest—and a national desire to deal in truth and cut out the hypocrisy, particularly if we could all laugh in the process.

So the times were catching up with my irreverence. People were ready for a woman who was a little bit dangerous, who might at any moment go over the edge in her improvised stream-of-consciousness delivery—a style that in itself was new and a break with the safe, conservative past. I was saying out loud what audiences wanted to hear. I was coming into sync with a public open and ready to identify with a woman's private pain—if it was eased by something ridiculous and silly. I was letting women know that they were not alone, that their troubles were shared. I was making them feel they were right.

At *Candid Camera* life soon became a little better because I was escaping from the office, getting into the show biz part. Allen Funt—still calling me Jeri, Jeannie, Jackie—sent me out with the film crews to act as "the bait" in stunts. We started at 8:00 A.M., which meant getting up at 6:00 A.M. in Larchmont, but I did not care. If I became the girl on *Candid Camera*, all America would know me. It was going to be wonderful. And Allen might have to learn my name.

On February 17, I was out preparing a setup in a luxury apartment building called Lincoln Towers. As I remember it, I was the rental agent, showing people an apartment furnished with only a chair, table, a mattress on the floor, a cup, saucer, fork, and knife and claiming it was the new, minimalist mode of living. Roy Silver telephoned me there in the afternoon. He said, "Get over here to my office. Shelley Schultz is putting you on the Carson show tonight."

I did not allow myself any emotions. I had been through the excitement before, been through the rush of adrenaline, and the dreams and knew the predictable end. Twice before I had been in the very same studio for Paar and twice I had been a failure. I wanted to think, *Wouldn't it be wonderful if tonight I became a star,* but I knew it was not possible.

I telephoned *Candid Camera* and said I was sick. I left the apartment, went to my car, and took out my black performing dress and the faithful hairpiece that had been on the parkway in the rain. At Roy's office I put on the dress and heard the story. The night before, Roy had watched an absolutely rotten comic on *The Tonight Show,* an idiot, and had gone crazy, storming into *The Tonight Show* offices the next day, screaming at Shelley Schultz and Art Stark, the producer. He told them they couldn't do that—put that asshole on and say I wasn't funny and turn me down. Roy said it was totally unfair—plus lots of other things I guess he could not repeat to me.

Shelley Schultz still said "No!" They had auditioned me so many times they had a file on me thicker than the Alger Hiss file at the FBI—and I was still not funny.

Roy said, "Put her on as a comedy writer. Use her in the death slot," which was the last ten minutes of the show.

They had had success with funny girl writers like Selma Diamond and Roy did have muscle—they would be coming back to him for Bill Cosby, so they had better pay attention. And certainly they wanted to shut him up. They said, "Okay, you got it."

Roy and I went to *The Tonight Show* and sat with Shelley Schultz and we worked out areas to talk about—the wig on the parkway, Mr. Phyllis, being single, Larchmont, my car, etc. I called my parents and told them I was on Carson. With Roy I went down to the bare, immaculate dressing room and suddenly a clutch of William Morris agents came crowding in plus a photographer flashing a strobe, commandeered by Roy to impress Johnny Carson and Art Stark and make them think something important was happening. The agents milled around, all in navy-blue suits, all short, all saying what Roy had told them to say: "She's a winner. Great career ahead of her. She's going to be a hit." Irvin Arthur showed up, beaming, escorting a client, and wished me luck. This made me wild with nerves because I wanted to concentrate on my lines, and instead it was gracious hostess time, saying, "Nice to have you here."

Roy shepherded me into makeup, where they made up my face just as though I was a real guest, which I thought was very nice of them. I had them anchor the hairpiece with extra pins, calming my fear that it would suddenly slip to the floor in the middle of the show.

The taping of the show began at 7:30 P.M. and I sat for an hour and a half in the green room, studying my routines written out on a sheet of paper, praying that Carson would ask me what I wanted him to ask. Are you single? How do you commute? I understand you're a New York girl—"Well, actually I'm from Larchmont, it's a very small town—the car wash is a Saint Bernard."

While I wrung my hands, Roy, my hip Nick Clemente of the sixties, was saying, "You're going to be fine, baby, honey, pussycat, angel. Nothing to worry about, sweetie. That audience is great. Listen to them out there." I could not hear a thing. I was a basket case. I felt set up for another defeat. I had so much to buck. I was not on the show because they wanted me. I was a favor to Roy, a favor to Bill Cosby. It was, "Oh, shit, Roy, leave us alone. She's on. She's on." I was a throwaway.

Finally they took me to the wings behind that stupid little curtain and I stood waiting in my shiny Jax dress from Second City, my pearls around my neck and, draped over one shoulder, making no sense with a short dress, the pathetic pink boa I wore at the Duplex to make myself a little show biz. I listened to Johnny Carson introduce me as a girl writer. ". . . wrote

'Topo the Mouse,' did Second City, currently writing for *Candid Camera*, she's funny, let's bring her on."

The stage manager sort of pushed me through the curtain and I did not even see Johnny Carson, because there was Milt Kamen. He had been the previous guest and was somebody who had been nice to me for years and knew me and would not be mean. I had a friend on my side.

I was startled to be actually on the set I had been watching for years with my mother and father. It was smaller than it looked on television and not as glamorous, and there was Johnny Carson, looking younger than he did on the screen and a lot thinner. I sat down and realized I was in *the* chair and it was gray, not the color I had thought on our black-and-white TV set. My hands went right to my lap, clutching each other for comfort, and I pressed my ankles and knees together —the way my mother had taught me they looked best. I focused all my attention on Johnny Carson, trying to block out the entire studio.

Suddenly from my right came Milt Kamen's voice. "I know her. I know her. Hey, I tried to call you."

Well, this was the new Joan Rivers, who had now paid her dues, and I was not thrown by Milt and knew how to play off him. I turned and said, "Please! I've been waiting for that call for two years. I lost twelve pounds. I never dared eat. I didn't want to answer the phone with my mouth full."

Milt laughed. Johnny laughed. The ice was broken. But I was still nervous, still not in control. I went on automatic. Those six years were paying off—the night after night after night of working to drunks, to Catskills audiences, to guys with their hats in their laps, to cheaters, to French-kissing "New Jerseys"—those layers and layers of knowledge and experience, an accumulated sixth sense, was carrying me through. I had learned to listen to the audience and feel its vibrations, learned not to be hesitant, because after saying and saying and saying these things at the Duplex—and getting laughter—I had the timing right and did not rush and could wait for the laugh I knew would come—and I knew, too, that if it did not come, I would not be destroyed, would not be physically maimed or die.

And the empathy that has always existed between Johnny Carson and me was there from the first second. He understood everything. He wanted it to work. He knew how to go with me and feed me and knew how to wait. I was very deliberate then, lots of shaking my head up and down and dropping in the punch lines almost as afterthoughts, lots of nervous gestures with the hands always ending up in my lap. He never cut off a punch line and when it came, he broke up. It was like telling it to your father—and your father is laughing, leaning way back and laughing, this warm face laughing, and you know he is going to laugh at the next one. And he did and he did and he did.

Right from the start he played with me the way he still does today, saying, "Look, if you say it's true, it's true. Who am I to argue?" He made it fun and that immediately spilled over to the audience. And the audience, bless them, had not been told that I was unfunny. Nobody had said to them, "She's too old and everybody's seen her and she'll never make it." And Carson did not know that everything was over for me and too late. I had not been a nuisance to him. He just noticed I was funny. At the end of the show he was wiping his eyes. He said, right on the air, "God, you're funny. You're going to be a star."

But those words did not register—did not register. I came off and everybody was grabbing and pulling and saying, "Terrific shot. Fabulous shot. You scored. Strong material. Fresh. Strong." Irvin Arthur came over and said, "Terrific shot. Very strong." I headed for the dressing room at the center of a rush of agents—these short men talking to me and walking backward, saying, "We can get her on the Mike Douglas show now." At the dressing room, Shelley Schultz put his head in the door and said, "Great shot. Johnny loved you."

But I had heard all that before, heard Bob Shanks saying after Paar, "Nice shot. Nice shot." I did not allow myself to believe it now, did not allow myself to go up or down. I wanted to get away in case I had not been good, in case Johnny Carson was going to change his mind tomorrow and draw a line through my name. I was not going to allow them to hurt me ever again.

Taking refuge in habit, I drove home as usual to Larchmont and told my family, "It went okay." I called Treva and said, "I think it went all right. He seemed to like me. Milt Kamen was there; that was nice." Everything was couched and turned and the edges taken off, phrased so that nobody would be disappointed and I would not be humiliated tomorrow when I had to say, "Carson didn't like me after all."

I sat with my family and we watched the show. Sure enough, it was a letdown. My mother said, "Nice." My father said, "Nice." I said, "Nice." Television is a great leveler. You never see glory watching someone you know, but this time I did hear Johnny Carson say, "You're going to be a star." Yet even that, after so much rejection, did not mean anything and the girl on the screen making America laugh seemed utterly remote from me.

After the show, nobody telephoned. But before I went to bed, my mother said, "Let me tell you something, Joan. If it did go well tonight and it means something, you've done it all on your own."

My father said, "What are you talking about? We've always encouraged her."

I got up the next morning at 6:00 A.M. and went back to work at the apartment in Lincoln Towers. The night before seemed misty and insubstantial, a half-remembered dream, and I thought nothing important had happened. Carson would go away like everything else, like Second City, like Falmouth, like the Paar show. I just hoped that perhaps we would get a booking out of it, hoped Roy would say, "Shelley wants you next March so we gotta go to work on new material." I thought that would be heaven.

I spent the morning in the Lincoln Towers apartment waiting for the *Candid Camera* crew to solve some problem in the setup. I was very tired. At noon I went down to a deli to get a bran muffin and coffee. Very nervous, I called Roy. He said, "Jesus Christ, where have you been? The phone has been ringing off the hook. The offers coming in, you won't believe." He said, "Have you seen the papers? Read Jack O'Brian."

I went out and bought a *Journal-American.* The title of the column was, "Rivers Stay Near Our Door."

Jack O'Brian said:

> Johnny Carson struck gleeful gold again last night with Joan Rivers, another comedy writer who was an absolute hilarious delight. . . . And her seemingly offhand anecdotal clowning was a heady and bubbly proof of her lightly superb comic acting; she's a gem.

I read it in a daze, alone and cold and exhausted, unable to believe that I had scored with the right people in the business. Nothing made sense. This was not my fantasy of becoming a star—sitting alone in a cold apartment reading a review. Becoming a star meant limos and champagne dinners. What was going on was impossible—that Roy's phone was ringing, that I was in the *Journal-American*—that it had really happened.

I called Roy back. He said to me, "You'll never make under $300 a week for the rest of your life. That's a guarantee."

I did not believe him. *Could not* believe him. I was not going to let down all my shields and armor and layers of accumulated protection, defenses it would take years to put back when disappointment came.

Roy went on, "You got whatever you want."

I said, "I want to quit *Candid Camera.*"

Before returning to Lincoln Towers, I went to my bank to cash a check—get the teller to register a check in my account right away, before it had cleared, so a check I had written would not bounce. They always gave me big trouble about that, saying, "I'm sorry, it's against bank policy." This time the girl said, "Of course. No problem. Right away. Oh, I loved you so much last night on Carson. You were so funny." This was not the phone call with Roy. This was not Jack O'Brian. This was me alone with a stranger whose eyes were saying, "I loved you."

I held in everything till I got back to that apartment. I went into the empty kitchen, sat on a stool, and stared at Jack O'Brian in the paper and thought about the girl at the bank. I had seen celebrity reflected back to me. She would go home and say, "You won't guess who came into the bank today—the funny girl on the Carson show." I had made her day.

I let myself believe. After six years, it really, really, really had happened. I was going to be able to make money . . . do what I loved doing. I would be able to entertain people and be happy doing it and survive doing it. And be my own self. Be a person. I began to cry with relief and anguish, crying for everything that had ever happened, finally letting out all the hurts, washing them away, shedding all my skins.

Roy Silver, Jack O'Brian, the bank teller, Johnny Carson, were saying to me now, "You're right. You've always been right. You were right when you were a kitty cat. You were right standing in the costume room at Ethical Culture wanting to be in those costumes." It had been thirty-one years of knowing, "That's what I should be doing. That's what I should be doing," knowing I was right while everyone was saying, "No, no, no, no. You're not right for it. You're not meant for this."

Thirty-one years of people saying, "You're *not* right." And, by God, I *was* right.

I went out and called Roy, who said again, "You got whatever you want. You name it, you got it." I called my mother, who told me that calls were coming there and the family was in an uproar. Everybody was saying, "Of course, we always knew." My father had known it all along. Irvin Arthur, so proud at the Carson show, he had known it. Jack Rollins—"Hey, it's just a matter of time." Well, the time had arrived—without him.

It was all over. Thirty-one years of people saying "No." That is a long, long time. And suddenly it was all over. All over in ten minutes. Ten minutes on television and it was all over.

Everybody at *Candid Camera* knew I was going to be fired and the coffee boy that morning had brought in one less container. I came back to the office in time for the six o'clock staff meeting. Allen Funt had found out about the Carson show and was furious—his face red, hands clenched—a dinky, apoplectic Buddha. He said he had heard I had done something. He cursed me for lying about being sick, screamed at me for moonlighting. When he had exhausted himself, I said, "There's nothing to talk about, because I'm giving notice as of the end of the week."

Allen Funt looked balefully at me and chomped down on a carrot stick. He chewed thoroughly and slowly. He swallowed. He said, "I think you're making a big mistake, Jill."

EPILOGUE

On July 15, 1965, Joan Rivers married Edgar Rosenberg. Their daughter, Melissa Warburg Rosenberg, was born January 20, 1969. In August 1983, Joan Rivers was named the first and only permanent guest host of *The Tonight Show Starring Johnny Carson*. She lives the life her mother longed to have— but still believes that next week everything will disappear.

ACKNOWLEDGMENTS

Reading this list, I was deeply moved. Your names, each with a special association, brought out all of the emotions that flowed through me during those extraordinary and crucial years we shared. I was grateful then that you were a part of my life—and grateful today that you have been so generous with your time and memories. My warmest thanks and appreciation.

Betty Aberlin
Lou Alexander
Steve Allen
Woody Allen
Bea Arthur
Carol Arthur
Irvin Arthur
Ben Bagley
Kaye Ballard
Billy Barnes
Sandy Baron
Charles Biasiny
Eddie Blum
Eugene Boe
David Brenner
R. G. Brown
Carol Burnett
Ruth Buzzi
John Byner

Ceil Cabot
George Carlin
Claiborne Cary
Dick Cavett
Chris Chase
Nick Clemente
Carol Cohen
Joe Cohen
Harry Colomby
Jim Connell
Bert Convy
Tommy Corcoran
Bill Cosby
Barbara Coughlin
Gene Dale
Rodney Dangerfield
Peter Daniels
John Davidson
Dom DeLuise
Charlotte Eth
Ida Eth
David Fitelson
Fannie Flagg
Jack Fletcher
Shelly Flower
Jeannie Fornadel
Budd Friedman
Sandy Gallin
Dick Gautier
Jackie Gayle
Harry Gittes
Dave Gordon
Ronnie Graham
Richard Grant
Don Gregory
Gary Haber
Bill Hahn

Frances Halpern
Dr. Lennie Heimoff
Florence Henderson
Buck Henry
Jerry Herman
Paul Hudson
Charles Joffe
Milt Kamen
Dori Kotzan
Miles Kreuger
Bernie Kukoff
Peggy Lloyd Larin
George Q. Lewis
Paul Lynde
George Maisel
Barry Manilow
Eman Marder
Mimmi Marder
Beatrice Marks
Anne Meara
Lillian Tobinson Mizrahi
Harry Molin
Dr. Meyer C. Molinsky
Julius Monk
Buddy Morra
Floyd Mutrex
Richard O'Brien
Tom O'Malley
Bernie Orenstein
Myron Orlofsky
Richard Pryor
Claibe Richardson
Les Roberts
Jack Rollins
Dick Roman
Arlyne Rothberg
Mort Sahl

Bill Sammeth
Ronnie Schell
Avery Schreiber
George Schultz
Bob Shanks
Roy Silver
Treva Silverman
Kenny Solms
David Steinberg
Howard Storm
Barbra Streisand
Danny Strickland
Jeffrey Sweet
Allan Thenen
Saul Turteltaub
Jeff Wald
Archie Walker
Jan Wallman
Rod Warren
Bob Waxman
Fred Weintraub
Ronnie Whyte
JoAnne Worley

INDEX